Color of Rape

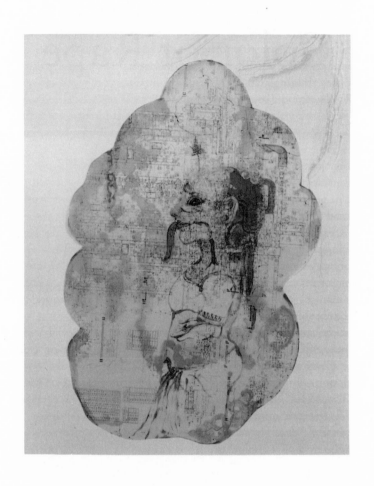

Purity, Rina Banerjee (2000)

Color of Rape

Gender and Race
in Television's Public Spheres

Sujata Moorti

State University of New York Press

Published by
State University of New York Press, Albany

© 2002 State University of New York

For information, address State University of New York Press,
90 State Street, Suite 700, Albany, NY 12207

Production by Michael Haggett
Marketing by Patrick Durocher

Library of Congress Cataloging-in-Publication Data

Moorti, Sujata, 1963–
    Color of rape : gender and race in television's public spheres / Sujata Moorti.
      p. cm.
    Includes bibliographical references and index.
    ISBN 0-7914-5133-X (alk. paper) — ISBN 0-7914-5134-8 (pbk. : alk. paper)
      1. Rape on television. 2. African Americans on television. 3. Rape—Press
coverage—United States. I. Title.

PN1992.8.R26 M66 2001
364.15′32—dc21

                                                                                2001042009

10 9 8 7 6 5 4 3 2 1

Contents

*To My Father
and In Memory of My Mother*

Acknowledgments

Over the course of this project I have gained a better understanding of the complex and subtle manner in which race and gender suffuse the terrains of citizenship and popular culture in the United States. Not only have I discovered that there are no easy answers to the vexing ways in which these categories of identity intersect, I have also come to appreciate the many different ways in which mainstream television tries to capture this complexity. In this, sometimes tedious and most often fascinating, process of learning I have had assistance from various quarters, some within the formal institutions of academe and the others from the informal kindness and generosity of numerous friends and colleagues. The extended nature of this inquiry means that I am indebted to numerous people for their enthusiasm, their zeal, and their patience. Often, seemingly offhand comments drove me back to examine the primary questions of this project and have provided intellectually exhilarating avenues. For these and boundless other insights I have not been able to thank everyone individually but my gratitude is unreserved.

Maurine Beasley, Evelyn Beck, Gina Marchetti, Jim Klumpp, Steve Barkin, Michael Gurevitch, and Richard Brown among numerous others at the University of Maryland taught me to pose difficult questions pertaining to democracy and citizenship. They have insisted upon and guided me through the process of critical thinking and their insights continue to shape my scholarship. Julie D'Acci, Anita Fellman, Rashmi Luthra, Lisa McLaughlin, Toby Miller, and Usha Zacharias have read parts of this manuscript, offered suggestions for improving it, and encouraged me with the research. Lisa Cuklanz, Sarah Projansky, Andrea Slane, and Patricia Priest have shared their ideas and their interest in television images of rape with ceaseless enthusiasm. They have offered a continuing dialogue and a community of scholarship. Rina Banerjee has helped me gain a better understanding of art. She and Andrea have spent long hours explaining the processes of producing artworks. Together these scholars have provided me intellectual sustenance and sharpened my interest in the politics of cultural representation. In almost all cases I have accepted their proposals, but if on occasion, I did through carelessness, disregard their warnings all errors of judgment and taste remain firmly with me.

Other friends and colleagues deserve my appreciation for their support. Mona Danner, Ed Jacobs, Carolyn Lawes, Jane Merritt, and Manuela Mourão have helped me stay focused and often borne with equanimity my distracted behavior. Amanda Bloodgood has doggedly helped me with the minutiae of research. Some of the arguments I develop in Chapter 5, "Testifying in the Court of Daytime Talk Shows," first appeared in *Social Text*. I would also like to thank the anonymous reviewers for their comments, which helped me examine my analysis with greater clarity. I am indebted to my editors at SUNY Press, Ron Hellfrich and Priscilla Ross, who have assisted me. My thanks also to Michael Haggett, Michele Lansing, and Lisa Chesnel who have worked assiduously with me and have helped me improve the manuscript.

Above all my family has been very generous with their time and patience. They have borne this project with forbearance and have offered me the serenity and sanctuary that writing requires. Amaresh and Usha have provided long-distance support and encouragement. Sanat and Raman have assisted me in countless ways, reading large portions of the manuscript and offering me kind nudges to complete it. Rina and Vas have offered their friendship and held my hand when needed. My father has diligently read the manuscript at numerous stages and has awaited its completion. Ananya has unknowingly brought much delight to this project.

Introduction

_____

In late December 1991, a pre-credits segment of *In Living Color* contained a skit with a woman dressed in a charcoal-gray suit and wearing a string of pearls, with a blue blob covering her face. The woman walks toward a seat in an area resembling a witness box in a courtroom. Once seated, she cheerfully endorses the merits of the Equity Card: "I may not remember why I took off my hose, or why I went for a walk on the beach with a member of the Kennedy family. I may have my bra and underwear scanned under a microscope for stains. But, I never leave home without my Equity Card." The woman's figure fades from the screen and is replaced with the image of the Equity Card, as an authoritative male voice-over underlines her endorsement: "If you leave home without hose, make sure you have your Equity Card. Call now and say that the woman with the blob asked you to call." This mock advertisement for a credit card is followed by a puffy-faced actor made up to resemble Senator Edward Kennedy, foregrounded against the Capitol, endorsing the Kennedy Carte Blanche Card. The senator praises the merits of his card by saying, "Kennedys not only get into the Senate, but also get away with anything." He is then joined by a figure resembling his nephew, William Kennedy Smith. Together, they assert, "When we get off, we get off scot free." The two-minute segment ends crudely with the senator urging Willie to put *it* in his pants, and then both men thrust their Carte Blanche Cards into the pockets of their pants.

The parodic, self-reflexive commentary on television programming represented in this skit condenses many of the central elements of a counter-hegemonic discourse. It mocks the consumer culture that underwrites television programming, including *In Living Color*. The skit simultaneously draws attention to the nature of celebrity culture—the ways in which stars are produced and anointed by the media and then are recruited to participate in an economy that can underwrite more spectacle-producing television programming. In addition, this black-authored program points out the particular ways in which (white) male privilege, the political and social advantages that have accrued around the Kennedy family, compares to the "equitable" status of women. In a reductionist stroke, it underscores that men and women are perceived differently, not just by society but also through legal and economic processes.

In many ways this skit provided one of the sharpest on-air analyses of the William Kennedy Smith case and its media coverage. The interpretation of the rape trial mockingly offered by the woman with the blue blob and the two Kennedy men opened new ways of discussing the event; it offers understandings that were unavailable in other television genres. The skit highlighted the spectacular nature of "celebrity" rape trials and showed how identities are constructed by others, especially for rape survivors. Above all, it revealed how the logic of television culture—the industry's practices and representational forms—could transform the violation of a female body into an asset to be traded in consumer culture. Simultaneously, it foregrounded who could speak and whose voices could be heard in television space; it introduced questions about the (racial and sexual) politics of enunciation. Even when the woman in the aforementioned skit speaks, in this case, to endorse the Equity Card, her utterance is supplemented by a disembodied male voice who lends authority and credibility to her claims.

Through indecorous humor, the skit propels the male body into the public arena in a manner uncommon on television. It brings to the forefront the privileges that have accumulated around particular configurations of white masculinity, the ways in which the Kennedys and other elite white males can "get away with anything." The segment combines social commentary with a critique of television practices in an ironic fashion that became emblematic of the situation comedies of the 1990s. The broad strokes of its criticism of white masculinity necessarily flatten some of the details, but the first time I saw it I marveled that an entertainment program from the denigrated Fox programming lineup would offer such biting commentary. Upon reflection, it becomes clear that it is precisely the devalued status of this network and of prime-time entertainment in general that allows this particular situation comedy to offer such an irreverent reading of a media event.[1]

The skit draws attention to the missing subjects of television rape discourse: the material effects of men's and women's different locations in a gendered social hierarchy, the ability of television's representational practices to shape popular understandings of events, and the logic of consumer culture that underpins television programming. It highlights too the fact that television programming is not monolithic but is a site where cultural meanings are contested, negotiated, and produced. Sometimes, as is the case with this *In Living Color* sketch, television programs open up the space for a counter-hegemonic understanding of social phenomena, at the very least one that does not emanate from the ideological center of society. Significantly, this particular commentary does not engage with the topic of sexual violence; the rape trial becomes a site for a critique of specific social practices. In many ways, this sketch offers a reading against the grain yet replicates aspects of network programming's engagement with rape, especially the focus on the processes surrounding sexual violence, and it encapsulates the possibilities for debate and discussion that are made possible by the cultural politics of television.

This book examines television rape narratives from the late 1980s and early 1990s, when a series of well publicized cases created a public arena for the discussion of sexual violence in a widespread fashion. Significantly, it examines how the categories of gender *and* race are represented in television images of sexual violence. Having recently arrived in the United States from India, I was taken aback by the diverse ways in which the topic of rape was discussed on television. In the state-run television system that then dominated India, such a discussion of rape would have been unthinkable; if it surfaced in the news, it would have been presented primarily as an assault shorn off the sexual specificity of the crime, and in prime-time entertainment it would have been produced spectacularly to authorize distinct valences of male citizenship.[2] I also was intrigued by the frank, impassioned discussions of pain and other intimate matters enabled by daytime talk shows. Traditional theories of democracy and the media did not provide the vocabulary within which to situate this diverse range of information that different genres of television programming provided about rape. The analysis contained in this book thus engages with the specific ways in which network television portrays rape, gender, and race and its ability to facilitate a democratic public sphere. I have inscribed my positionality in this awkward manner not to follow programmatically a feminist sensibility of situating the self but also to instantiate my stake in the arguments I put forth in this book.

TELEVISION AND PUBLIC SPHERE THEORIES

This book examines a single topic across several television genres—network news, prime-time entertainment, daytime talk shows, alternative programming, and video art. It is not concerned with the authenticity of representational practices or with which genre more authentically represents the facts. The analysis instead focuses on the kinds of debates and discussions about rape that the different genres enable, on the contestation and negotiation that underpin cultural understandings of sexual violence, and on the sedimented discourses of gender, race, and sexuality that shape television narratives.

In the United States, as numerous scholars have pointed out, the topic of rape has been entwined with the issue of race.[3] The analysis conducted in this book necessarily engages with the ways in which gender and race are imaged in television portrayals of sexual violence. It reveals the manner in which seemingly unconnected discourses of gender, race, and sexuality cohere to create unified narratives about rape.

In situating television narratives within democratic structures, this analysis is guided by political and media-centered theories of democracy. Most scholars concur that a discussion and debate of issues of common concern are central to the formation and maintenance of democratic societies, as I elaborate on in Chapter 1. In modern societies, in the absence of face-to-face communication, mass media have become sites where such discussions are enabled. Jürgen Habermas's *The Structural Transformation of the Public Sphere* (1989) is credited with reinvigorating studies about the media's role in promoting democratic debate and discussion. The English-language translation of this book has promoted a wide-ranging debate over the ability of the media to facilitate the functioning of the public sphere, an autonomous arena of democratic debate and discussion. Media theorists though have tended to view the news as the primary site of information production and dissemination, hence, the public sphere. By including prime-time entertainment, daytime talk shows, and alternative programming, this book broadens the scope of existing public sphere theories.

I have deliberately limited my analysis to programs aired on the "free" commercial networks—ABC, CBS, NBC, and Fox—between 1989 and 1993. Cable, syndication, satellite, pay-per-view, and other services have become increasingly important to television's representations of gender and race. But if a prerequisite for democratic debate is free access to information, then examining these "pay" television sites would necessarily eliminate economically disenfranchised citizens. If television is to function as a forum that facilitates debate and discussion, its programming should theoretically be available to all of the citizenry.

I have emphasized those television images aired between 1989 and 1993 to maintain the fidelity of the arguments I make. Network news coverage of the three rape cases I analyze in this book propelled the topic of sexual violence into the national spotlight and provided a salience and legitimacy to other television genres' engagement with the topic. In the chapters that follow, I do not offer a comparative analysis of the narratives put forth by different forms of programming. However, I do point out the intertextuality between them, the ways in which they borrow imaging practices from each other and speak to each other. The focus on a five-year period allows me to underscore the ways in which the same topic is addressed from a multiplicity of perspectives and the markedly different debates and discussions facilitated by a wide range of television programming. It also allows me to capture the structure of feeling of this historical moment. I am not suggesting that this period is unique, nor do I want to privilege the news as the originary site of this widespread engagement with sexual violence. Instead, as I indicate below, many of the practices and tendencies I isolate in this book prevailed before and continue to structure television images. The analysis I offer is neither programmatic nor prescriptive. Rather, it is designed to highlight the need to broaden conceptions of the public sphere and of television's role in facilitating democratic communities.

TROPES OF DIFFERENCE

I have chosen rape narratives as the exemplary site from which to make this intervention into theories of the public sphere for two reasons, both of which are informed by feminist and critical race theories. In their examination of rape, feminist scholars have valorized knowledge produced by women and other subordinated groups. They have pointed out that so-called feminine discourses, those that foreground emotions, affective relations, and the pain experienced by individuals, produce different forms of knowledge than those produced by rational-critical reasoning. Building on these insights, feminist television scholars have highlighted the ways in which the devalued genres of daytime talk shows, soap operas, and prime-time entertainment enable "feminine" discourses. Similarly, critical race theories have pointed out how devalued television genres are key sites where cultural understandings of racial identity and marked bodies are circulated and produced. These studies broaden the scope for scholarship beyond the news.

The women's movement of the 1970s has been largely responsible for redefining sexual violence as a public concern and not as a private, individual problem. As I illustrate in Chapter 2, feminist theories postulate that rape is a violent manifestation of the systems of subordination and domination that are prevalent in society. They point out that the ideological nature of the public/private divide that has characterized theories of democracy has kept the "private" topic of rape outside of the public arena of democratic debate. In addition, feminist and critical race theories point out the gender and racial exclusions that are characteristic of the public sphere. Their work insists on the inclusion of domestic issues in the arena of public debate.

The analysis in this book thus foregrounds two key issues that emanate from feminist and critical race theories. First, my examination of rape narratives permits me to evaluate network programming's ability to accommodate a "private" topic and make it available in a public forum. Second, by studying the same topic across different genres, I am able to assess which ones are able to foster democratic community formation. Even as my analysis highlights the gender- and race-based fault lines of the public sphere, it reveals that no single genre is able to include unproblematically the marginalized voices of women and racialized subjects. The debates and discussions that television programs enable are partial and limited. The analysis reveals that genres that foreground the affective over the rational, such as daytime talk shows, are able to negotiate discourses of gender and race more productively than those that deal only with rational-critical information. Gender, race, and sexuality are socially constructed categories that derive their significance from cultural practices; their meanings are constantly negotiated, contested, and materialized in the everyday lives of women and men. Unlike the news, the devalued genres of prime-time entertainment and daytime talk shows introduce the body, desire, and emotion into the public arena. They highlight how individuals cope with issues pertaining to gender, race, and sexuality rather than present them as abstract ideas.

In this book, I have limited my analysis to television representations of female victims and heterosexual rape. While studies have pointed out that men are raped and that sexual violence is prevalent in gay and lesbian communities, women continue to be the predominant raped subjects. By limiting myself to heterosexual rape, I am able to specify the ways in which women and feminine discourses are included in the public sphere of debate and discussion. Since racial difference constitutes the ways in which individuals experience rape, I examine constantly the ways in which television representations produce the intersections of race and gender. In the chapters that follow I return insistently to questions of how black men are portrayed in television rape narratives, how white women are depicted as rape survivors, and how these images compare with the images of black women as rape survivors. I contend that historical anxieties about black sexuality continue to shape contemporary television representations. Consequently, the myths of the black male rapist, black male bestiality, and black female promiscuity inform the images of black women and men in rape narratives as well as the black male and female experience in the legal and criminal justice arenas.

The metanarratives of the public sphere and of feminist theories of rape provide the theoretical underpinnings of this book. As a key structure of democratic communities, the public sphere has been conceptualized around the unmarked white male humanist subject, one that can participate in ratio-nal-critical debate. Feminist theories, on the other hand, have foregrounded gender as a central axis of collective identity formation, often ignoring race. Using a cultural studies approach, I identify how the intersection of these two metanarratives shapes the debates and discussions about rape, gender, and race that are made possible by television programming. Here I do not outline the specific theories I mobilize in my analysis. As an interdisciplinary project, I have used a range of theories; in the individual chapters, I specify the theo-ries that structure my examination.

The analysis in this book can be described as emerging from a cultural studies perspective, informed by insights from feminist and critical race the-ories. Cultural studies is a multidisciplinary, and some argue an antidiscipli-nary, domain of scholarship that is concerned with understanding the rela-tionship between culture and power and culture and society. It is not a unified body of work but a "set of approaches which attempts to understand and intervene in relations of culture and power."[4] Grounded in everyday practices and the analysis of a whole range of artifacts—artistic forms, texts, mass-produced commodities, and so on—cultural studies scholars identify the processes of meaning making in a particular community or culture.

As is true in most other domains of scholarship, feminist and critical race theories have been instrumental in highlighting the gender- and race-based assumptions that underpin these analyses. The gaps and absences of this interpretive mode of analysis also have been highlighted by poststructuralist theories that reject a unified grand narrative. Poststructuralist thought privi-leges multiple, fragmented, and contestatory narratives about society. In the realm of television studies, these theories allow us to read against the grain and to recuperate meanings and worldviews that have been marginalized or rendered absent. This approach has been particularly useful in highlighting the ways in which narratives of race, gender, and nationalism, among others, are presented on television. My examination of rape narratives is informed by these broad analytical modes.

Methodologically, the arguments in this book cohere around three areas: (1) the rhetorical forms and genres associated with public discussion of private topics; (2) the ways in which gender and race are imaged and nar-ratively inscribed; and (3) the unexamined racialized identities that under-pin theories of knowledge, sexuality, and sexual violence. Reading through and across network programs each chapter foregrounds a problematic domain in television discourses of rape. Through an exploration of these sites of cultural discourse production, the chapters that follow broaden understandings of the public sphere and offer a critique of the unexamined racialized identities that underpin theories of knowledge and sexuality. I repeatedly examine who is considered the "ideal" viewer of individual programs. Is it male? Is it a white male? Is it female? Is it a white female? Or, is it a nonwhite spectator? I argue that these assumptions mold the knowledge about rape that is made available in television programming. In turn, this shapes the nature of debate and discussion, the nature of the public sphere, facilitated.

It is necessary that I clarify here my use of the term *discourse*. I do not use it to refer to the textual properties of television programming. Borrowing from poststructuralist theories, I use the term to refer to the processes of meaning making within particular historical, social, and political conditions. This allows me to draw attention to which statements are made and which ones are left out, rather than to how they are made. Locating discourses within the conditions of their production and circulation helps point out the ways in which social and cultural power functions. I derive these understandings of discourse from Michel Foucault's writings.[5] He characterizes it as a historically, a socially, and an institutionally specific structure of statements, terms, categories, and beliefs. In his broad range of writings, Foucault shows that the production and circulation of meaning involve conflict and power, meaning is contested and negotiated within overlapping, multiple "fields of force." Power enters this process through the claims to knowledge made by disciplinary and professional organizations and institutions. In the analysis I conduct in this book, I use *discourse* to refer to the ways in which television programming draws on institutional, organizational, and social discourses to provide authority to and to legitimize their truth claims.[6]

CONTESTS BETWEEN RACE AND GENDER

The analysis in this book bridges the information-entertainment divide but maintains the specificity of television's major genres. In the chapters that follow, I highlight the particularity of each genre of television programming but introduce the topic here to clarify a central argument that I put forward in this book. The use of the term *genre* to refer to television products is specific to the medium and should not be conflated with its use in literature or film. It is an artificial construct that highlights the production practices and routinized rhetorical, visual, and narrative strategies associated with specific clusters of programming. For the most part, these categories are determined by the location of the program within a television schedule.

News and news magazines are programs that assert their nonfictional status primarily through rhetorical strategies of objectivity, a surveying from above that classifies and categorizes events. These programs focus on issues pertaining to the public arena and address them within a rhetoric of abstraction that is distanced from emotions, body, affect, and desire. Ideas here are supplemented by empirically verifiable data, and news workers often work hard (consciously and unconsciously) to disguise their storytelling practices and to offer their representations as a transparent window to the world.

Prime-time entertainment self-consciously inscribes its fictional status by highlighting an issue or an event from several different perspectives. Many of these programs present themselves as social realist texts by addressing issues emanating from the news. The narrative movement in this genre, however, often is impelled by highlighting the emotional and affective responses of individuals to the issue. Daytime talk shows straddle the fiction/nonfiction divide. They discuss issues traditionally isolated in the domestic arena. Daytime talk shows make no attempt to present abstract arguments, yet they are not fictional programs. Instead, the dominant mode of engagement is through the experiential voice of the layperson. These shows reveal how and what "ordinary" people think about an issue.

As my analysis reveals, the classification of programs as fictional and non-fictional is fragile and does not provide a productive way of thinking about the television apparatus. Each genre borrows techniques, ideas, and presentation strategies from one another, but these practices of nomination permit them to valorize specific modes of representational practices. Scholars such as Raymond Williams and Nick Browne have argued that the technology of television and/or the economic underpinnings of the medium require that we study the flow of programming rather than a genre or an individual program.[7] In this book, I argue that each genre is able to facilitate only a narrow range of debate and discussion about the issue of rape. It is the totality of television programming that makes possible multiple and variegated understandings of issues. I outline below what this means in the context of this book.

The first section of my analysis addresses news and other information-based programming traditionally associated with the public sphere of democracy. Feminist theories have had a marginal influence on their representational practices. Network coverage of the 1989 interracial Central Park jogger's case, the intraracial William Kennedy Smith case in 1991, and the intraracial Mike Tyson case in 1992 reveal the cultural conceptions of racialized masculinity that underpin understandings of rape. News coverage illuminates understandings of prescribed and proscribed white and black masculinity, and these meanings are derived primarily by erasing the female experience of sexual violence. The next section explores the fictional programming of prime-time entertainment, particularly cop shows and legal dramas. The focus on justice and retribution allows these narratives to present women primarily as victims or as misguidedly postfeminists. The debates they enable focus on either a deracinated female experience of trauma or on the ways in which racist stereotypes shape nonwhite male sexuality.

Having marked the problematic ways in which most television programs represent rape, my analysis turns to sites that contain tentative but emancipatory impulses. Unlike other programming, the testimonial nature of daytime talk show discussions allows television to foreground ordinary women's experiences of rape. The organizational structure of daytime talk shows permits them to engage in and to incorporate feminist perspectives on sexual violence most elaborately. Further, the public articulation of pain allows the participants to forge a collective identity around a gender- or race-based oppression. The fragmented and repetitious narratives of daytime talk shows facilitate the formation of an affective public sphere, an arena where the body, emotions, and subjective experience are central to debate and discussion. These programs not only give women and marginalized voices a forum to articulate their experiences, they also recognize the validity of these experiential voices. However, the need to maintain audience ratings forces this genre to highlight conflicts, and it undercuts any emancipatory potential. Alternative programming, such as the made-for-television movie *The Fallen Champ*, and art exhibits based on network video clips critique hegemonic discourses and illuminate how television representations could create a space of self-definition for marginalized communities, one that articulates subjugated nonwhite and woman-centered knowledges. These projects self-consciously effect a strategic essentialism between gender and race as they point out the ways in which television representations silence and marginalize subjects. Narratives that offer a critical analysis of media practices, such as television's grammar for imaging rape, gender, and race, often find themselves at an impasse. Their criticism can emerge only from the repertoire of images already in circulation. They can direct our attention to absences, but to give voice to the unrepresented such critiques have to turn to sources outside television. For instance, I argue in this book that nonwhite women's experiences of rape often remain invisible in television narratives. Alternative sites of programming, such as video art, can represent this idea only by turning to images outside television or they have to focus on some other aspect of the rape narrative and refer to the elisions tangentially. Alternative programs, however, are the only products that illustrate how media images themselves inform cultural understandings of rape. As even this brief summary illustrates, none of the television genres individually engages with the complexity of sexual violence. When taken together, though, I argue that the multiple understandings that the different genres promote facilitate a wide-ranging debate about rape, gender, and race.

Five years after the events that I analyze in this book, rape has returned, briefly, to the media spotlight. Popular culture, particularly television, responded to a series of events that reinvigorated the debate about rape. Many contemporary media images echo the themes of backlash and post-feminist ideology that I discuss in Chapter 2, while others present a renewed feminist perspective of the issue. The emergence of *Law & Order, Special Victims Unit*, an hour-long television show devoted to the apprehension of rapists, is emblematic of both the changes in attitudes toward sexual assault and the resilience of some problematic features. The fact that a weekly episodic television show has been dedicated to focus on the crime is significant. Many trends are laudable here: the show presents sexual assault in the home and on the war front, highlighting its pervasiveness, and it also foregrounds the difficulties in apprehending and prosecuting assailants. Nevertheless, viewers understand the despicable nature of the crime primarily through the responses of the two cops; rape has once again become a backdrop against which the talents of this male-female cop duo are showcased. Finally, I would argue that rape itself is reduced into an object and a spectacle. We do not receive the female experience of sexual violence, it is always mediated through legal discourses or framed by the concerns of the criminal justice system. *Law & Order, Special Victims Unit* highlights the significance of this topic and simultaneously undercuts its relevance by reducing rape to a narrative device that could augment audience ratings.[8]

I have enumerated this development at some length to illustrate how the trends that I identify in television representational practices and the debates that they engender continue to be replicated today. As my analysis reveals, television programming can facilitate a wide range of debate about sexual violence, provided we take into account multiple genres. In the following section, I provide a very brief chapter outline and then return to the significant features of my findings. A short note about the frontispiece is illustrative here. The multimedia installation by Rina Banerjee, "Purity," captures evocatively the ways in which the figure of the female is constituted through multiply intersecting social discourses. Purity highlights how social understandings of gender and race are inflected by historical conceptions as well as institutional discourses such as medicine or the nation-state and inscribed on the female body. Woman functions as a "transmission point," permeable and penetrable yet persistently "veiled." This structure of feeling underpins the television discourses of woman in the rape narratives that I examine; woman as rape survivor emerges as both wholly knowable and unfathomable.

The frontispiece and the cover image together represent the spectrum of imaging practices that exist in television space. Some genres, such as the news, silence and occlude women of color's experiences of rape. Other genres, most notably video art, adopt a representational grammar that reveals the embodied female subject as the site where multiple social, institutional, and cultural discourses come to reside. These forces, in turn, shape women's experiences of violation. This range of portrayals makes possible multiple avenues for debate and discussion.

CHAPTER OUTLINE

Chapter 1, "Television and Theories of the Public Sphere," provides the structuring framework for the analysis conducted in this book. I offer a brief genealogy of democratic theories and the roles that they assign to the media. The majority of the chapter though focuses on Habermas's formulation of the public sphere and on the interventions that feminist and critical race theorists have made to broaden its parameters.

Chapter 2, "The Feminist Subject of Rape," once again addresses the theoretical issues underpinning this book. I isolate feminist engagement with the topic of rape since the 1970s to highlight which aspects of these complex, nuanced theories are appropriated by the media and with what effect. A central argument I make in this chapter is that contemporary understandings of rape, including feminist, emerge from particular insights into the unified modern subject. Consequently, they tend to privilege gender over race in their understandings of sexual violence, and this racial blindness is highlighted in television representations.

In Chapter 3, "The Right of Sight Is White: The Singular Focus of Network News," I analyze network news coverage of three "celebrity" rape trials and point out how the white masculine gaze of the news shapes the field of the visible. In all three rape cases—Central Park, Mike Tyson, and William Kennedy Smith—network news coverage focused on the accused. The masculine vision that dominates the news locates rape victims on the margins of stories that center on their physical violation. The raped woman becomes a symbolic cause to discuss other social issues, such as inner-city violence or political privilege. When news narratives focus on women, often only during trials, stereotypes of female sexuality predominate. I argue primarily in this chapter that the subject positions occupied by men and women in rape narratives are unstable, constantly shifting, and relationally determined. The only consistent feature is the demonization of black masculinity. Such images of race and gender underscore how power and access to material resources shape an individual's participation in the public arena.

Analyzing various episodes of prime-time entertainment in Chapter 4, "White Men Do Feminism: Multiple Narratives of Prime-Time Rape," I argue that fictional narratives are able to better capture the dynamics of sexual and racial hierarchies that characterize sexual violence. I isolate three predominant modes of representing fictional accounts of rape: as allegories, as inversions of cultural stereotypes about racialized sexuality, or as undermining the relevance of feminism. Working within discourses of crime and punishment, the programs often present a female-centered understanding of rape, but most feminist understandings of sexual violence are espoused by male characters. In prime-time rape narratives, the men are staunchly feminist, while the women are postfeminist or antifeminist. In an equally problematic trend, several of the narratives deploy racial difference and racism as the generative moment of their story lines. However, they rarely show how race and gender work together to shape individual experiences of sexual violence. For instance, an *L.A. Law* episode begins with an African-American lawyer arrested on rape charges because he was jogging in a white neighborhood where the crime had occurred. The continuing hold of the black male rapist myth propels this story line. But as the narrative enlarges on the theme of police corruption rape slides out of view. Fictional narratives might allude to the legacy of a racist past, but apart from a cursory gesture they fail to depict how it affects the lives of nonwhite people who experience rape.

Chapter 5, "Testifying in the Court of Talk Shows," examines how the extravagant plurality of daytime talk shows contributes to the formation of a counter public sphere. The format and structure of daytime talk shows allow them to form an imagined community that coalesces around either gender or race. Even though they operate within the gender/race binary, daytime talk shows are significantly different because of the nature of the debate that they facilitate. Through the public articulation of ill-defined topics, these shows accommodate bodily and affective aspects of human existence within the realm of debate and discussion. Further, the storied voices of participants illuminate the effects of social inequalities on public deliberative practices. The affective public sphere these shows facilitate permit the inclusion of ordinary voices, and those who are normally marginalized on television.

The final chapter, "Fragmented Counternarratives," turns to alternative programs to provide a more optimistic outlook for the formation of a counter public sphere. By examining a range of artifacts—the made-for-TV movie,

the documentary *Fallen Champ*, network educational efforts, and video art—
the chapter points out how the commercial logic that saturates television
space requires that we grasp at fragments. These artifacts may focus only on
race or gender, but they highlight repeatedly how television images shape our
understandings of sexual violence. They offer a criticism of television imaging practices and suggest an alternative grammar.

In the public spheres enabled by television rape representations, discourses of gender and race are strategically separated. The programs either
address rape as it affects (white) women or as an effect of black masculinity,
rarely as a site where gender and racial discourses intersect in problematic
ways. This valorization of either gender or race allows television programming to continue to hail the white male subject as the normative citizen of
democratic debate and discussion. While Habermas believed that people
could participate in the public sphere as if they were equal citizens, this study
points out that gender, race, and class shape *who* speaks about rape in the
public arena and *how* they speak about it.[9] Further, television rape narratives
replicate the focus on the unified modern subject characteristic of the majority of feminist theories on the topic. Although television programming may
have become sensitized to the different ways in which gender mediates the
experience of rape, it continues to present the white experience as universal.
When race is introduced, television narratives often resort to stereotypes and
fail to highlight the ways in which race and gender intersect to produce interlocking systems of domination.

The analysis shows that television should not be conceived of as constituting a monolithic public sphere; the different genres enable many public
spheres, some counter public spheres, which are key to democratic community formation. Also, the analysis reveals that "irrational" subjects such as
rape cannot be discussed only within the contours of rational-critical debate.
Genres that promote feminine modes of participation and discussion and
foreground the subjective experience of sexual violence advance new knowledges about the phenomenon. Discourses of subjective experience alert us to
the ways in which identity issues, particularly inequalities in status, shape
deliberative practices.

1

Television and Theories
of the Public Sphere

If you're not on television, you are nobody.
—Suzanne Stone, *To Die For*

The statement in the epigraph is uttered in the movie *To Die For* by the protagonist who hopes to be a television star. She enters the field with no obvious training, but her physical appearance allows her first to be a "weather girl" on the local news and then a news anchor. The movie underscores the power of nomination bestowed on television: the medium does not just recognize individuals and events but also endows them with cultural significance and legitimacy. An accompanying, and perhaps an overpowering, subtext is the disdain expressed toward television as a shallow, superficial, inauthentic medium of communication. This double theme has been repeated in other Hollywood movies and even in television programming. Commonsense understandings of the medium and of the scholarship conducted on it shuttle between rationalizing the cultural authority of television and condemning its ability to trivialize "serious" issues. Nevertheless, all agree that television representational practices have a significant structuring influence on our everyday lives.

In his seminal work *Imagined Communities*, Benedict Anderson theorized that print-capitalism was a key element in the formation of the nation as imagined community; print media allowed people to share affective bonds with those they had never encountered and thereby engendered a communal sensibility.[1] While there have been no explicit studies that theorize the ways in which the technology of television has sustained and altered the concept of imagined community, numerous scholars have pointed out the medium's role in constituting shared imaginations.[2] They have attested to the power of its visual elements, the ability of the medium to seemingly transport viewers. Television provides a "window out to the world and into the home," and in so doing, it informs people's conceptions of the private sphere and their modes of engagement with the community. Television programming represents a "dramatisation of consciousness," Raymond Williams asserts. Its programs produce a flow that attempts to link viewers.[3] In this book I explore not just the real and imagined communities that television enables, but I specifically interrogate the ways in which the medium can facilitate democratic community formations. In this chapter, I underscore theories that help inscribe television's role in this democratic project. I also point out why rape becomes a useful site to intervene in this arena, one that highlights the ways in which television programming mobilizes gendered and racialized bodies (men, women, white, and nonwhite) and inscribes them within democratic communities. The double theme that I have already referred to, television's capacity to bestow social legitimacy and to trivialize issues, is a key consideration as I outline the need to include the medium in discussions of contemporary democratic formations.

DEMOCRATIC SUBJECTS

In the United States, television's relationship with women has been complex and problematic. Feminist scholars in particular have pointed out that television, like other mass media, has targeted the female viewer as the primary consumer for the household and hence the key source of revenue for the industry.[4] These studies point out that the medium has facilitated the formation of a particular imagined community, one that allocates specific roles for women and the feminine. Examining the historical moment of television's arrival into the American household, diverse scholars have pointed out that the apparatus reconfigured the domestic space. Until recently, television programming reproduced the ideological separation of the public and private realms, firmly positioning the home as the space of femininity and leisure and the public world as a place of masculinity and work.[5] Arguing that television solicits a gendered viewer, feminist scholars have interrogated consistently the medium's relationship to women's everyday lives. They have teased out the connections between television programs and the larger social and cultural milieu in which the programs are viewed. In television's representational practices, women's bodies have borne the burdens of the entire body politic, these scholars argue. My interest in this book lies in tracing how television programming solicits (white and nonwhite) women as subjects of democratic communities. I do not just underscore the gendered nature of the imagined communities facilitated by television but specifically explore where women fit into the democratic debates and discussions enabled by its programming.

Informed by critical race theories, other scholars have pointed out that the medium has helped reproduce and naturalize stereotypes about racial difference yet also has provided a space within which identity politics can be reconfigured. Rather than simply condemn the negative images of race that are presented, these scholars have paid attention to the cultural politics enabled by television programming, the ways in which the U.S. racial order is constructed, reproduced, and challenged. For instance, Herman Gray argues that television is both a "resource and a site in which blackness as a cultural sign is produced, circulated, and enacted."[6] These scholars, like many feminists, point out that race cannot be separated from issues concerning gender; they should be seen as intersecting categories. Avtar Brah succinctly states that "it is crucial to make explicit that racism is always a gendered phenomenon. . . . Not only are men and women from one racialized group differentiated from their counterparts in another racialized group, but the male from a subordinate group may be racialized through the attribution of 'feminine' qualities, or the female may be represented as embodying 'male' qualities."[7] Impelled by these concerns, I examine how racialized and gendered people are addressed in television programming. I highlight the specific locations allocated to gender- and race-based identities within the social order and the body politic.

Analyzing television representational practices, cultural studies scholars attest to the medium's structuring influence. For instance, in their recent ethnographic study, Andrea Press and Elizabeth Cole illustrated how women's attitudes toward abortion are shaped by television programs. They argue that television is an active participant "in our social conversations about political and cultural matters, influencing our ideas, opinions, and values."[8] The women's voices they document highlight the links between television programming, community, and politics. A more explicit articulation of the medium's significance to society can be found in the normative principles enshrined in television industry regulations. I am referring here to the idea of the "public good" that television programming is supposed to serve. Since the advent of radio, broadcasting regulations in the United States have proclaimed that the airwaves belong to the public and that all electronic mass media are expected to serve the public interest.[9] This concept also is key to theories of democracy, where it is assumed that the media will serve as the knowledge brokers of society, providing citizens with all of the materials necessary to make informed choices. These expectations go beyond the assertions made by cultural studies scholars. Indeed, they function as prescriptive guidelines for the maintenance of democratic societies. By teasing out the connections between individual programs, community, and politics, I explore the ways in which television imaging practices could facilitate democratic participation in a manner that encompasses marginalized groups and ideas.

It is now commonplace to acknowledge that democratic formations have traditionally been the domain of men and that theories of democracy have been formulated around the white male as the universal subject.[10] Women and racialized subjects have not been central to these theories; they are marked as different. Today, institutional processes of democracy, such as elections, include women and others who historically were rendered absent. My analysis in this book explores the specific ways in which these "different" subjects are incorporated into television representational practices. Through this examination I foreground the location ascribed to differences in the democratic formations that are facilitated by television programming. I do not evaluate the medium's ability to provide information but instead focus on the kinds of democratic debates about difference that the programming can facilitate. As Stuart Hall said in another context, "Because there are many different and conflicting ways in which meaning about the world can be constructed, it matters profoundly what and who gets represented, *what* and *who* regularly and routinely gets left out, and *how* things, people, events, relationships are represented."[11] The analysis conducted in this book does not focus on the quantity of information that television programming provides. Instead, it examines the nature of debate that contemporary network television facilitates about one topic: rape.

CENTERING WOMEN AND RACE

Since at least the 1970s, feminists have revealed that rape is not an individual problem but one that belongs to the public realm and requires structural explanations. Statistics gathered by state institutions and scholars substantiate the prevalence of this crime. However, only after repeated and insistent demands made by the women's movement has society been willing to acknowledge that this issue is not just a crime but one that highlights the social and material conditions of women's lives. Scholars have pointed out that although men are subjected to rape, women continue to be the predominant victims, and above all, the fear of sexual assault structures most women's everyday lives. I elaborate on these ideas in the next chapter, but I introduce them here to point out the significance of examining television rape narratives. Analyzing the ways in which this issue is imaged in television will provide us with insights into the position assigned to women in the community the medium serves. As I have already mentioned in the Introduction, the issue of rape in the United States is deeply embedded in cultural ideas of racial difference. Rape thus provides an excellent site from which to examine television's capacity to facilitate democratic processes of debate and discussion about gender and race. Rape narratives allow us to examine where women and issues pertaining to women fit into our imagined democratic communities. In this book, rape serves as the site through which to evaluate the structuring influence of television programs on social understandings of women, sexual violence, and racial difference.

This book examines rape narratives across various genres of television programming, thus with a twofold purpose. The first is to analyze the social understandings about gender, race, and sexuality that television rape narratives encode. As numerous scholars have illustrated, television provides us with texts of the here and now, texts that emanate from the ideological center of society.[12] I examine television as a site where race- and gender-based discourses are produced, contested, and erased. The rape narratives I analyze allow me to foreground the historical and social factors that shape contemporary conceptions of sexual assault, the multiple intersections of race and gender embedded in our understandings of sexual violence, and more generally how the category of race inflects cultural understandings of masculinity and femininity. The second purpose of this project is to evaluate the range of information about rape—and, by extension, about gender and race—that various genres of television programming provide viewers. Examining a single topic across genres permits an assessment of the type of program or combination of programs that best serves the democratic enterprise of fostering debates and discussions that are inclusive of differences.

The analysis in the following chapters illustrates the complex manner in which television rape narratives propel the female body into the public arena. The presence of this topic on television and the centrality of the female subject within it are inherently destabilizing of the social order; together they contribute to an interrogation of previously established boundaries of the public. The topic of rape allows me to foreground as well the intimate connections between (racialized) sexuality and citizenship.

A primary assumption underlying this analysis is that the ways in which we understand the terms *feminine/masculine* or *white/nonwhite* and the ways in which we use them are socially constructed. These words neither signify genetically determined properties that can be easily pinned down, nor are they binary categories. Instead, the meanings attached to these complex categories are constantly in flux, differing across cultures and time. Their significance is dependent on social, political, and economic factors, and often meaning is derived from the context in which these words are used. Hence the meanings ascribed to them are relationally derived and subject to debate. Such a postulate about the culturally constituted significance of gender and race theorizes that the influence of biological differences and indeed sexuality itself is constructed over time through discourse. I elaborate on this concept in my chapters on the analysis of specific television narratives.

This chapter focuses on the role assigned to television in democratic societies and locates the structuring framework for my analysis and arguments. I situate this chapter within broad narratives of democracy and the specific roles they assign to the media. My discussion centers on Jürgen Habermas's conceptualization of the public sphere and the kinds of debates it has invigorated among media scholars. Next the chapter traces feminist scholarship that has drawn attention to the ideological nature of the public/private divide inherent in these understandings of the public sphere. Feminist and critical race theories have necessitated an examination of the normative subject of the public sphere and have drawn attention to the exclusions and marginalizations that underpin definitions of democratic participation. They facilitate a connection between the ways in which identity issues, particularly inequalities in social status, shape public deliberative processes. These interventions have endowed a racial and gendered identity to the public sphere. The chapter ends with suggestions that would make the narrative of democracy more inclusive of differences.

DEMOCRACY AND THE SUBTEXT OF COMMUNICATION

In general, democracy is interpreted as a form of government in which all citizens participate actively in decision making and in assisting with the process of governance. Most contemporary references to democracy trace their antecedents to Athens; discussions and debates in the Athenian marketplace are held up as exemplars of democratic practice.[13] The evocative rhetoric surrounding this concept embodies many contemporary desires for the good society. In his remarkable book *Keywords,* Raymond Williams provides a historical outline of the changing meanings of the term *democracy,* which has been always polyvalent, depending on different interpretations of the words "people" and "rule."[14] Tracing an abridged history of the word, he reveals that until the nineteenth century, democracy was considered an unfavorable condition, primarily associated with negative connotations. Contemporary definitions, connoting a benign, popular collective rule, are at some distance from these earlier understandings.

A recurring leitmotif among various theories of democracy is the importance accorded to communication. Diverse theorists have emphasized the pivotal role that communication plays in maintaining an active, participating democracy. They contend that the dynamics of democracy are intimately linked to the practices of communication; they allow citizens to make well-informed electoral choices. The mass media, in particular, are vested with the responsibility of providing citizens with all of the information they need about specific issues. In addition, the media are expected to serve as a two-way channel of communication between the state and citizens; they are to inform the public about the state's activities and at the same time convey citizens' opinions to the state. Despite these normative expectations, as John Keane points out, the media's role in modern democracies has become equivalent to the transmission of decisions from the governors to the governed.[15]

Working within a definition of democracy that centers on the electoral process, scholars such as Walter Lippmann, have lamented over the media's inability to perform the instrumental function of transmitting information about state activities. He argues in *The Phantom Public* (1927) that mass media provide only partial and often distorted information, affecting the public's ability to effect well-informed electoral choices. Writing an epitaph for the public, Lippmann recommends abandoning the ideology of popular democracy in favor of a democratic elitism. Other scholars, notably John Dewey and C. Wright Mills, have provided a more expansive definition of democracy as a way of life, a process of building a community by sharing ideas and making decisions together, and not just as a political practice.[16] Scholars examining the media from a cultural studies perspective have found this particular formulation a useful way to theorize the role of the media in democratic societies. They have examined both news/information and entertainment/fiction as central elements in establishing a democratic community.[17] In particular, television, more than any other medium, "has gained a prominent position" within such a configuration, Peter Dahlgren argues.[18]

In this book I want to hold onto the urgency that these writers evoke when underscoring the media's role in the democratic project. I simultaneously want to shift the angle of vision by interrogating the specific ways in which gendered and racialized subjects are included in the democratic project through representational practices.

Modern Agora

While cultural studies scholars have underscored the ways in which television and other mass media shape our sense of the world around us, it is Jürgen Habermas who has most explicitly made the connection between the media and democratic community formations. In the corpus of his work, he has forwarded a discursive model of democratic society, one where communication is central to maintaining and sustaining democracy. These ideas were introduced in *The Structural Transformation of the Public Sphere* and later expanded on in his other works, particularly in *Inclusion of the Other* and *Between Facts and Norms*.[19] Working across disciplines, Habermas traces the historical circumstances under which the liberal public sphere, an autonomous arena of debate and discussion, came into being.[20] He defines the public sphere as a forum where people meet as equals and debate issues of common concern in a rational-critical manner and then guide the state.

Written originally in 1969 but translated into English only in 1989, *The Structural Transformation of the Public Sphere* traces the rise and fall of the bourgeois public sphere and is limited to a feature characteristic of a specific epoch. Habermas contends that the bourgeois public sphere emerged in the late seventeenth century at the historical moment when the growth of capitalism transformed the relations between the state and civil society.[21] It developed as the space between government and society, an autonomous forum where individuals participate in the making, exchange, and mobilization of political opinion. It is conceptually different from the state and the official economy; its participants assemble to discuss matters of common interest, to criticize the state, and to make the state accountable to the citizenry. The public sphere is essential to representative democracy since it is an area where private individuals exercised formal and informal control over the state—formal control through the election of government and informal control through the pressure of public opinion.[22]

Tracing the seventeenth-century institutional location of the public sphere, Habermas identifies tea shops in England and literary salons in Europe as its original sites.[23] Here individuals outside of government evaluated state activities with a critical eye and functioned as a counterweight to the state. As in the ancient Greek city-states, the people who participated in the seventeenth-century democratic process were circumscribed within a very narrow segment of the populace. Only those who had access to specific cultural products—books, journals, plays—could participate in "democratic" debate and articulate the concerns of society. Houston Baker describes it as "an associational life of male property owners gathered to exchange rational arguments and critical opinions shaped and mirrored by novels and the press."[24] Habermas acknowledges that the bourgeois public sphere was elitist and included only the literate. He recognizes its exclusionary and ideological character, but he does not retreat from promoting its norms as the constitutive basis for democratic participation.

In the second half of this narrative, Habermas accords the newly emerging newspapers the status of enabling the public sphere, replacing tea shops and literary salons. The development of capitalism and of improved printing technologies facilitated, however, the transformation of the press into the mass media. Newspapers were now accessible to non-elite sections of society, and these groups could now participate in democratic formations. Originally, according to Habermas, newspapers served as a forum for rational-critical debate and discussion. Soon the demands of profit making took over, and newspapers became a mass medium: purveyors of information and entertainment for a larger audience. The expansion of the public sphere, Habermas contends, was accompanied by a degeneration in the quality of debate. It was no longer governed by rational-critical arguments. Further, with the rise of consumer culture, the emergence of a mass media governed by the logic of the market, and the institution of the welfare state in the nineteenth century, relations between the state and society became intertwined. The distinctions between civil society and the state became blurred. With the loss of this critical boundary marker, the public sphere as an autonomous forum becomes untenable. This blurring of boundaries can be witnessed in the changed role of the media: they no longer transmit information and disseminate discourses among participants in a larger public body but have become sites for the consumption of information. Habermas contends that the media have failed in their function of facilitating democratic debate and are primarily responsible for the debilitated version of democracy that currently prevails, one marked by a culture-consuming rather than a culture-debating public.

Habermas's formulation of democracy as a function of communication rather than institutional structures has reinvigorated the debate about the role of the media in society.[25] Scholars have acclaimed Habermas's historical analysis and his formulation of an enabling model of democratic society. At the same time, they have been critical of the assumptions that underlie his formulation of the bourgeois public sphere. Habermas is concerned primarily with the rise and decline of a historically specific and limited form of the public sphere; he fails to critically scrutinize the assumptions of his model, these scholars believe. Most of the criticisms leveled against his conceptualization can be divided broadly into three categories: its utopian underpinnings; its specific gender-, race-, and class-based exclusions; and Habermas's reliance on a monolithic construct. In what follows, I explore first the exclusions that are constitutive to the liberal public sphere, then the historical rebuttals to Habermas's conceptualization, and finally suggestions for redefining this concept.

UTOPIAN CONSTRUCT

Habermas defines the bourgeois public sphere as an autonomous forum where people meet *as if* they are equals and debate issues of common concern in a rational-critical manner. He contends that critically reasoned argument is more important than the identities and status of participants. Michael Schudson and Nancy Fraser, among others, believe that such a version of the public sphere is utopian. They contend that the idea of a free discursive space where people can participate as though they were equals is an enabling account that can be achieved only by obscuring material inequalities and political antagonisms among participants. Habermas may present the public sphere in a rhetoric of accessibility, but it is actually constituted by a number of significant exclusions. He assumes that the public sphere is or can be a space of zero-degree culture; interlocutors are expected to set aside characteristics such as differences in status and to speak to one another as if they were social and economic peers. Fraser reminds us that social inequalities taint deliberative practices, but because he brackets out power and interest, Habermas is able to posit the bourgeois model as the ideal public sphere. Rita Felski concurs that the bourgeois public sphere is blind to the actual and material conditions that render its own existence possible; it holds fast to the idea that the people are adequately represented by the male, property-owning public. These critics cast the bourgeois public sphere as utopian, because it is structured by issues of power and inequality that remain unaccounted.[26]

In the analysis that follows, I argue that television representations of rape, gender, and race underscore the specific modalities through which identity issues shape who is included in the public domain, how they are presented, and with what consequences. This aspect of the book highlights the blind spots that underpin the conceptualization of the public sphere.

Approaching the utopian elements from a different perspective, Michael Schudson questions the applicability of Habermas's bourgeois model to the United States. He argues that there exists no historical evidence suggesting participation in democratic debate and discussion was any different in an America of the past than it is today.[27] Records reveal that people attended public rallies and debates, but there is no trace of what people attended to during these meetings. American politics and culture, Schudson insists, have not declined from some golden age in the past. Further, he observes that, unlike the Habermasian model, the American press has never served as an autonomous vehicle of political conversation; the colonial press "was not a permanent source of political conversation; its politicization was a sometime thing," he contends. In this book I examine the possibilities for discussion television programming makes available; I evaluate the claims to representation that are built into television narratives.

REDEFINING THE PUBLIC SPHERE

Perhaps feminist scholars have made the most sustained and far-reaching criticisms of Habermas's formulation. These have stemmed from two main concerns: the masculine ideological underpinnings of the public sphere and the physical exclusion of women from it. The two issues are related, but I am separating them for clarity. These criticisms that point out the masculinist bias center on the public/private divide, the privileging of rational-critical debate over other modes of communication, and the reliance on an autonomous sphere.

As feminists have done in their critique of the social order, they have taken exception to Habermas's reliance on a rigid public/private distinction. The bourgeois public sphere Habermas traces rests on an assumption that social activities can be divided neatly, belonging to either the private realm or to the state, and that the debate in the autonomous public sphere only deals with issues pertaining to the state. Several scholars, particularly feminists, have found this critical divide untenable. Working from a range of disciplines such as sociology, political science, and philosophy, feminists have pointed out the centrality of the public/private split to their disciplines and have contested the binary. Pointing out the arbitrary and artificial nature of the demarcation, these scholars have underscored how gender as a category remains consistently unproblematized in theories of democracy. In political science, the public/private split has been used to seal women's experiences and participation wholly into the private sphere, while men's activities are allowed to straddle the two spheres. In traditional definitions of political engagement, which tend to focus on the process of participating in elections, women always remain on the periphery, argue Janet Siltanen and Michelle Stanworth. Such a conceptualization of democracy derives from traditions of thought that are, in both their theoretical and empirical dimensions, rooted in masculine experience, they add.

Echoing this sentiment, Eva Gamarnikow and others observe that in sociology and political science the public realm is privileged and constructed as the exclusive domain of male and masculine activities, while family life is relegated to the private sphere.[28] They argue that the public/private split becomes a metaphor for the social patterning of gender and throws into sharp relief the power relationships in society. It is assumed that the public/private split is not only coincident with gender but also that the division directly affects only women's, not men's, consciousness.

Like other political science theorists, Habermas constructs the public-private divide as a place marker that designates issues as being either relevant or irrelevant to the state. In such a construction, issues relating to the family are categorized as belonging to the private realm and hence irrelevant to democratic society. Such a definition of the public realm limits the number of issues that can be included under the purview of democratic practice, feminists have argued.[29] The bipolar public/private structure is an arbitrary, cultural construct that not only limits the range and content of issues included in the public arena, it also reproduces a gendered discourse of domination, they contend. Primarily, they argue that the public sphere should be an arena of collective self-determination. Its boundaries should be set by the participants who determine what constitutes the common concern. There can be no a priori boundaries to the public sphere. Issues of identity or of the family cannot be bracketed from discussion.[30] A central argument that these critics put forth is that the public/private distinction rests on the idealized representation of the universal citizen as an autonomous (white) male.

Cautioning against a totalizing assumption that all women and women's issues have been limited to the private domain, feminists who engage in issues pertaining to women of color point out that the categories of public and private "are not simply gendered categories, they are racialized categories as well." Examining the sexual violence experienced by black women, Fraser points out that in the United States, "historically, blacks have been denied privacy in the sense of domesticity. . . . At the same time, they have lacked the public standing to claim state protection against abuse, whether suffered at home or at work."[31] In the African-American community and for other racial minorities there is no private sphere protected from state intervention. Social workers, the police, the legal system, and other state agencies intervene on a scale that does not permit a private familial world insulated from the state.[32] These scholars argue that theories of the public sphere, whether feminist or not, should take into account the ways in which race and gender intersect to produce multivalent and shifting definitions of the private and public domains.

A corollary to these arguments of the public/private split critiques another aspect of Habermas's formulation of the bourgeois public sphere: his assumption that the public and private realms are independent of each other. Several scholars, including feminists, have contested this supposition. They argue that the fault line separating the two realms is leaky. Their central argument is that relations inside of the family and household are shaped by public policies, just as conversely relations in the workplace and in politics are molded by inequalities of sexual power. Carole Pateman explains succinctly that "the private sphere . . . underpins the public world of politics; what happens in one shapes and constrains what is likely to occur in the other."[33] The feminist movement in the United States has repeatedly asserted this interdependence of the spheres and has encapsulated the idea in the slogan, "The personal is the political." As Carol Smart and Barry Smart observe, the women's movement has helped redefine our understandings of several "private" problems: these problems are not the result of individual psychologies or a result only of personal circumstances. Instead, the women's movement has illustrated that these problems are located clearly in the public sphere.[34] Ignoring this symbiotic relationship only legitimizes a repressive ideology, they argue. As Seyla Benhabib remarks:

> Any theory of the public . . . presupposes a distinction between the public and the private. These are the terms of a binary opposition. What the women's movement and feminist theories in the last two decades have shown, however, is that traditional modes of drawing this distinction have been part of a discourse of domination that legitimizes women's oppression and exploitation in the private realm.[35]

The dichotomization of social issues that characterizes Habermas's definition of the public sphere only helps remarginalize concerns that are of immediate relevance to women. Indeed, the bourgeois public sphere that Habermas presents as an exemplar is based on a rigid public/private split, and the exclusion of women's concerns serves as the very precondition and possibility of democratic community, these scholars argue. Within Habermas's definition of the public sphere, issues such as rape, sexual violence, and wife battery cannot be countenanced as "public" concerns. These phenomena are marked as individual problems that are not amenable to rational discussion and therefore relegated to the private realm. His conceptualization fails to consider how issues in the public realm that foster the disparity in gendered power and social location enable such instances of private male domination.

Reconceptualizing some of the structuring terms of democratic theories, feminists insist that politics comes into play wherever elements of social life are contingent; it is an activity that may take individual or collective forms centered around a struggle over power. Power, on the other hand, is defined as the capacity to perpetuate or transform a given order; it is structured by asymmetrical access to resources and the ability to mobilize them. Political struggles are, therefore, both constituted by and the result of the organization of relations of "public" and "private" life. Conventional analyses of gender and politics ignore the extent to which the private domain is implicated in the political process. The private world—the world of personal relations and marriage, of friendships and family, of domestic routine and child care—is, as feminists have persuasively demonstrated time and time again, political as well as personal. Understanding the relationship between public and private is itself a political issue, they argue. Such a reformulation of both politics and the public and private realms allows us to introduce the issue of rape or sexual violence in general as a concern that belongs to the "public" agenda.

The public-private distinction has allowed Habermas to ignore the gendered and racialized nature of the bourgeois public sphere and to marginalize the impact of identity politics. Primarily, he assumes that social equality is not a necessary social condition for democracy. According to Fraser, Habermas believes that issues of culture and identity do not influence a person's ability to participate in the public sphere.

Notwithstanding Habermas's caveats, the public sphere indeed involves identity, but does so with more emphasis on actions and their consequences rather than on the nature or characteristics of the actors. Feminist research has shown how issues belonging to the so-called private realm are shaped by a battery of policies in the public arena, and it also has illustrated how policies relating to the private arena limit an individual's ability to participate in the public sphere. Gender, race, and class shape the ways in which individuals can participate in deliberative processes and cannot be bracketed out.

Numerous scholars also have found problematic Habermas's characterization of rational-critical debate as the only valid mode of participation in the public sphere. Interrogating the assumptions that this term encompasses, critics have pointed out that Habermas fails to define rational-critical debate and seems to uncritically assume a mode of thought characteristic of the Enlightenment. This unproblematized and crucial reliance on rational-critical debate, scholars argue, has resulted in Habermas locating the nascent newspaper of the eighteenth century as the repository of the public sphere and hence of all of the values required for democratic participation. Joan Landes, Mary Ryan, and Susan Herbst point out that Habermas's reliance on rational-critical debate privileges masculine modes of talking and locates other modes of discursive participation in the realm of the "private." Similarly, Susan Bourque and Jean Grossholtz argue that, "Rational political behavior is defined by the male pattern: it is by definition the expression of male values, and irrationality is by definition the expression of female values."[36]

In her examination of the French Revolution, Joan Landes traces the concurrent development of an austere, masculine speech with the bourgeois public sphere. At the same moment that women and groups associated with the body (primarily racialized subjects) were excluded from political participation, a rhetorical mode that excludes the body, affect and desire also came to be dominant within the public arena. Habermas privileges this problem-solving discourse in the public sphere, equating abstract modes of speech with citizenship. Iris M. Young elaborates, "By assuming that reason stands opposed to desire, affectivity, and the body, the civic public must exclude bodily and affective aspects of human existence."[37] Similarly, Laura Kipnis contends that the very substance of the bourgeois subject is constructed through sanitized modes of address.[38]

So far I have outlined the conceptual blind spots in Habermas's formulation of the public sphere. These arise primarily from his reliance on categories that assume the (property-owning) white male as the normative citizen. These assumptions have significant effects; primarily, they shape the type of evidence that Habermas gathers to provide his account of the bourgeois public sphere. I now summarize some of the arguments that feminist historians have made about the validity of Habermas's historical subject.

HISTORICAL ALTERNATIVES

In *The Structural Transformation of the Public Sphere*, and in his later writings, Habermas repeatedly points out the physical exclusion of women from the public sphere. Nevertheless, he maintains the validity of his formulation and does not believe that the occlusions destabilize his theory.

Addressing issues inherent to the public/private split, feminist historiography has drawn attention to the gendered nature of the public sphere. Feminist historians point out that Habermas's account of the bourgeois public sphere relies on records that were framed by a male perspective, which tended to elide women's presence in the public sphere. Feminist reconsiderations of historical social formations reveal that women shaped and influenced public discourse often using idioms of motherhood and domesticity, language that is identified with the domestic sphere. For instance, Mary Ryan argues that nineteenth-century voluntary associations provided U.S. women access to

political participation. Examining the contributions that these women's organizations made to public discourse, she concludes that traditional historical
accounts of democratic political process rest on a class- and gender-biased
notion of the public sphere, one that privileges the bourgeois public's claim
to be the public.[39]

Similarly, Susan Herbst examines the ways in which European women
participated in the public sphere of the late eighteenth century.[40] Her analysis centers on the activities of women pamphleteers in English politics, the
ways in which women shaped and influenced the proceedings of the French
literary salon, and American women's participation in the Civil War. Underscoring the gaps and absences in Habermas's narrative, Herbst argues that
women played a key role in shaping public discourse, although their contributions remained unacknowledged. Both Ryan and Herbst conclude that the
bourgeois public sphere is a masculine ideological construct that served to
legitimate an emergent form of class rule. In theorizing the public sphere,
Habermas failed to take into consideration the gendered nature of his basic
premises. He privileges masculine sites of political participation and locates
other modes within the realm of the private.

Tracing the history of women's participation in the French Revolution,
Landes points out as well that it is not just the public sphere but also the discourse of modern rights and republican virtues that exclude women. She
argues that Habermas's theory, with its reliance on Enlightenment rationality,
has been organized around a male norm and pays insufficient attention to the
specificity of women's lives and experiences. "The equation of modernity with
particular public and institutional structures governed by men has led to an
almost total elision of the lives, concerns, and perspectives of women."[41]

The versions of history offered by Habermas and feminist historiogra-
phers are affected significantly by the gender of their normative subject. Similarly, critical race theorists have pointed out that the normative subject of the
public sphere tends to be the white male. Warren Montag examines the diary
of an eighteenth-century Scotswoman to point out that the universal subject
of the public sphere is assumed to be not just male but also white. In Enlightenment discourses, nonwhites oscillated between being characterized as non-
human and human. This sensibility is reflected in the bourgeois public sphere
as well. The Black Public Sphere Collective has formulated a wide-ranging
criticism of the racial blind spots that mark Habermas's formulation and has
offered ways to conceive a public sphere that is more inclusive of differences.
Baker concludes that "the idea of the bourgeois public sphere as one com-
pelled by reason alone, free of class and status distinctions and resolutely challenging state authority, is tremendously attractive. Even in a discussion of

Habermas's model, however, it is obvious that the idea of such an apparatus is far more compelling than its shadowy exclusive manifestation in history."[42] Both feminists and critical race theorists draw attention to the rhetorical strategies that permit the white male to appear as the bodiless, normative participant of the public sphere. They point out that whether the normative subject is assumed to be male or female, white or nonwhite, has important consequences for the kind of narrative that unfolds. Gender and race affect the factual content of historical knowledge, what is included and what gets left out. Rather than examining the public sphere as a monolithic construct, a multiplicity of competing and overlapping public spheres, the historical evidence that these scholars provide reveals the usefulness of conceptualizing the public sphere in plural. I return to this idea in the last section of this chapter.

GENDER AND THE MEDIA

Critics of Habermas have sought to include in the public sphere discussions about issues of common concern that normally would not be classified as constituting rational-critical debate. In addition, feminists and critical race theorists have pointed out that dialogues and fragmented, repetitious narratives constitute an engendered form of knowledge building, which should be included in theories of the public sphere.

These reformulations have immediate consequences for scholars examining television. They dilute the focus on the news and permit an extension of the public sphere to other products and channels of participation. Various television genres may serve different functions, but together they shape our perceptions of the world around us. News, talk shows, and entertainment programs are not likely to represent an event or to talk about it in the same way; each genre highlights different aspects, but all contribute to our understanding of events.[43]

For instance, James Curran argues that traditional perspectives of the media overstate the rationality of public discourse. Entertainment usually is omitted because it does not conform to a classic liberal conception of rational exchange. Curran contends that media entertainment is one means by which people engage at an intuitive and expressive level in a public dialogue about the direction of society. Entertainment, he suggests, should be seen as an integral component of the media's informational role. It can provide a way of exploring, experimenting with, and expressing a concept of self in relation to others. Media fiction and other products also provide a way of mapping and interpreting society.[44] This need to include entertainment and fiction within the realm of the media's informational capacity has been highlighted by numerous other scholars, feminist and otherwise.

Lisa McLaughlin, in her study of the O. J. Simpson trial, reveals how "media spectacles" are able to address the issue of difference. She argues that the Habermasian model, with its reliance on rational-critical debate, is unable to adequately account for difference as a subject of debate. Rather than condemn media spectacles, she points out that television coverage of the O. J. Simpson case facilitated a wide-ranging debate about the legal system and legal practices. Further, the case raised awareness, however briefly, about domestic violence.[45] Her study points out that even seemingly "irrational" spectacles are able to facilitate debate and discussion and contribute to citizenship. The analysis in this book is informed by such an examination of media spectacles, as sites that could potentially address difference.

Scholars such as Ien Ang, Tony Bennett, and Janice Radway, among others, have analyzed media products traditionally classified as fiction to reveal that these texts too, like the news, engage in a discussion of social, cultural, and political issues. Jane Feuer and Ellen Seiter, for example, argue that soap operas and prime-time melodramas such as *Dallas* and *Dynasty* are potentially emancipatory sites for debate and discussion. These theorists have sought to free the public sphere from a limited definition of rational-critical debate and, by extension, from the news. Each suggests that our understandings of events are shaped by numerous media products, even those that do not fall under the information genre.[46] More recently, focusing on prime-time entertainment programs, Andrea Press and Elizabeth Cole point out that women's stances about abortion and their community are shaped by television images. In their ethnographic study, they reveal that women's responses are multivalent, but that the shared feature is the significant role television images have on cultural conversations.[47]

This book extends this notion and argues that genres outside of the news—prime-time entertainment programs and daytime talk shows—are often more useful sites for debate and discussion of race, gender, and sexuality than are news programs. I argue that our diverse understandings of these complex categories cannot be completely characterized in rational discourse. For instance, when the news attempts to provide an "objective" account of events relating to these categories, it ends up reproducing bipolarized hegemonic understandings. This happens primarily because reporters rely on institutional voices, such as the police or representatives of government. We rarely hear peoples' interpretations of events and categories. Instead, through the institutional voices, we hear definitions that emerge from the ideological center of society. Further, in the interests of objectivity and balanced journalism, reporters tend to juxtapose institutional voices with more institutional voices, ones that counter the others' positions.

This positioning of two dramatically opposed and always contrary views does not reflect the multilayered understandings that comprise the social understandings of issues. Neither does this discourse depict the cultural contestation and negotiation that at any historical moment characterize social understandings of rape, gender, and race. Further, news discourses rarely make explicit the social, historical, and cultural myths that structure contemporary understandings of the terms. Fictional programs and daytime talk shows at least hint at these historical underpinnings. Besides, with their partially open-ended structure, they provide the audience with a greater latitude in accepting or rejecting the understandings promoted by their narratives. In general, we hear the same event described from multiple perspectives in noninformation genres; these perspectives are articulated by a variety of individuals, each of whom is differently located on the social landscape by class, race, gender, or religious affiliation. These two elements—the lack of authoritative closure to the narrative and the multiple interpretations of any event—allow fictional genres to reveal some of the complex ways in which contemporary understandings of culturally constructed categories instantiate social, historical understandings. Fictional programs are able to introduce into the public arena issues pertaining to the body, affect, and desire. The news, on the other hand, relying on official sources of information, can only re-produce dominant understandings of cultural categories; it is unable to include voices from the margins that may provide a radical departure from hegemonic perspectives.

In conceptualizing non-news genres as facilitating better democratic debate and discussion of gender and race, feminist reconsiderations have been particularly useful to this project. These women-centered critiques reveal how gender and race remain problematic categories in current definitions of popular power. They suggest how cultural categories that shape identity are a necessary part of the public sphere and need to be redefined through debate and discussion.[48]

In general, feminists have sought to expose the foundations of a theory of democracy that not only marginalizes but often erases and occludes women's concerns (i.e., issues of the private realm) from the notion of democratic community altogether. Even as feminists have trenchantly criticized Habermas, they also have pointed out that aspects of his formulation can be used to theorize a more emancipatory democratic politics. They have argued that his discursive definition of the public sphere frees politics from the iron grasp of the state, which has effectively defined the public in masculine terms. They have contended that Habermas's enunciation of the public sphere is formulated in such a magnanimous way that female subjects and their opinions are a legitimate part of the common good. Rather than abandon the idea of democracy itself as an inherently exclusive enterprise, feminists have sought to reinscribe the term and to redeploy it so that issues that have been traditionally erased from the terms of participation in democratic debate and discussion are now instantiated in any discussion of community. In line with this approach, feminists reiterate C. Wright Mills' mode of distinguishing between issues that are relevant to a democratic society and those that are not. Mills characterized personal issues as "problems appearing more or less randomly or infrequently and which permit individualistic explanations, and public issues, problems which afflict many people systematically over time and space and therefore require not psychological but social structural explanations."[49] This reformulation brings under the purview of democratic debate issues such as rape that were traditionally considered "private" and not an issue of common concern.

RAPE—A PUBLIC CONCERN

Feminists have revealed that rape is not an individual problem but one that afflicts many people systematically over time and space and requires social structural explanations, hence it is an issue that belongs to the public realm. Statistics gathered by state institutions and scholars substantiate the prevalence of this crime. However, only after repeated and insistent demands made by the women's movement has society been willing to acknowledge that this issue is not just a crime but one that highlights the social and material conditions of women's lives.

Until two decades ago, rape remained a taboo subject for the media, an "always-already" private issue, hence outside of the realm of debate and discussion. While films have consistently thematized rape, in the press and on television, sexual violence appeared rarely until the 1970s. With the impetus provided by the women's movement, the media have started to explore the social, political, and cultural structures that permit such an operation of gendered dominance. If one were to follow Habermas's argument of rational-critical debate and focus on television news, rape remained an invisible subject until the 1980s. If and when issues of rape erupted into the arena of newsworthy items, they were located within the public sphere in disguise, so to speak. References to rape pointed to spectacular instances of violence, to legal transformations, or to social structural changes that helped accommodate rape as a crime of violence; issues of gender politics were always ignored.

If we expand the public sphere to include other genres, however, one sees that since the late 1960s television entertainment has engaged in the issue of rape. Of course, rape often served merely as a titillating subject, but there were instances of more substance, such as in an episode of the cop show *Barney Miller*, which portrayed marital rape, or in *Lou Grant*, where a reporter was raped in the "safe" space of her apartment. These narratives may not have dealt with all of the issues that feminists sought to foreground, and sometimes they reified numerous myths about rape, but at least they put the topic within the realm of the "public" and possibly allowed people to debate and discuss their reactions and understandings of the issue. Further, the two shows cited above contradicted the imagery of rape created in the news; the portrayals conformed to statistics, showing the frequency of acquaintance rapes rarely accompanied by violence. Then, as now, news discourses of rape focused on exceptional cases, or on instances of extreme violence and brutality, so we received a very lopsided version of rape as an event that afflicts few people and as a crime committed by abnormal men.

Like entertainment programs, daytime talk shows as a rule have dealt with issues that are considered "taboo" on the news. Thus rape has been a topic that has been discussed and debated from a variety of perspectives on these programs. In this sense, we can say, television news followed the lead provided by these "non-information" genres and only in the 1980s started to delve into the treacherous arena of gender politics as related to the issue of rape. The news, for the most part, still continues to frame the issue within traditionally acceptable newsworthy terms, say as a sociological feature, political event, or a case involving a celebrity. Rarely does the news deal with the multiple and complex gender politics at which rape directs our attention. These news narratives also hint at, but rarely make explicit, the ways in which race is inevitably imbricated in contemporary discourses of sexuality. It is only by analyzing all of the genres together or, in Williams' words, studying the flow of programs that we can obtain an understanding of rape, gender, race, and sexuality reflecting the complex nature of our meanings for these terms and the frameworks within which we debate and discuss these issues.

RECOVERING SITES OF DEBATE

So far I have pointed out the problematic aspects of Habermas's formulation of the bourgeois public sphere. Feminist and critical race theorists though have cautioned against abandoning the concept and instead call for a broader definition of the public sphere. Historical studies by Ryan, Landes, and

Herbst reveal that even during the eighteenth and nineteenth centuries, the bourgeois public sphere coexisted with several competing publics. Women participated in political activity, but through a series of idioms and communicative modes not recognized as public activity. Geoff Eley points out that the bourgeois public sphere as a "natural" arena of rational-political discourse was founded on a field of contestations. Within it, people vied for space and definition and contested meanings, and in the process some were excluded altogether. These contestations occurred in class-divided societies that were structured by numerous inequalities. The emergence of the bourgeois public sphere reveals the processes by which a hegemonic ideology gained legitimacy. The bourgeois public sphere gained currency because it was comprised of members of the dominant class who could claim intellectual and moral leadership through specific communicative practices.[50]

Rather than deploy the bourgeois public sphere as an ideal we should aspire to replicate, these scholars contend that public participation in governance and decision making can be better understood by conceptualizing multiple, competing public spheres, counter public spheres, where differences are recognized rather than banished. Counter public spheres do not seek a universal rationality, Felski contends. They are directed toward an affirmation of specificity in relation to gender, race, and class.

The women's movement comprises one such counter public sphere. Feminists have used publicity—the media, films, videos, the lecture circuit, and so on—to build a forum where women can withdraw to form a collective identity, and simultaneously they have used communicative networks to point out to the rest of society the specific ways in which patriarchal ideologies are produced and circulated. The feminist public sphere is defined in terms of a shared identity; it does not claim a representative universality. According to Felski, the feminist public sphere serves a dual function. "Internally it generates a gender-specific identity grounded in a consciousness of community and solidarity among women; externally it seeks to convince society of the validity of feminist claims, challenging existing structures of authority through political activity and theoretical critiques."[51]

These scholars argue that the complex interpenetrations of state and society in late capitalism prevent us from postulating an ideal public sphere that can function outside of existing commercial and state institutions and at the same time claim an influential and a representative function as a forum for oppositional activity and debate. Instead they believe that multiple public spheres should be seen as carving out a space for discussion within a social sphere dominated by the logic of the market. Thomas Holt, for instance, believes that black popular culture is a product of the political economy of a global advanced capitalist order, but it has the potential to be a space for critique and transformation of that order.[52]

Within a conceptualization of multiple overlapping public spheres, the media must be conceived of as enabling one of several coexisting public spheres. In the following chapters I argue that conceptualizations of the public sphere should expand to include communicative practices that cannot be described as rational-critical debate. Simultaneously, I point out that television programming is a site that participates in the maintenance of hegemony. Consequently, it becomes crucial that we consider it as facilitating one of competing public spheres. The title of this book refers to this multiplicity of public spheres, in television and in society.

Considering the centrality of the media in the effectiveness of the women's movement, Lisa McLaughlin draws attention to the striking absence of feminist analyses of the media as a public sphere. The media are important actors in the maintenance of hegemony but as the successes of the women's movement testify also are a site where contestatory ideas can be forwarded. This analysis of television rape narratives attempts to counter this "major shortcoming."[53]

The analysis in this book examines only instances of heterosexual rape where females are the victims. This allows me to specify the ability for women's voices to be heard and included in the public arena of debate and discussion. Further, most scholars of the public sphere have identified it as a space that valorizes masculine concepts of rational-critical, objective debate. My study assesses the ability of such a theoretical structure to include a public issue that is defined primarily by feminine characteristics: emotion, pain, and subjective perceptions. Finally, in the United States, understandings of rape are intertwined with the issue of racial difference. This analysis permits as well an evaluation of the public sphere's ability to integrate racialized subjects.

2

The Feminist Subject of Rape

A horrific social stigma accompanies rape in Kosovo, bringing lifelong shame to a woman and her family. It is the biggest problem that rights groups face as they begin to collect information on whether Serbian forces used rape as a premeditated tactic.

—*New York Times*[1]

An Italian court of appeal overturned the conviction of a driving instructor, ruling that it is impossible to rape a woman wearing jeans.

—The Associated Press[2]

These two statements reveal the contradictory ideas that continue to mark the field of rape. People respond with horror and revulsion at the spectacular and routinized use of sexual violence in war zones, whether it is in Rwanda, Bosnia-Herzegovina, or Kosovo, to name just a few instances from the 1990s, calling for legal punitive measures. Nevertheless, in instances of "everyday," individual rape, the Italian court of appeal's ruling reveals the manner in which entrenched attitudes about female sexuality continue to inform legal (and commonsense) understandings of sexual violence.[3] The statements underscore the success that the women's movement in the United States and elsewhere has achieved in raising public consciousness about the crime— international war crimes tribunals have been vested with the responsibility of ensuring that rapists are punished—and its inability to alter attitudes that underpin such behavior. I do not intend to level differences in the ways in which sexual assault is understood in the United States and elsewhere; nevertheless, I do want to mark how the media are able to be critical of certain interpretations of rape when they emerge from "out there" but are reluctant to turn a similarly critical view when covering sexual violence "at home." In this chapter I trace some of the feminist writings that have enabled this change in public awareness about the crime, and I highlight the problematic issues in these theories that could account for the inertia that resists change in individual attitudes.

Since the 1970s, feminist scholarship on rape has resulted in new understandings of sexual violence and the social hierarchies that underpin it. In this chapter I provide an overview of the multiple understandings of rape promoted by different strands of feminist theories, emphasizing those that locate it as a form of violence embedded in interlocking systems of gender, race, and class oppression. The narrative of feminist rape literature that I outline shows that the majority of contemporary understandings emerge from a conceptualization of universal woman, a female counterpart to the modern male subject. Consequently, most feminist theories tend to privilege gender over race. I highlight the exclusions and erasures that are enabled by such a formulation and show how feminist theories can move beyond this impasse.

Necessarily, the field of feminism that I map in this chapter is partial. While I tend to highlight the lacunae, the history of feminist engagement with sexual violence is more complicated. I have tried to provide here a sense of the issues that have been taken up and popularized by the media, primarily explanations for rape that resonate with dominant ideas of individualism, national values, and femininity. As we will see in the next four chapters, this has important consequences for the kinds of rape narratives that prevail on television, as well as its representational practices. The more complex feminist ideas that engage with the intersections of gender, race, class, and other issues of social identity tend to be marginalized. I discuss the consequences of these erasures in the last section of this chapter.

There is no single definition that can encompass the many meanings associated with the word "rape." At different sociohistorical moments, it has signified different things to different people—in ancient civilizations, rape was considered a violation of man's property, and today some would theoretically define all heterosexual intercourse in a patriarchal society to fall under the rubric of nonconsensual sex.[4] Legally, in the United States, while there are variations across jurisdictions, rape is defined as intercourse with force or coercion *and* without consent.

In terms of social definitions, on the one hand, rape is understood as a charge that can be easily made against men but one that is difficult for them to deny. We see this belief echoed in the Italian judge's ruling. In this school of thought, an act is considered rape only if the victim is above reproach and the perpetrator is a psychopathic, armed stranger who forces the woman to have intercourse. The woman should resist the attack actively and must bear the physical marks of resistance. On the other hand, since the 1970s, the U.S. women's movement has attempted to redefine rape as a social problem that reflects inequities in gender relations. In this school of thought, rape is a ritualistic reenactment of the daily patterns of social dominance.[5] Within a patriarchal society, sexual violence is a visible dimension of a more generalized and routinized system of women's oppression. It should be viewed as a behavior pattern derived from societal relationships among women and men, most feminists suggest.

Despite the different definitions, few contest the high incidence of rape in the United States, although there is little agreement on the actual numbers. Figures vary dramatically from 1.5 million to 106,593 rapes per year. According to a 1992 government-sponsored study, *Rape in America*, every 44 seconds a woman is raped in the United States (or 1.3 women are raped every minute). Conducted over a three-year period, the national study revealed that 683,000 adult women were raped in 1990. If women under eighteen and children are included, the number of rape victims would be over 1.5 million annually.[6] These alarming statistics seemed to confirm some of the most dismal portraits painted by feminists. The study also reveals that one in eight women has been raped at some time in her life (12.1 million women in the United States have been raped once in their life); 84 percent of rape victims do not report the crime to the police (only one in six raped women report the crime); rape by strangers is the exception (nearly eight out of ten women know their attackers); overall, 62 percent of all victims were younger than eighteen—29 percent of the victims were younger than eleven, and 32 percent more were between the ages of eleven and seventeen.[7]

The figures cited in this study are six times the number previously estimated by the federal government, and as a result the survey has been critically scrutinized. The FBI's Uniform Crime Report reported 106,593 rapes in 1991, which translates to about one rape every five minutes.[8] Meanwhile, the National Crime Victim Survey reported 171,420 rapes in 1991, which is about one rape every three-and-a-half minutes.[9] The discrepancies in these figures are attributed to the different definitions of rape employed and the validity of data-gathering methods. Further, both the Uniform Crime Report and Justice Department statistics only take into account the rapes that are reported to the police, and since sexual violence is considered one of the most underreported crimes, it would be safe to surmise that the actual figure is higher than those estimated by official sources. Notwithstanding the dispute over statistics, it is commonly acknowledged that rape is the fastest growing crime in the United States. According to the FBI, during the 1980s the incidence of rape increased at four times the rate of other crimes. This ascending trend in rape rates has been a constant since the 1960s. Even in the 1990s, when overall crime rates dropped, rape still continues to be the fastest growing crime. Several reasons are attributed to this continued upsurge: better crime reporting, broadened definitions of rape, and the higher incidence of the crime per se.

The magnitude of this crime and the fear that it instills in all women transforms this issue from an individual problem into an issue that sociologist C. Wright Mills would characterize as belonging in the public realm; it afflicts many people and requires social structural explanations. While rape has always been a topic of interest to criminologists, sociologists, sociobiologists, and psychologists, scholarly interest in the area has expanded enormously following the feminist focus on sexual violence. In an effort to understand the phenomenon, academic discourses on rape have spiraled: studies now exist on the medical and psychological effects of rape, the psychological causes of rape, the psychological motives of the rapist, the social conditions of the victim, the history of rape, the legal processes, and so on. Reading the vast literature available, one comes away with a kaleidoscopic image of the crime. Studies contradict one another, and no single definition of any of the issues exists. Consequently, the perception of rape varies according to which, among the complicated array, available discourse one turns to. "What rape essentially reveals, in the present context, is the profile of the multiple agencies which embrace rape as their object of knowledge, a profile whose main feature, historically considered, is undoubtedly that very multiplicity."[10] Or, according to Mieke Bal, rape is an "obscuring term" that fails to address the cultural status of the event.[11]

In this chapter I outline only feminist understandings of rape; I follow a roughly chronological order to mark the shifts in concerns and solutions that feminists have offered. By the term *feminist* understanding of rape, I refer to perspectives that promote women-centered experiences of sexual violence, knowledge that emerges from and foregrounds women's voices.[12] Since feminism is itself an interdisciplinary field, I have necessarily been selective in summarizing the diverse strands of rape theories. I then turn to the criticisms that women of color have offered and explain why we must pay attention to these theories that insist that feminism should examine gender, race, and class as interlocking systems of oppression that shape the ways in which people experience rape.[13] By offering this genealogy of the feminist subject of rape, I highlight the ways in which discourses of sexuality, power, and knowledge shape understandings of sexual violence. Through such a narrative I want to highlight how the media, especially television, have appropriated selective aspects of feminism. I conclude this chapter with an overview of the U.S. media's engagement with feminism, especially sexual violence.

It is important that I clarify some of the language that I use; the word "survivor" refers to women who have experienced rape. Anti-rape activists point out that the word "victim" removes agency from women and "contributes to the idea that it is right and natural for men to prey" on women.[14] In the following chapters I use the descriptor "rape victim" though when television programs present the woman as passive and lacking agency.

UNIVERSAL WOMAN

The women's movement of the 1970s is largely responsible for transforming individual acts of sexual assault into a phenomenon that belongs in the public domain; it made the crime against women a prime focus of its campaign. Most scholars identify the 1971 Speak Out on Rape, organized by the New York Radical Feminists, as a defining moment that brought into public view the obstacles that rape survivors face in obtaining justice. Anti-rape activities from this period included take-back-the-night marches, speak-out rallies, consciousness-raising sessions, the organization of rape crisis centers, the patrolling of neighborhoods, and the production of educational pamphlets. Consciousness-raising groups were the fertile ground in which a feminist consciousness of sexual violence was articulated and promoted. According to Catharine MacKinnon, in these sessions women explored their feelings and individual experiences of rape. Then, through a collective scrutiny of these experiences, they built feminist theory.[15] The majority of the literature that emerged from this historic moment captures evocatively the energy and vitality of the movement. The legacies of this early part of the movement are visible today in television, especially in daytime talk shows, which often have self-consciously modeled themselves on the format of consciousness-raising groups.

Writings about rape from the early period consist primarily of individual women's accounts of violation, providing a personal face to the crime. Through an enumeration of various women's personal experiences, these writings attempted to raise public awareness about the prevalence of sexual violence and to mobilize women into political action; the writings were an integral part of the larger anti-rape movement. Susan Griffin's article, "Rape:

The All-American Crime," epitomizes these trends. She captures powerfully the manner in which rape and the threat of rape shaped her life and those of other women. "I have never been free of the fear of rape. . . . [I] have thought of rape as part of my natural environment—something to be feared and prayed against like fire or lightning." She supplements this first-person narrative with the experiences of other women. Collectively, these narratives become the site from which she elucidates a broad understanding of the phenomenon. She isolates gender-role socialization and cultural factors as the primary causal factors.[16]

Writings by Andra Medea and Kathleen Thompson, Diana Russell, and others make the violence of rape tangible and enumerate the various myths and stereotypes that have accumulated.[17] Rape must not be viewed as the actions of perverts but must be seen as a social issue related to broader gender relations, they argued. Through the citation of everyday women's voices, these studies illustrate a paradoxical social dynamic that was at play: most women testify to a pervasive fear of rape, and yet many feel that it cannot happen to them.

Like Griffin, other writers from this period isolated patriarchy as the central determinant of sexual violence. For instance, Medea and Thompson identify rape as the logical extension of "male-aggressive, female-passive" gender-role socialization patterns. Hostility toward women and the dehumanization of females are condoned by a sexist society, they assert. Further, they characterize as mini-rapes actions such as wolf whistles and unwanted hugging and pinching, actions that remind women that men see them as sexual objects. From these understandings, anti-rape activists developed powerful and broad definitions of the crime. "[R]ape is the deprivation of sexual self-determination. Rape is a man's fantasy, a woman's nightmare. Rape is all the hatred, contempt, and oppression of women in this society concentrated in the act."[18] Rape is characterized as a demonstration of power, of a will to assert authority and to dominate, an attempt to (re)establish male dominance by physical violence.[19] These definitions focus on how women and men are stratified into socially defined gender roles. They point out that beliefs about women's position in society are transmitted across generations, and that males are socialized to be aggressive and dominant while females are socialized to be passive. In the case of rape, male aggression is tolerated as appropriate sex-role behavior and therefore as a variant or slight extension of socially condoned, normal sexual relations. Rape is thus a product of a patriarchal society, where women's subservience is reinforced by social and cultural institutions.[20]

The elucidation of these ideas identifying patriarchy as the central cause of rape helped produce a collective identity for women, one based on a shared sense of oppression. In an effort to mobilize women into anti-rape activity, most of these books offered concrete suggestions to translate awareness into action. Sections of these books resemble how-to manuals; they describe in detail the various steps that need to be undertaken to develop anti-rape activities and organizations.

At this early stage of the anti-rape movement, the studies focused on women's victimization alone and envisaged power relations in a rather static one-way model, where men are perceived to have all of the power, and women are the "objects" over whom men seek to exercise control. Despite their focus on universal woman, these early studies are clearly aware of the ways in which understandings of rape are imbricated in racist structures. Many of them include cautionary gestures, pointing out the ways in which people of color experience rape differently. The following section from Medea's and Thompson's *Against Rape* encapsulates this awareness:

> When pressing for a better rate of arrest and conviction, it is very important to remember that, in this country, rape and racism are too closely intertwined to deal with one without the other. In many states the rape laws have been used almost exclusively to keep black men away from white women. This is a fact and one which must be faced when asking for more and better prosecution. Your demand may be answered only by more prosecution and conviction of black men. We would not, of course, suggest that black rapists should not be convicted. We simply warn against allowing your anti-rape group to be used as a tool of the racist and "law and order" forces at work in our society.[21]

Nevertheless, these understandings are integrated rarely in the theories of rape that the individual authors develop; this is a theme that I develop later in this chapter. The early anti-rape writings generated a universal identity for woman, one that centered on oppression. They helped develop a collective identity, mobilized women, and promoted cultural understandings of feminism. As I enumerate in the later chapters, it is this strand of feminism, one that foregrounds a universal identity for woman, that dominates television narratives of rape.

While the early books illustrated the pervasiveness of rape, Susan Brownmiller's book *Against Our Will* is often credited with producing a mainstream awareness of the crime and demonstrating the seriousness of the problem. In this groundbreaking book, Brownmiller provides a historical lineage for the crime and argues that it has been the chief weapon of male domination in all societies. She lays bare the manner in which rape has been codified in patriarchal societies. Historically, societies have acknowledged that sexual assault is a crime, not against women but against men. From the Old Testament to feudalism, Brownmiller contends, rape was primarily treated as a theft of property, and women in their roles as daughters or wives were treated as men's chattels.[22] Since rape destroyed a woman's property value on the marriage market, as punishment often the rapist had to marry his victim and provide her father with financial restitution. In other cases both the victim and the rapist were meted the same penalty—death by stoning or drowning, or they were ostracized and excommunicated—and the woman was considered culpable since she did not prevent the rape. During this period, rape was perceived as a crime of passion. This was not a static vision across history. Perceptions of sexual assault changed during the sixteenth century, when it was recognized that women, rather than their fathers, were the injured party. Abduction was made a distinct felony, and the crime of rape came to be seen as sexual ravishment, which in turn was viewed as the theft of chastity and virtue rather than of body and chattels.

The shifts in historical definitions of sexual assault, Brownmiller asserts, are nevertheless framed by the male fear of false accusations. This fear has been included in popular folklore since the biblical days of Joseph the Israelite and Potiphar's wife and is based on the assumption that women are scheming, lying, and vindictive. In Chapter 6 of this book, I illustrate how these popular narratives influenced artistic representations of sexual violence and laid the foundations for the representational grammar on which television images of rape are based. Like other writers from the early 1970s, Brownmiller portrays the crime as being functionally integral to patriarchy. "Essentially the rapist performs a myrmidon function for all men by keeping all women in a thrall of anxiety and fear," she writes.[23]

Sylvana Tomaselli and Roy Porter caution against such a narrative of a homogeneous, unchanging tale of all peoples being indifferent to the crime. They argue that rape was historically neither passed over in silence nor made light of or endorsed. There is ample evidence in myths and art objects that rape played a crucial role in the accounts and explanations of the rise and fall of cities, the causes of wars and revolutions. Analyses of Western civilization that posit an unchanging patriarchy, they insist, are reductive and presume that both sex and rape are a constant, and that our culture and attitudes toward both remained untouched by the passage of time. Examining the experiences of African-American women, several other scholars, including Hazel Carby, bell hooks, and Jacquelyn Hall, contend that rape should not be regarded as a transhistorical mechanism of women's oppression but as one that acquires specific political or economic meanings at different moments in history.[24]

Despite these shortcomings, Brownmiller's book brought into play two significant issues in the debate over rape. She argues that a rape culture was fostered by patriarchy and compounded by anatomical differences between men and women and is the cause for the "creation of a male ideology of rape." Brownmiller introduces in the debate the issue of physiological differences between men and women. This strand of her argument popularized a biologically essentialist view of rape, papering over the complex operations of power that enable male sexual violation of women.[25] Television narratives have popularized this essentialist view. For instance, in daytime talk shows, rape is commonly addressed as a phenomenon that results from a lack of communication between the sexes, because men and women communicate differently. Similarly, news magazines that focus on apprehended rapists tend to privilege the view that their behavior is biologically determined.

At the same time, the book situated the crime within a global context, including instances of its prevalence in war zones such as Bangladesh. This aspect was later developed by scholars to reveal the ways in which culturally constructed discourses of sexuality shape the ways in which power inequalities are materially manifested. For instance, anthropologist Peggy Reeves Sanday looked beyond the United States to develop cross-cultural accounts of rape. Comparing the prevalence of rape in various societies, along with a range of cultural factors, she categorizes cultures into those that are comparatively rape free and those that are comparatively rape prone. On this sliding scale, the United States ranks as a rape-prone society, while several "tribal" societies are categorized as rape free.[26]

Other writers from the late 1970s and early 1980s developed themes that were raised in *Against Our Will*. Most significantly, these writings advanced a more complex, nuanced vocabulary for the crime. The anti-rape movement illustrated that rapists were typically perceived as armed men in ski masks who attacked unaware women, what Susan Estrich has characterized as "real rape."[27] Women's individual accounts though revealed that rapists were often nonstrangers—they could be friends, relatives, husbands, just about any man. *The Rape in America* findings support this understanding. The survey showed that only 22 percent of the victims were assaulted by someone they did not know, and that the "typical" rape victim would be a girl or a teenager raped by someone she knew.

In the post–*Against Our Will* period, writers started to characterize rape as either stranger rape or acquaintance rape to refer to nonstranger cases. According to Margaret Gordon and Stephanie Riger, in some jurisdictions, rapes are classified as nonstranger cases if the victim is known to the rapist, even if the victim does not know the rapist. Within this broad legal definition, rapes committed by stalkers would be classified as nonstranger cases. Most feminists though have adopted a narrower view, limiting acquaintance rape to those instances where the woman knows her assailant.[28] Further, they distinguish date rape as a crime that occurs when a woman is initially willing to be in the company of a man who turns violent. Some feminists believe that the term *date rape* originated in the media and subtly casts doubt on the credibility of the sexual assault charge.[29] Mary Koss characterizes date rape as a *specific* form of acquaintance rape, one where the complainant and the defendant had some level of romantic interest between them and a relationship in which consensual sexual intercourse would be seen as appropriate.[30] These differences are collapsed, as we will see in the Mike Tyson and William Kennedy Smith rape cases, when the media refer to all acquaintance rapes as date rapes. The media focus on the "date" aspect facilitates a narrative that presents women as sexual objects.

Revealing more differences within the category of nonstranger rapes, scholars such as Russell examined the specific characteristics of rape in marriages. Robin Warshaw and Mary Koss turned to college campuses, where the experience of rape is significantly different; here the sexual violence often is committed by groups of men, resembles initiation rituals, and is accompanied by alcohol consumption. More recently, scholars such as Vikki Bell have started to examine incest as a specific form of rape.[31] These iterations of sexual violence underscore the feminist assertion that the experience of rape is not uniform or homogeneous.

Even as feminists developed a more precise nomenclature for rape, their writings continued to give voice to individual experiences of sexual violence. This branch of feminist research allowed women to identify ways in which to resist or minimize injury, reduce the probability of completed rape, and ascertain factors differentiating the women who report rape and those who do not.[32] In addition, these writings allowed scholars to chart the aftermath of rape—the physical, emotional, and psychic costs of sexual violence—and the extent to which medical and police practices ignore the trauma. These studies of rape trauma syndrome are useful to facilitate social change by drawing the attention of policy makers. They ascertained the extent to which a rape leads to temporary or extended stress, and the fiscal costs entailed by the state. For instance, when interviewing women who have experienced rape and those who have not, Gordon and Riger conclude that the crime must be considered a serious national problem, as it severely restricts the activities undertaken by women.[33] (This aspect has been picked up by television news, as we will see in later chapters.) Apart from naming the problem, studies on the effects of sexual violence reveal the specific ways in which power inequalities in society are materialized along gender lines.

To clarify further the crime of rape, each of these writings exposed certain myths that persist about the crime, the rape victim, and the rapist.[34] Together, the following are some of the clarifications offered:

1. Rapists are insane; they are perverted, or sick, and belong to the margins of society. Menachem Amir's 1971 study, *Patterns in Forcible Rape*, shows to the contrary that men who rape are not abnormal. This study reveals that in terms of psychological profiles, rapists are no different than other men.[35]

2. Rapists are motivated by lust and have uncontrollable sexual needs; sexual assaults occur when a sex-starved man is overcome by his needs and acts impulsively in a sexually repressed society. Amir's study once again refutes this myth. His analysis reveals that most rapes, especially gang rapes, are planned.

3. Rape is natural behavior, and men must learn not to sexually assault women. This is a corollary from the previous myth that men have greater sexual needs than women do, and that their sexuality is more urgent than women's.

4. Women secretly want to be raped. This myth suggests that women desire rape, that despite protestations and struggles, the victim has actually wished for her own violation. The anti-rape literature's enumeration of individual women's responses to sexual assaults refutes these assumptions.

5. Women provoke rape. The victims are believed to have enticed their assailants by their dress, behavior, and sexuality. They also are believed to have behaved carelessly prior to the crime, thus it is the woman's responsibility to avoid rape. The debate about acquaintance rape suggests that if a woman goes to a man's house or room it implies that she is willing to have sex, and if she refuses, that she is inviting rape.[36]

6. Women mean "yes" even when they say "no," and women cannot be forced to have sex against their will.

7. Only "bad girls" or "loose women" are raped. This myth once again suggests that women invite rape and provoke their rapists. It also assumes that bad things do not happen to good people.

8. Women "cry rape" for revenge. According to this myth, sexual assaults are a figment of female fantasy. Further, women use the charge of rape to avenge themselves, to cover accidental pregnancies, or simply to get attention.

The writings that dominated feminist anti-rape literature during the late 1970s and early 1980s, the post–consciousness-raising period, enact a subtle shift from the earlier focus on engendering a collective female identity through the articulation of a shared oppression. The recommendations that feminists offered were no longer limited to the provision of rape victim services or activities that would help redefine women's rights to their bodily and psychological integrity. Instead, they were directed at enacting institutional and social changes that would in the long run redefine gender roles and alter cultural attitudes.

REDEFINING THE BOUNDARIES OF THE LAW

Concerned over the low prosecution rates of rapists, scholars began to pay attention to legal definitions of rape and the treatment of rape survivors in the courtroom. Most scholars attribute the low reporting of rape to the skewed nature of court trials; women who have experienced sexual assault repeatedly assert that institutional insensitivity is a major deterrent.[37] Very few rape cases come to trial, and even among those that do go to court, the victim and the accused are treated unequally, scholars assert.[38] The differential treatment manifests itself in the victim being questioned about her sexual history and other details of her past, while the accused is not subjected to the same questions. During the trial, lawyers present details of the woman's sexual history to insinuate that she is a liar who consented to sex and later cried rape. (In the chapters that follow, we see these trends enacted in television narratives.) These scholars point out that the law and the legal process foreground male interests. According to Brownmiller, the male fear of a false rape charge is written in all state laws.

Examining the content of rape law, feminist legal scholars have pointed out that rules governing the conduct of rape trials originated in the archaic English common law. Specifically, they were shaped by an opinion written by English barrister Sir Matthew Hale in 1671. He believed that rape was a charge easily made and that it was difficult for a man to defend against, so it had to be examined with greater caution than any other crime. Since U.S. law relied on this opinion at least until 1974, in any rape trial the state had to offer evidence that the act was committed forcibly and against a woman's will.[39] The woman's credibility could be established only through physical evidence and the corroboration of witnesses. In effect, the rape survivor had to prove her innocence and credibility; she had to provide evidence that she resisted.

Protesting these laws, the women's movement demanded rape law reform.[40] Beginning in 1974, various states started to alter their legal definitions of rape and the conduct of the rape trial. While the reform efforts have been uneven, many states have replaced the common-law term *rape* with the terms *sexual assault* and *sexual abuse*. The crime is now defined as intercourse under circumstances that presume both criminal intent and nonconsent. These redefinitions have theoretically shifted the burden of proof from the victim to the accused. Rape is now defined in terms of the assailant's conduct and the use of force rather than the woman's behavior.[41] Other common reforms include limiting cross-examination of the woman about her sexual history and disallowing what used to be a routine cautionary instruction by the judge to the jury that rape is an easy charge to make but a difficult one to defend against. All states technically have included rape within marriages in their definitions of the crime.[42] These efforts attempt to shift the focus to the violent aspects of the phenomenon, redefining rape as a criminal rather than a sexual act.

Female lawyers who work in offices prosecuting rape testify to the changes enacted in the criminal justice system. Linda Fairstein and Alice Vachss, both New York prosecutors, recount in separate accounts the increased prosecution of rape charges. They both point out though that the various reforms have not facilitated the ways in which women are perceived by the legal and criminal justice institutions. The woman's conduct is still the focus of rape trials, and the outcomes hinge upon whether the woman can be classified as "good" or "bad," Vachss writes. A "good" victim tends to be a PTA mom, while a "bad victim" is a street kid with a drug problem.[43] If she is a "good" victim, everybody agrees that a rape occurred, and the only question pondered during the course of the trial is the identity of the culprit. If she is deemed a "bad" victim, court processes are directed to determine if there was a rape at all, using legal standards of consent and evidence. In these cases it becomes unclear who is on trial, the victim or the accused. Vachss and Fairstein concur that despite rape shield laws, the woman's past is often raised in an attempt to discredit her, and that a similar scrutiny of the accused often is absent.

Similarly, Sue Lees points out that in rape trials the jury is expected to evaluate the accounts of the defendant and complainant according to different criteria. "In the defendant's case his character or reputation depends on his lack of previous convictions and his occupation. In the woman complainant's case her lack of previous convictions are not referred to as enhancing her reputation. Instead, it is her sexual character and past sexual history that are considered crucial."[44] The conclusion that one can draw from rape trials is that "a woman's prophylactic against such men [rapists] should be to retreat into passive, demure, and chaste behavior, and ensure they had proper patriarchal protection."[45]

Capturing the central features that permit such an ambivalence toward rape, Carol Smart points out that the "law is based on a binary system of logic: truth/lie, innocence/guilt, and in cases of sexual violence, consent/lack of consent. In a courtroom, only one party's claims can be judged truthful, yet the participants often interpret the event quite differently. The subtleties and ambiguities involved in rape cases are generally excluded from legal discourse."[46] These problematic aspects of the legal definition of rape trials are reproduced in television news narratives, but prime-time entertainment programs have productively employed this ambivalence as a generative moment in their story lines.

While most scholars have focused on the formal structures of the law, others such as Gregory Matoesian, Zsuzsanna Adler, and Andrew Taslitz have paid close attention to the language of rape trials to reveal the subtle ways in which male domination is exerted in the courtroom. Paying attention to the dynamics of talk-in-interaction, Matoesian points out that within courtroom definitions of criminal facticity, women's experience of violence (and nonconsent) is delegitimized, decriminalized, and transformed into consensual sex. Examining the British legal system, Adler concludes similarly that the rhetorical strategies deployed in the courtroom transform sexual violence into consensual sex.[47] Writing from his perspective as a lawyer, Taslitz documents the loopholes available to circumvent rape law reforms. He believes that the progress made in this arena is modest. Concurring with the scholars I have enumerated already, Taslitz asserts that a central problem is the adversarial nature of the rape trial. "It is based on competition. It assumes that a battle between warring adversaries will yield truth." And gender role socialization skews the participation of men and women in the courtroom, the ways in which they narrate the event, and the ways in which their accounts are believed.[48]

Most feminist scholars concur that rape law reform efforts have been only moderately successful. Although activists were successful in effecting changes in legal definitions, societal attitudes about rape have been slower to change. The reforms enacted are symbolic rather than substantive.[49] Among feminist scholars, MacKinnon has offered the most sustained critique of existing laws as well as feminist efforts at law reform.

In a series of writings, MacKinnon has developed a cogent analysis of the legal process and primarily concludes that, like the state, the law is male. Legal definitions of rape are framed inextricably by patriarchy and privilege a male point of view. The "injury of rape lies in the meaning of the act to its victim, but the standard for its criminality lies in the meaning of the act to the assailant."[50] Specifically, she points out the fallacy in the law that defines rape as intercourse with force or coercion *and* without consent. It is the conjunction "and" that becomes central to MacKinnon's argument; if intercourse were characterized by force alone, it would be considered sex. She draws attention as well to the meaningfulness of women's consent in a patriarchal society. MacKinnon believes that an adequate definition of sexuality should acknowledge the "eroticization of dominance and submission."[51] Through her various writings she raises the problematic issue of a feminist's ability to know the world differently when living in societies that are gendered to the ground. By this she refers to the gamut of cultural, social, and institutional practices through which gender identity is constituted within patriarchy: the ways men and women are socialized to speak, the ways in which we understand their actions, and the ways in which we understand terms such as *sex* and *consent.*

Most feminist scholars though have distanced themselves from MacKinnon's position on sexual violence; many argue that marking rape as paradigmatic of all heterosexual sex dilutes the violence women experience. They believe as well that such a totalizing position provides women with little agency and in effect reproduces them as "always-already" victims.[52] Others have pointed out that MacKinnon's analysis prioritizes gender over other forms of oppression, which I develop in the next section of this chapter as a common failing of much of the research I have listed here. MacKinnon's analysis of rape emerges from an interrogation of the positions society ascribes to women as public citizens, how women are imbricated in the state as subjects of the law. Agreeing with some of the points raised by MacKinnon but approaching the issue from a philosophical perspective, Keith Burgess-Jackson suggests that rape be defined as coerced sex rather than nonconsensual sex. He believes that only such a formulation would take the "focus on a rape case off the victim, which means it is no longer a defense to a rape charge that the accused *believed,* however reasonably, that she consented."[53]

In the 1990s, in what many described as a backlash against feminism, several writers asserted that the women's anti-rape movement only facilitated the victimization of women. Using their personal experiences, authors such as Katie Roiphe and Christina Hoff Sommers point out that the feminist attention to sexual violence has produced a "victim" culture.[54] They accuse feminists of generating false statistics and exaggerating the extent of sexual violence. In particular, they criticize MacKinnon's theories for impugning all men and heterosexuality, thereby casting women as "beleaguered, fragile, intuitive angels."[55] These authors believe that feminism turns women into victims. Roiphe forwards the view that feminism "transforms perfectly stable women into hysterical, sobbing victims." Sharon Lamb, who distances her ideas from Roiphe's and Sommers's, on the other hand, argues that the media are largely responsible for equating feminism to an exclusive focus on victimization.[56] Many feminists describe Roiphe, Sommers, and others as espousing a postfeminist perspective—the belief that society has already met the challenges posed by the 1970s' movement, that men and women now have equal access to material resources, and thus any discourse that foregrounds gender is divisive and destructive. The postfeminist perspective assumes the validity of some feminist claims though. According to Sommers, "good feminism" is concerned with equal pay and equal rights. Postfeminists question all other feminist goals. Since the 1970s, the trajectory of feminist anti-rape writings has moved from a belief in the subordination of all women to one where some now believe that all women have reached the promised land of equality with men.

This branch of anti-feminist feminism, or what Chris Atmore calls "media feminism," has gained significant visibility in the media.[57] While Roiphe, Sommers, and others position themselves as postfeminist, media discourses on rape, as I illustrate in the last section of this chapter, conflate feminism and these writers' positions. Such a conflation of terms has important consequences for the kinds of rape narratives made available on television. The singular focus on one aspect of a broader critique of patriarchal systems and the attention paid to individual narratives allow the structural and systemic changes that feminists have long demanded to slide out of view.

SPEAKING FROM THE MARGINS

Amidst these disavowals of feminism, one group has increasingly drawn attention to the ways in which both the majority of feminist theory and especially postfeminist writings minimize the differences that separate women from each other. Emerging primarily from women of color, this body of literature points out that race, class, sexual orientation, and a whole range of other factors mediate the ways in which women experience the effects of gender.[58] These criticisms do not imply that women of color have been estranged from the anti-rape movement or are unconcerned about issues of sexual violence. As I illustrate in this section, women of color have had a long history of involvement in anti-rape activities, but this participation has been shaped and inflected by racist structures. Specifically, women of color have from the early 1970s pointed out the racial blind spots of feminist theories of sexual violence. Initially, women of color emphasized that feminist anti-rape strategies facilitated the sustained repression of people of color by various institutions. Increasingly, though, the criticism has shifted to point out possible ways of effecting a multicultural anti-rape movement, one that takes into account the specificity of the experience of marginalized groups.

A note of caution is required here. Although I am singling out women of color for pointing out the racial blind spots in feminist theories, the history of the women's movement and feminism is more complicated. Some white feminists have for a long time pointed out the exclusive focus on white women's experiences of rape. As I have already noted, since the early 1970s, writers such as Medea and Thompson have drawn specific attention to the ways in which rape affects racialized communities. In what follows, I do not intend to produce a narrative that implies that feminism in the United States has gradually evolved to a more enlightened understanding of rape by including the voices of women of color. Instead, I have intentionally isolated the critique offered by women of color to foreground their silencing and absence in media representations of feminism and images of sexual violence.

Most narratives of anti-rape activism tend to suggest that women of color have only recently intervened in feminist debates of sexual violence. But Angela Davis reminds us that black women have been involved with anti-rape activities since at least the turn of the century. Then and now, black feminists and women of color have consistently articulated a position that centers on the ways in which race and gender intersect to define the ways in which individuals experience rape. They argue that an anti-rape movement can be successful only if participants understand the ways in which rape has been historically materialized across the racial divide and scrutinize the ways in which a racialized sexuality was deployed during and after slavery.[59]

During the eighteenth and nineteenth centuries, the rape of enslaved black women by white men was routinized and normalized. The sexual violation of a black woman was justified by presenting her as a sexually promiscuous and lusty Jezebel. The argument forwarded was that a white man would not have to force a black woman to have sex, because she was always willing. Any reluctance was believed to be feigned, and easily overcome. In the absence of official data, figures on the number of black women who were raped can only be approximated. However, it is commonly acknowledged that this was a widely prevalent practice.[60]

Michele Wallace, Jacquelyn Hall, and Hazel Carby have pointed out that during the nineteenth century, rape was part of a complex structure that upheld a system of racial and economic exploitation of slaves, both men and women. Rape was a weapon both of domination and repression; it extinguished black women's will to resist and also demoralized African-American men. "The sexual access of white men to black women was a cornerstone of patriarchal power in the South."[61] The systematic rape of innumerable black women has, however, remained silenced. The issue has been explored in some African-American fiction, and more recently it has been recuperated in histories of the slavery era.[62]

Apart from rape, black women's bodies were regulated through a series of ideological mechanisms. As numerous scholars have pointed out, during slavery and later in the Reconstruction period, the black woman was ideologically constructed as the antithesis of the white woman. Specifically, Sander Gilman argues that white people sexualized their world by projecting onto black bodies a narrative of sexualization disassociated from whiteness. Analyzing representational practices, he points out the spectacular objectification of black female bodies that contributed to the stereotype of uncontrolled sexuality. Through these practices, black sexuality itself became an icon for deviant sexuality, he contends, a trend that continues to find expression in contemporary society.[63] As my analysis in the following chapters reveals, these ideas about black sexuality continue to frame television depictions of racialized bodies.

Black men too were similarly characterized as being hypersexualized, but this stereotype did not develop fully until the late nineteenth century. Ideas pertaining to black male sexuality are condensed in the myth of the black rapist that took shape in the Reconstruction period. Even as African Americans tried to establish their families and communities outside of the system of slavery, the black male was presented as a threat to white womanhood and hence to society. In the post–Reconstruction Era, black men were ideologically constructed as lascivious, sexual monsters who preyed upon white women, and white society countered this threat of racial-sexual transgression through thousands of lynchings.[64] Elizabeth Pleck contends that politicians from the South have repeatedly used the threat of the black rapist to play upon racial and sexual fears, to justify lynching, to defend segregation, and to disenfranchise black voters. The threat of interracial sexual assault was the product of unstable race relations before and after the Civil War. "When whites felt that blacks threatened white power and privilege, they responded by crying rape."[65] The myth of the black rapist continues to resonate today and has been repeatedly trotted out in moments of political crises, uniting white Americans across class divides.[66] Davis argues that the image of black men as rapists "strengthened its inseparable companion: the image of the black woman as chronically promiscuous. And with good reason, for once the notion is accepted that black men harbor irresistible, animal-like sexual urges, the entire race is invested with bestiality. . . . The mythical rapist implies the mythical whore—and a race of rapists and whores deserves punishment and nothing more."[67]

During slavery, black women's rape remained invisible, however, in the post–Reconstruction Era, the alleged threat that black men posed to white womanhood transformed rape into a hypervisible domain, a site where discourses of national identity and citizenship were inscribed. As Hall argues, while rape is a primary instrument of male terror, it also has served to maintain other forms of domination. It has affected black women and black men profoundly, although each group experiences its effects differently. In the post–Reconstruction South, rape was inseparable from lynching. The violence committed on women's and men's bodies was linked to and secured the maintenance of white patriarchy; together, rape and lynching upheld white men's control over (white and black) women and black men. Despite the social and economic changes that occurred during the twentieth century and the radical transformation in race relations, the legacy of these attitudes continues to inform contemporary understandings of African-American women and men. Micaela di Leonardo believes that, "The Southern rape complex has moved north as the media highlight black sex crimes against white women (a small percentage of all sexual assaults) and white male yahoo violence against perceived black miscegenation."[68]

Within this historical context, black women's participation in the anti-rape movement can be traced to the turn of the century, when they were mobilized into action to protest lynchings. For instance, Ida B. Wells investigated over 700 lynchings and found that accusations of rape had been made in less than one-third of them.[69] Her writings revealed that the black male rapist myth provided a flimsy cover for the maintenance of white domination. Most African-American women's challenge to sexual violence emerges from similar anti-lynching activities initiated by the Black Women's Club Movement.

Unlike the 1970s' anti-rape movement that centered on women's victimization, black women's protests against sexual violence originated in their concern over lynching. When examining African Americans' material lives in the late nineteenth century, ironically, Sir Matthew's edict becomes relevant: indeed, rape is a charge easily made but difficult to defend against. This idea is captured very well in the Scottsboro case. I have chosen to isolate this particular case because trends established in press coverage of this rape trial continue to shape media portrayals of rape and rape victims, especially in cases involving African Americans. "The Scottsboro case was not only a landmark case in the history of civil rights but also in the history of rape coverage."[70] Helen Benedict and Brownmiller concur that press coverage of the 1931 case pitted race against gender, and as my analysis in this book reveals, this trend persists in contemporary television coverage.[71]

To summarize their accounts, the Scottsboro case involved two poor, white women, recently laid off mill workers from Huntsville, Alabama, who took a ride on a freight train to Chattanooga, Tennessee, "for a bit of adventure." On their trip back to Huntsville, they boarded a train with many black and white male youths. Somewhere along the route, a fist fight broke out, and the white men were forced out of the train. When news of the fight reached the train's next destination, Paint Rock, Alabama, along with the knowledge that two white women were still on it, a posse of seventy-five white men, talking of rape, waited for the train. As soon as it arrived, nine of the black youths, ranging in age from thirteen to twenty, were arrested. The two women tried to run away but were cornered by the posse. When asked if they had been raped, one woman replied in the affirmative, while the other refused to answer. The two women were placed in jail on possible vagrancy and prostitution charges, and it was believed that they acceded to the rape accusation under pressure from the police. After a three-day trial, eight of the nine youths were sentenced to death, and the ninth received a life sentence, because he was a juvenile.

At this point, the American Communist Party, the International Labor Defense, and the civil liberties movement organized demonstrations to protest the rape trial. They managed to have the convictions overturned on the grounds that the jury was all white. A second trial was set, and one of the women recanted her story, declaring that she had lied about being raped, while the other stuck to her original story. The second jury again convicted all of the youths. This conviction too was set aside by the judge, on the grounds that both women were lying, and that women of that "character" tend to lie in general. A third trial resulted in a conviction yet again, but after several appeals, the death penalty was revoked for all but one of the accused. The remaining Scottsboro "boys" served long prison sentences.

In this account, the myth of the black rapist played a key role both in the apprehension and repeated conviction of the accused, even in the absence of any physical evidence. Significantly, press coverage of the case did not focus on the deployment of the black rapist myth; instead, it focused on women's proclivity to lie. Since then, media coverage of rape has emphasized the possibility of false accusations, which has resulted in binarized images of the woman as a virgin or vamp. The separation of race from gender in discussions of rape continues to shape popular conceptualizations of sexual violence.[72] The anti-rape feminist movement has engendered a similar disjuncture in its analysis of sexual violence, foregrounding oppression based on gender. It has been left to women of color to point out that the twin myths of black male bestiality and black female promiscuity continue to inform contemporary understandings of the crime, even if they are invisible referents. The dynamics that Brownmiller and Benedict isolate in the press coverage of the Scottsboro case continue to inflect contemporary television narratives.

Numerically, women of color have been underrepresented in the women's movement, particularly during the 1970s. Most of the participants in the early women's movement traced their activism to the activities of the New Left. The birth of feminism within the New Left occurred at the moment the black movement was becoming separatist. Sara Evans believes that this historical conjunction explains the whiteness of the women's movement. Paula Giddings concurs, and adds that as the women's movement expanded, it included more middle-class women who lacked the racial and class consciousness of the earlier participants. African-American women were alienated by the interpersonal racism prevalent within the movement. This estrangement was compounded by the "shrill tone" the movement adapted toward men.[73]

African-American women's muted participation in the anti-rape movement is particularly striking, because they are more likely to be victimized than white women, Patricia Hill Collins notes. Several black feminists have addressed this absence and attribute a set of reasons that can be broadly grouped into two categories: anti-rape activities focused on white women's concerns ignoring race, and these activities unconsciously supported racist operations of institutional power. According to women of color, the anti-rape movement did not take into account the specific ways in which racialized women experience sexual violence.[74]

Roz Pulitzer, a member of the Manhattan Women's Political Caucus, which was lobbying on rape issues, said that she did not expect black women to get very involved in the issue of rape. She explained:

The splits between the concerns of white women and our concern was so great that strategically we had to have a black organization to give the women's movement credibility in our own communities. . . . At the same time that the black woman does not want to be another foot on the black man's head, she is trying to point out that a lot of interactions that go on between black men and women are very oppressive. It's a very difficult situation to deal with. You're

caught up in the reality of these things being wrong and you're
caught up in the reality that it is a racist society too—it's almost as
if you have to take sides.[75]

This sense of validating race over gender has been a consistent theme and
reflects the ways in which black women's victimization has repeatedly been
marginalized within black communities.

Since the horror and brutality of lynchings, black men's experiences of
racism have been considered more profound than those experienced by
black women. Further, the operations of the criminal justice system,
wherein black men are treated with greater harshness than white men, allow
African Americans to view rape as a form of racist oppression rather than
sexual oppression. African-American women have had to hierarchize race-
based oppressions as being more significant than gender-based oppressions,
or else be considered race traitors.[76] They are unwilling to participate in a
movement whose demands could result in more repressive action against
their families and communities. Instead, they have had to formulate anti-
rape activities that would not lead to frame-up rape charges. Often this sensitivity to the African-American male experience in repressive institutions
has led to the silencing of women's voices. The history of false accusations
of rape by white society and the racist oppression of black men often are
highlighted, as opposed to the history of victimization among black
women. According to Musa Moore-Foster, the myth of the black rapist has
served as a twofold barrier to dialogue about both the nature of race and
gender relations outside of the black community and the quality of gender
relations within it.[77] As I elucidate in my analysis of news narratives on the
Mike Tyson rape case and Barbara Kopple's *Fallen Champ*, these attitudes
help explain the lack of public support for the accuser within the African-
American community. In the absence of this historical context, television
coverage of African-American support for the boxer leads to a "they just
don't get it" evaluation.

Even as women of color in the 1970s were raising awareness of the ways
in which race and rape intersect to affect black men and women differently,
men in black communities undertook initiatives to curtail the problem
through extra-legal measures. Medea and Thompson point out that, in 1974,
"a black, male-run radio station in Chicago (WVON) is receiving and broadcasting descriptions of rapists throughout the community. In response, black
policemen volunteered to investigate these cases in their off-duty hours."[78]
Subsequently, two more black stations in Kansas City and Louisville insti-
tuted similar Operation Crime-Stop programs.

These initiatives circumvent one of the central charges that African-American women have launched against the anti-rape movement: the crime must be addressed, but the better prosecution and incarceration of rapists should not reinforce the oppression of people of color. In Operation Crime-Stop Programs, the community rather than state institutions is mobilized to end violence against women. As I have mentioned already, anti-rape movement leaders were aware that African-American women were unwilling to participate in a movement that could lead to more repressive attacks on their families and community, yet the white women who predominated had the "privilege of forgetting or noticing the operations of race."[79]

As an antidote to such racial blindness, Angela Davis urges feminists to locate sexual assault within the larger social and political context rather than focus on individual instances of victimization. Violence against women is related to domestic racial violence as well as to global imperialist aggression. Further, she insists that masculinity itself should be understood not as a biological or psychological characteristic but as one that is produced under conditions of capitalism. The important question to answer is, "Do men rape because they are men, or are they socialized by their own economic, social, and political oppression . . . to inflict sexual violence on women?"[80] However, Davis cautions against a mechanical relationship between behavior and existing power structures; she demands instead an understanding that reflects the complex interconnectedness of race, gender, and class oppression, or what Hill Collins calls the "matrix of domination."

Davis argues that an effective multiracial anti-rape movement can be forged only when participants recognize the enduring and pivotal role that the myth of the black rapist continues to play in our understanding of sexual violence. Others such as Kimberlé Crenshaw, Aída Hurtado, and June Jordan argue that people of color are mobilized differently by the discourses of rape—the medical, legal, criminal, and media discourses conjugate sexual violence differently when the rapist is a person of color, or when the rape survivor is a person of color. These theorists do not isolate patriarchy but examine the ways in which discourses of race, economic factors, and cultural systems together make sexual violence possible.[81]

Concerns about race may initially seem unnecessarily divisive. "Racial issues are not explicitly part of the politicization of gender, [but] public controversies show that racial policies are often linked to gender violence in the way that the violence is experienced, how the interventions are shaped, or the manner in which the consequences are politicized and represented." When racial politics are separated from gender politics, we get an incomplete understanding, one that distorts and often excludes women of color. Specifically,

Crenshaw calls for an intersectional framework to uncover the manner in which "the dual positioning of women of color as women and as members of a subordinated racial group bears upon violence committed against us." She describes intersectionality as a provisional concept that points out the different ways in which women of color are situated between categories of race and gender when the two are regarded as mutually exclusive.[82]

Black feminism argues that racial subordination and sexual subordination are mutually reinforcing, that black women are marginalized by politics of race and gender, and that a political response to each form of subordination must at the same time be a political response to both. Feminism should oppose racism and misogyny simultaneously.

FRAGMENTING WOMAN

The narrative of the anti-rape movement that I have provided reveals the shifts within feminist understandings of sexual violence and the solutions they offered. In the first phase, through a narration of personal accounts, anti-rape activists emphasized the violence of the crime. These writings were meant to clarify a common misconception that rape was the eruption of male sexual desire; they showed instead that it was a violent act embedded in unequal power relations. However, the writings from this period produce a universal woman, one who is the object of male rapacity and can only respond through fear. "The rhetoric of these works serves the dual purpose of deindividualizing rape and placing it firmly in the social and political arena, and of rendering fear an essential part of femaleness."[83] Later analyses develop a broader vocabulary for the crime and try to reintroduce the sexual aspect into the crime. The anti-rape movement, in this phase, points out that the sexual nature of the crime made it unique. Later analyses have fragmented the feminist subject of rape—they have clarified that patriarchy is neither totalizing nor a discourse that operates uniformly across race and class. Women of color and some white feminists have been particularly productive in developing this aspect of feminism. They have pointed out that a patriarchal, capitalist society mobilizes many rape subjects. Revealing the silences within feminist theories, they point out that women can be both dominated and dominators.

Feminist scholars have deployed Michel Foucault's theories of sexuality, power, and knowledge to avoid either/or dichotomies, to stop framing issues concerning women as either unequivocally liberatory or wholly repressive. His theories have sharpened awareness of the ways in which structures of knowledge help form our sense of the very objects they claim to analyze. Before I turn to media coverage of feminism, I make a detour through Foucault's theories, because they provide a very productive intervention into the "difference impasse."[84] They also offer us ways to reconceptualize theories of rape around the intersecting discourses of gender, race, and class.

Writing across a range of domains and social practices, Foucault develops a sophisticated account of the ways in which power and knowledge are linked. In this chapter, though, I limit myself to the first volume of *The History of Sexuality*, which is immediately relevant to this analysis. He puts forth two interrelated points, which are significant to my analysis. First, Foucault's historical exegesis on the cluster of practices surrounding sexuality allows him to assert that sexuality is not a property of the body, nor is it a preoccupation with sex. Since the beginning of the nineteenth century, Western society has discussed sexuality as the expression of the individual. However, Foucault classifies it as a discursive formation. Sexuality has historically been produced and deployed through the operations of power-knowledge networks; it intersects with a larger set of ideas, of the consciousness of the body, of bodies.

Second, most histories of sexuality tend to follow a freedom-repression-limited freedom trajectory. These point out that in pre-capitalist, pre-industrial societies, sexuality and sex were practiced and talked about without adhering to any rules. Within these narratives, the Victorian Era is marked as a period of repression, when talk about sexuality was restricted, and sex itself was tightly controlled. The contemporary era is one of partial freedom, trying to shake off the repressive tendencies of the Victorian Era. The women's movement and its efforts to rewrite sexual politics are emblematic of this effort to "unrepress" sexuality. Foucault rejects such a linear characterization, and points out that the Victorian Era did not repress sexuality but was marked by an explosion of discourses apropos sex. The modes of talking about sex were altered though. The church and the confession became the central sites for the discussion of sexuality, and the Victorian Era is identified as the historical moment when a whole new cluster of practices surrounding sexuality emerged. In the twentieth century, discourses of medicine, psychology, science, religion, and media, among others, constitute sexuality and shape the ways in which we understand them.

These changes can be traced to the ways in which power operates in relation to sex. Power does not operate, according to Foucault, as the legal formulation of "thou shalt not," laying down the law concerning the licit and the illicit. Instead, power is more productive, producing subjects with sexualities. Beginning in the eighteenth century, the power that constitutes sexuality came to reside at four central processes: the hystericization of the female body, the pedagogization of children's sex, the socialization of procreative behavior, and the psychiatric analyses of perverse pleasures. The operations of power with regard to sex in the last century, Foucault contends, have altered the ways in which we understand the body.

It is necessary to clarify some of the vocabulary used here. In Foucault's theories, power does not reside in any particular individual or institution, and its operations cannot be separated from the operations of knowledge. Power relations, however, are not equivalent to class relations as they would be in, say, traditional Marxism; they mark the struggles whereby social groupings with different interests engage with one another.

While in earlier books Foucault described power more familiarly as a source of domination, in *The History of Sexuality* he conceptualizes people's experience of subordination and domination as an effect of power. Here he describes power as a "network of relations, constantly in tension, rather than as a privilege that one might possess. . . . In short, this power is exercised rather than possessed."[85] It is all encompassing, a web that enmeshes the entire field of the social; it emerges—it is produced—in specific instances, in concrete sets of relations. Among the relations in which power is produced, Foucault suggests, are certain coordinates of knowledge: there is no power relation without the constitution of knowledge, nor any knowledge that does not presuppose at the same time power relations.

The power-knowledge network can be observed only through an examination of discourses surrounding a phenomenon. The term *discourse* in Foucauldian theories refers to historically, socially, and institutionally specific structure of statements, terms, categories, and beliefs. Discourses function as sets of rules and define social practices, such as what constitutes insanity, and "what it is possible to speak at a given moment."[86] He specifies that we cannot imagine a world divided "between accepted discourses and excluded discourses or between a dominant discourse and the dominated one; but as a multiplicity of discursive elements that come into play in various strategies. . . . Discourse transmits and produces power; it reinforces it, but also undermines it and exposes it, renders it fragile and makes it possible to thwart it."[87]

In *The History of Sexuality*, Foucault reveals the ways in which sexual deviancy and criminality are constituted through the operation of discourses. These formulations are useful in making sense of the historical shifts in understandings of rape. As Brownmiller has documented, in ancient Greece and Rome, sexual assaults of women were not viewed as violent crimes but as property crimes. Later, rape was addressed only in terms of its relevance to political processes.[88] In both of these phases, woman as subject is absent from the prevailing discourses of rape. Instead, she figures only as an object in male-centered discourses. During the late eighteenth and nineteenth centuries, sexual assaults disappeared from the stage of public debate, both as a crime and from the realm of politics, and it was discussed primarily as an individual problem and a crime of passion. Public reflections on the crime were suddenly absent, Roy Porter has shown. The shifting discourses on sex and sexuality could partially explain the silence during the last phase. Discourses of rape are moved out of the public realm and located within the domestic arena.

In her study of rape between 1770 and 1845 in Britain, Anna Clark points out that the rise of capitalism and the concomitant social changes altered definitions of the crime as well as who could be considered a rape victim. The emergence of a wage-earning working class and the expansion of the middle class were accompanied by shifts in definitions of female sexuality and acceptable feminine behavior. Consequently, white, middle-class women were perceived as the primary victims of rape, while the violence that working-class women experienced was erased. Specifically, Clark points out that in nineteenth-century England, the threat of rape helped secure women's location in the private sphere.[89] Women's isolation in the domestic arena also shifted understandings of rape; only chaste women were "rapable." The raped woman was spoken for and by numerous institutional voices—the judicial system, the criminal system, and the media—and effectively silenced.

Like Clark, many other feminists have employed Foucault's theories quite productively to underscore the ways in which women's bodies and sexuality are constituted by social institutions and prevalent discourses. Foucault himself, though, evades an analysis of the gendered specificity of social formations, especially sexuality. He addressed the topic of rape once in a public forum in 1977, and these remarks drew sharp criticism from feminists.[90] Specifically, he disagrees with feminist definitions of rape and their demands for more stringent prosecution of rapists. Foucault believes that rape should only be regarded as a violent crime, "whether one punches his fist in someone's face or his penis in the sexual organ makes no difference." Defining rape as a sexual crime would mark certain parts of the body with an excess of significance, as being more sexual than other parts of the same body. To escape the operations of power, he contends, rape should be desexualized. He also believes that the feminist focus on punishing rape would result in a repression of sexuality. "In no circumstances should sexuality be subject to any kind of legislation whatever." Having desexualized rape, he also calls for its decriminalization.

While acknowledging the hazards of "fetishizing" one part of the body, Monique Plaza and Catharine MacKinnon argue against Foucault. "If we say these things [rape, sexual harassment, pornography] are abuses of violence, not sex, we fail to criticize what has been done to us through sex."[91] They concur that social sexing makes rape sexual. Other feminists agree that Foucault's points are valid only as long as one fails to examine power as it upholds a nonegalitarian social structure between men and women. Feminist criticisms of Foucault also have pointed out that his conceptualization of power as an all-encompassing network of relations precludes the possibility of resistance or social change.[92]

Similarly, his theories and analyses elide race, but scholarship on this absence has been limited.[93] Nevertheless, numerous critical race theorists and postcolonial scholars have deployed Foucault's theories to mark the specific operations of discourses of alterity and the ways in which racialized subjects have been constituted. Robert Young provides an excellent analysis of the ways in which Foucault's theories of sexuality, institutions of surveillance, and specialized knowledge formations clear the space for an intervention into the arenas of race and colonialism. Abdul JanMohamed points out that Foucault remains deeply Eurocentric and fails to examine discourses of racialized sexuality, the intersection of discourses of race and sexuality. Discourses of racialized sexuality shaped the operations of power in the United States during slavery and in the colonial context. These two historical periods—colonialism and slavery—are central to the formation of modern Western subjectivity but remain unproblematized in Foucault. These two strands point out the limitations of his theories.

Despite these marked erasures, feminists, critical race theorists, and postcolonial scholars borrow elements from his theories, because they destabilize the conceptualization of a universal subject. For feminists, they permit a formulation that displaces the concept of woman with a multiply articulated female subject. This has been a difficult enterprise though. Early feminist theories attacked Enlightenment thought as concealing a masculinist bias beneath the appearance of neutrality and objectivity.[94] At the same time, feminists continued to think about power and knowledge within categories of thought that already existed. These are, in part, assumptions about reality and truth, cause and effect, and freedom and the nature of human agency. Consequently, the majority of feminist rape theories were formulated around the universal subject of Enlightenment, this time though she was female. Susan Hekman points out that Foucault's methods radically redefine the autonomous subject of modernism. His theories can thus be potentially useful in formulating a fragmented, multiply intersected subject of rape. It permits us to understand how discourses of sexuality and race intersect to constitute radically different discourses of rape. Racialized social subjects can thus be seen as experiencing rape differently because of the operations of power networks.[95]

The anti-rape movement was based on a conceptualization of the universal woman, a unified subject whose primary identity was determined by gender; she functioned as a female counterpart to the male liberal humanist subject. The universal woman constituted by these analyses replicated a series of exclusions and erasures analogous to those of the Enlightenment subject. Women of color have drawn attention to these lacunae, as I have just illuminated. Feminist critiques of the anti-rape movement have called for a transformation of the universal woman into a subject position that includes fragmented and multiply intersected identities.

Susan Friedman points out that the feminist agenda against racism requires not only an examination of power and privilege, it also requires relational narratives that interrogate the manner in which cultural discourses of race affect what we see, say, write, and do.[96] A Foucauldian approach that analyzes the specificity of mechanisms of power and develops a strategic knowledge permits a freeing of difference. It requires "thought that accepts divergence; affirmative thought whose instrument is distinction; thought of the multiple—of the nomadic and dispersed multiplicity that is not limited or confined by the constraints of similarity."[97] This freeing of difference is appropriate for formulating a multicultural feminism, one that realizes that the oppressions women face are varied and multiple, requiring specific resistances designed for the particular situations that different women experience.

Foucault's deconstruction of power releases feminism from rigid conceptions of, for example, universal patriarchy, racism, or heterosexism, as Hekman points out. By seeing power as everywhere and at some level available to all, it can encourage us to overlook women's systematic subordination of other women, as well as systemic domination by men. Using Foucault's ideas, and more broadly poststructuralist ideas, of power, knowledge, and sexuality means acknowledging the multiplicity of difference and claiming the end of woman as a universal category. As I have indicated, Foucault's position on gender and rape is very problematic. However, I am suggesting that feminists deploy some of the insights that his writings and those of poststructuralism to think about rape in a manner that allows for the integration of a multiplicity of identities simultaneously. This can facilitate the multicultural feminism that women of color have long been seeking, one that can acknowledge the ways in which discourses of race and class intersect with those of gender.

TELEVISUAL FEMINISM

The previous section outlines the complex ways in which feminist thought is now conceptualizing sexual violence, perspectives that highlight the ways in which the operations of power structure knowledge about sexual violence as well as the ways in which different groups experience rape. This, along with women of color's critique of feminism, helps us reconceptualize the subject of rape in a manner that does not emerge from and address an essentialized woman. While the first section of this chapter helps us understand the brand of feminism the media most frequently refer to (and appropriate), the other two sections lay the groundwork for the arguments I present about the nature of debate and discussion that television rape narratives could potentially facilitate.

I conclude this chapter with a brief exegesis on television representations of feminism. In the chapters that follow, I develop the specific studies that engage in the topic of rape. Here I outline some of the key issues that characterize the public image of feminism that television has made available. From the earliest books of the anti-rape movement, feminists have addressed the problematic ways in which the media image rapes and represent women. These criticisms have had an impact on media practices. Indeed, over the last three decades, portraits of women and gender-related issues have altered significantly. Women are no longer presented only as victims or objects of male desire. I would argue that by discussing rape as sexual violence, television genres have, on the most basic level, introduced what was once a private issue into the public forum.

As several scholars have noted, the media in the United States tend to privilege narratives of the individual over stories that might offer insights to structural and social issues. Television has been no different in addressing issues brought to our attention by the feminist movement. Whether fictional or nonfictional programming, television narratives have consistently focused on stories of individual achievement or individual victimization, ignoring the logic and structural demands of feminism. Examining the modalities through which the media frame and present women and gender-related issues in a *Signs* forum, "Feminism and the Media," several scholars arrive at the disheartening assessment that the media "have neither the language nor the vision to speak of systemic or cultural problems and solutions. Rather, commercial media focus on individual resistance and individual deviance."[98] Consequently, only those aspects of feminism that resonate with dominant ideas of individualism and femininity appear on television. Indeed, the coverage of the women's movement itself focused on individual figures such as Betty Friedan or Kate Millett rather than on the politics they advocated. While the spotlight on individual women's achievements is important, this aspect is developed at the expense of discussing "systems of gender, race, and economics that allow violence and other inequities to continue."[99]

A significant effect of the women's movement has been the attention that television has provided to problems arising from and within the domestic

sphere. While it is difficult to make easy correlations between media representations and social change, scholars such as Wendy Kozol point out that the
media are partly responsible for establishing violence against women as a public policy issue. Nevertheless, she says that media representations of gender-
related issues are flawed, because they ignore "the overall context of patriarchy,
male domination, systems of racialized inequality, and above all capitalism,"
thus producing a very skewed, limited sense of female agency. Effectively, television's storytelling practices have reversed the feminist maxim that the personal is the political and have reduced the political to the personal.[100]

The slippages that occur between television representations of feminism
and the ideas articulated by the movement have had significant effects. Most
feminist politics function through public testimony and the witnessing of
female struggles, as I have already noted. When framed by a logic of individualism, these powerful demands are reduced to complaints of victimization. It
is this portrayal of feminist demands as an endless litany of women's victimization that the postfeminists, to whom I referred earlier in this chapter,
address. Lauren Berlant believes that media practices permit women's voices to
become visible only when they operate within the genre of the complaint.[101]

While nonfictional programs have privileged narratives of the individual,
prime-time entertainment and daytime talk shows have been marginally
more successful in communicating ideas initiated by the women's movement.
For instance, even as they depict female autonomy as success in a "man's
world," they also have developed narratives where female friendships are celebrated. However, by the mid-1980s, prime-time entertainment began to
privilege a postfeminist perspective, one that recovered the normativity of the
heterosexual family and celebrated women's traditional roles within the
nuclear family. By 1989, when my analysis begins, this was the terrain,
marked by a reliance on the individual and postfeminist thought, that the
narratives of rape I examine were developed.

3

The Right of Sight Is White

The Singular Focus of Network News

In the previous two chapters I outlined the dominant theories framing the analysis in this book, specifying the problematic ways in which both theories of the public sphere and feminist analyses of rape address issues pertaining to gender and race. In the next four chapters, I examine different domains of television programming to outline the specific ways in which these conceptualizations are materialized, and the nature of debate and discussion that they foster. In this chapter I interrogate news programming, which is most commonly associated with the public sphere. Through my analysis, I show that the gendered division of public and private issues results in news coverage that shifts attention from sexual assault to a discussion of masculinity. News coverage effects this through a sustained examination of the accused men. While this focus on men and masculinity could be seen as promoting a feminist explanation of rape, as the analysis in this chapter reveals, network news tends to reiterate stereotypes of racialized sexuality, particularly female sexuality. My examination of three well-publicized rape cases, however, cautions against a monolithic reading of the news and argues that despite their focus on the accused men, news workers have incorporated *some* aspects of feminist rape theories. Significantly, the feminist theories that news workers appropriate facilitate a focus on gender alone and enable a racially blind coverage of rape. My analysis reveals that, despite their procedures and rhetorical strategies of objectivity, the news in the United States is enunciated from a white, normative standpoint. Network coverage of interracial and intraracial rape cases reveals the specific ways in which whiteness has arrogated the right of sight in television news.

Here I examine a range of information-based programming: the majority of the analysis is based on network news coverage but includes news programs such as *Nightline* and *20/20* and the specific ways in which they narrate instances of rape. I analyze here three "celebrity" rapes—the Central Park jogger rape case in 1989, the William Kennedy Smith rape charge in 1991, and the Mike Tyson rape case in 1991—to mark the different ways in which news-based programming presents sexual assault, the accused, and the woman who experiences rape. I have followed a chronological order; this allows me to reveal the limited repertoire of rape narratives that news workers deploy. Further, the order reveals that, notwithstanding the numerous on-air critical analyses of television practices, network images of race and gender remain fairly static and elucidate a high degree of resistance to change. In the analysis that follows, I foreground the meanings privileged, and I identify those that are rendered absent; by examining these assertions and elisions, I assess the ability of the news to facilitate a public sphere of democratic debate. Through my findings, in three specific cases I do not intend to generalize to the whole body of television rape coverage; rather, my intent is to use these instances to mark the ways in which gender and race shape who can participate in the public sphere enabled by television and how they speak.

The three cases I examine here are inherently different. The Central Park case fits most closely stereotypical understandings of sexual violence. It was an interracial gang rape, accompanied by an inordinate amount of violence. Media coverage focused on the brutality of the crime and the racial transgression of white female sexuality. The William Kennedy Smith and Mike Tyson charges fit the acquaintance rape mold—they were intraracial and derived their media salience primarily from the celebrity status of the accused. Considering these significant differences, I do not compare network presentations of the three cases; rather, I read them through and against each other to foreground the nature of the public sphere facilitated by network news. The analysis reveals the specific ways in which the intersections of gender, race, and class inflect understandings of rape, particularly which aspects are discussed in the public sphere enabled by television news. I contend that race- and gender-based definitions of sexuality and sexual assault and the gendered definitions of public and private domains are imbricated in any understanding of television as public sphere. The analysis here reveals that television's ability to promote democratic debate and discussion about sexual violence is stymied, because network news narratives hail the white male subject as the normative citizen of the public sphere.

Despite the variations in network news coverage of these rapes, in all three instances news narratives effect a strategic separation between the discourses of gender and race. I argue that it is precisely this strategy of focusing either on race or gender, but rarely their intersection, that allows news workers to produce such different rape narratives. When the rape coverage is concerned with nonwhite participants, the news tends to foreground race-based assumptions of sexuality; this is strikingly visible in the interracial Central Park and Mike Tyson cases, where black masculinity is demonized. Indeed, racial difference becomes the primary explanatory framework for the crime. When the coverage is concerned with white participants, the news foregrounds gender-based assumptions of sexuality. In these instances, it is the accuser, and more generally, woman, who comes under scrutiny, and news coverage reiterates numerous patriarchal myths about sexual violence. The inability to capture the complex ways in which race and gender mediate social experience reveals the normative standards of the television gaze: from a white masculine perspective, race or gender is the axis of difference around which understandings of rape are constructed.

In all cases, whether it involves white or nonwhite participants, the news presents a limited understanding of rape, one that reproduces dominant understandings. This perspective is effected by the news focus on the accused. News workers appear to have responded to feminist criticism of the binarized portrayals of rape victims by shifting their attention to the accused rapist. While the celebrity nature of the cases may account for the attention paid to the accused, a close analysis reveals that the news produces masculinized narratives of rape. These reports are more about masculinity, what is proscribed and prescribed masculine behavior for black and white males, than about sexual violence. The woman who brings the rape charges slides out of view; her violation is transformed into a symbolic cause for the discussion of other issues, such as inner-city youth violence, athletic socialization, or political privilege. On the few occasions she becomes visible, news workers see her from the accused male's point of view, and she is cast as crying rape. News narratives mobilize this false rape charge by focusing on superficial details such as the scene of the assault, the events immediately prior to and after the assault, and the circumstances leading to the assault. This reporting style (inadvertently) transforms these details into causal factors for the rape. The complex theories of rape postulated by feminists are seen rarely in television news coverage of rape. Network news narratives locate rape survivors on the margins of stories that center on their physical violation. Indeed, I argue that they become bit players with walk-on parts in their own biographies. Equally important, the white standpoint from which these narratives are enunciated allows the female body to become a site for inscribing cultural anxieties about nonwhite, particularly African-American, male and female sexuality. Together, these factors shape the nature of the public sphere of debate enabled by news programs.

A striking absence in my analysis is network news coverage of interracial rape cases where black women are victimized. During the period of my analysis, in New York City, the St. John's University gang rape trial occurred. A Jamaican-American student charged six white fraternity students with rape. While local news covered this case and the 1991 trial quite extensively and sensationally, especially the acquittal of the defendants, network news coverage was absent.[1] This silence replicates the historical silencing of black women's rape. Earlier in 1987, similarly, the Tawana Brawley case drew little attention from the networks. In this instance, too, local news covered extensively Brawley's charge that she had been abducted and raped by six white men, including a police officer. Jonathan Markovitz notes that the national media did not treat her allegations as newsworthy until considerable doubt arose about their reliability. Even then network coverage was limited to the striking ways in which Brawley's attorneys mobilized the African-American community in New York City. Overall, the media presented Brawley as the stereotypical "sexually duplicitous and available black woman" rather than as a potential subject of sexual victimization.[2] A grand jury dismissed her charges and, subsequently, in 1998, the police officer won a libel suit against Brawley's attorneys. Given the absence of network coverage of these rape cases, I have not included them in my analysis. Cognizant that this lacuna could replicate the historical silencing of African-American women's experiences, in my analysis I highlight the consequences of this lack of representation of black female victimization in interracial rapes.

SPEAKING FROM SOMEWHERE

Before I proceed with the analysis of the individual cases, I must elucidate how I deploy the terms *white* and *masculine* to describe the enunciative modality of the news. I contend that although news workers work hard to produce the news objectively, to speak from nowhere, they indeed speak from somewhere, a space that is marked by the socio-sexual identity of news institutions. As cultural studies scholars, particularly Stuart Hall, have demonstrated, the information presented by the news is situated, grounded in its conditions of production.[3] It is shaped by who speaks the news and by where it is spoken. When I assert the situated nature of the information provided by the news, I am not referring to the sex or racial identity of individual reporters or news anchors. I am arguing that news narratives of rape are shaped by institutional structures, social practices, and the relations of power embedded in news workers' activity. A central point I am making is that we understand sexual violence through specific practices of signification, within particular discourses. The news worker covering rape encodes it in a manner that endows the event with particular meanings. This does not imply that this is the only meaning of rape permitted by the report. Instead, I argue that this is the meaning of sexual violence that is privileged.

Scholars such as Helen Benedict and Wendy Kozol have persuasively revealed that the male point of view saturates news coverage of women and gender-related issues. Others such as Helán Page contend that the white public space from which the U.S. media operate renders blackness hypervisible.[4] I develop the significance of these two insights on the politics of enunciation later in this chapter.

A Masculine Gaze

I refer repeatedly in this text to a masculine perspective; this does not refer to the sex of the speaker but instead to the male-centered worldview that is foregrounded by the news.[5] A masculine understanding of rape could be best understood as a patriarchal definition that privileges a male-centered view of sexual assault. This perspective would attempt to explain what leads a man to rape and how a rape charge affects a male, and would perceive of consent and resistance in primarily male-defined terms. Significantly, a masculine understanding of rape would focus on the institutional processes, such as trials and criminal procedures undertaken by the police, and would tend to view rape as a private/individual problem rather than as a social concern.

In contrast, as I have pointed out in the last chapter, the anti-rape activities in the United States have attempted to reconfigure this understanding by substituting a woman-centered definition of rape, one that foregrounds the perspective of the rape survivor, the violence committed on the female body, and the emotional and physical trauma associated with experiences of sexual assault. Patriarchal understandings present rape as anomalous behavior, and the rapist is understood to be pathologically abnormal. Feminists, on the other hand, emphasize the structural conditions that engender sexual assault, such as the institutions and structures that stratify men and women into socially defined gender roles, the dominant cultural artifacts that dehumanize and objectify women, and the educational system that effects gender role socialization.

THE TRANSPARENCY OF WHITENESS

The white perspective from which news narratives emerge defies easy definition. Whiteness is not a racial identity marker, but as Ruth Frankenberg,
John Fiske, David Roediger, and others suggest, a position of privilege that
presents itself as universal.[6] Whiteness is "everywhere in American culture,
but it is very hard to see," George Lipsitz asserts. It is a point of space "from
which we tend to identity difference," Hazel Carby clarifies.[7] Similarly,
Roediger declares, whiteness is defined only negatively, by what it is not, a
rule of norm established only after the phenomena that it came to define as
inadequate or abnormal.

Working from these concepts, critical race theorists have attempted to
delineate relations of racial representation, the specific ways in which whiteness constructs nonwhite peoples as other. They are specifically interested in
displacing the unmarked and seemingly transparent status of whiteness. They
unravel the ways in which whiteness emerges as embodying rational, legitimate, normal, and natural characteristics. For instance, examining television
coverage of the Anita Hill–Clarence Thomas hearings and the 1992 uprisings
in Los Angeles, Fiske points out that whiteness in the media "comprises the
construction and occupation of a centralized space from which to view the
world, and from which to operate in the world. This space of whiteness contains a limited but varied set of normalizing positions from which that which
is not white can be made into the abnormal; by such means whiteness constitutes itself as a universal set of norms by which to make sense of the
world."[8] These analyses reveal the privileges that are accrued to positions and
subjects marked white.

In his analysis of whiteness, Roediger borrows Mary Louise Pratt's concept
of the imperialist gaze to capture the frames and relations of racialized power.
Examining travel writings from colonial South America, Pratt argues that the
imperialist gaze is characterized by a desire to classify and categorize; it also is
marked by a particular surveying from above.[9] Within the U.S. context, Roediger argues that the imperialist gaze can only take us so far. Here it is necessary
to engage with the specificity of the historical legacy of slavery and its construction of racial identity. This caution is particularly relevant in discourses of
sexuality. As numerous scholars have pointed out, since slavery, the black body
has been menacingly sexualized; while the black male has been cast as sexually
rapacious and a threat to white women, black women have been presented as
promiscuous.[10] This constellation of ideas continues to prevail and shapes contemporary understandings of rape, both in terms of how intraracial rape among
white and black people is understood as well as interracial rape.[11]

I use the term *whiteness* to interrogate the ways in which racial subjects are constituted through representational practices. Specifically I examine what the news characterizes as deviant and abnormal behavior and, by extension, what is presented as normal sexual behavior. Together, the terms *white* and *masculine* permit a recognition that issues of sexuality and race always appear in "articulation, in a formation, with other categories and divisions and are constantly crossed and recrossed by the categories of class, of gender, and ethnicity."[12] This formulation permits as well an analysis of the ways in which difference is constituted across the categories of gender, race, and inevitably class. Insisting that conceptualizations of the public sphere should take into account how gender and race intersect to create multivalent and shifting definitions of the public and private, Nancy Fraser has suggested that when examining the public sphere defined by the news, it is important to interrogate whose words count and what determines the official public story of what really happened. "Who has the power to decide where to draw the line between public and private? What structures of inequality underlie the hegemonic understandings of these categories as well as the struggles that contest them?"[13]

Taking into account these theories, in what follows I underscore what is specifically discussed about rape, the ideologies that have been collected about the subject, and which assertions are made about it and which are disallowed. Foucault's mode of analyzing discourses as structuring knowledge and social practices helps highlight the relations of power that make possible these particular meanings of rape. The operations of power relations in network news discourses can be understood by examining whose perspective is represented in the narrative and by examining the causal relations made: who is represented as doing what to whom. The following analysis reveals the distinctive relations of power implicated in television discourses of rape and sexuality. Network narratives of rape emerge from an unexamined position of whiteness, valorizing specific understandings of sexual violence and determining whose voices dominate in these narratives and whose voices are marginalized.

SEX AND VIOLENCE: MEDIA STAPLES

Historically, violent crimes have been the staple fare of the media, and several scholars have pointed out their enduring newsworthiness.[14] Despite the prevalence of sex crimes in the news, there have been few systematic studies of media representations. The majority of scholarship has examined the possible effects of programs/articles on the behavior and attitudes of the audience.[15] In this section I highlight the limited qualitative analyses of news coverage of rape, and I point out the interventions that I make.

Helen Benedict's *Virgin or Vamp* provides a comprehensive and detailed analysis of newspaper coverage of sexual assaults in the United States. While she focuses on the coverage of five cases that occurred during the 1980s, her book situates this analysis within a historical pattern of press practices. During the first half of the twentieth century, the news coverage of sexual assaults was riddled with stereotypes about the pathological rapist and the "vaguely disturbed" victim. Benedict contends that the consciousness-raising activities that accompanied the second wave of the women's movement may have extended to the press in the 1970s, elucidating a less stereotype-ridden portrayal of the crime. In the 1980s, however, the coverage was comprised primarily of stereotypical understandings of the crime. Any feminist influence on the reporting process had been countered by a backlash against women's concerns, she argues. This backlash is evident in press portrayals of rape victims and rapists. Benedict argues that reporters tend to cast victims in a dichotomous fashion either as virgins or vamps. The victim as virgin is portrayed as being pure, innocent, a person attacked by monsters, while the vamp as victim is depicted as a wanton female who provoked the assault with her sexuality. Similarly, the accused rapist is presented either as a depraved and perverted monster or as the boy-next-door who is the antithesis of the pathological rapist. This trend did not improve in the 1990s. Benedict points out that most news coverage continued to ignore feminist analyses of rape and thereby repeatedly presented the crime as an incomprehensible act. Examining local television news coverage of rapes, Marian Meyers reaffirms these patterns. She asserts that the victim is often cast as either the "good" girl or the "bad" girl, a situation analogous to Benedict's virgin or vamp.[16]

Examining the influence of rape reform efforts on news practices, Lisa Cuklanz arrives at an analogous conclusion. News practices fail to integrate feminist understandings of sexual assault in their coverage and offer only fragmented depictions of rape reform history.[17] Sylvia Walby and Keith Soothill, among other British scholars, find similar trends in the United Kingdom's press coverage of sex crimes. While paying an inordinate amount of attention to brutal rapes, newspaper coverage casts doubt on the pervasiveness of the crime, they add.[18]

While my analysis echoes many of the themes highlighted by this scholarship, I also suggest that television news coverage of sexual assaults is far more paradoxical and complicated than these accounts suggest. By examining the intersections of race and gender, my analysis reveals that depictions of white women and African-American women are significantly different and cannot be reduced to virgin/vamp categories. Instead, I argue that since these racialized and gendered identities are relationally constituted, in any given case the figure of the raped woman could, at different moments, occupy both categories of virgin and vamp, or neither.

THE SPLIT SUBJECT

The various studies I have listed above explore the linkages between media portrayals of rape and feminism. The intersection of race and gender and the manner in which it inflects rape coverage, however, have rarely been systematically examined. Critical race theorists have pointed out the stereotypes that have accumulated around the relatively rare phenomenon of interracial rape. Historical anxieties surrounding the transgression of racial boundaries continue to inform media representations of African-American sexuality. The politics of racism thus cannot be separated from the representations of rape and the social understandings of it, critical race theorists argue.[19]

The majority of work in this area has explored the ways in which media portrayals demonize black masculinity. For instance, Jack Lule and Michael Awkward conclude in separate analyses that newspaper coverage of the Tyson rape case presented the black male as posing a sexual threat not only to white women but to society as a whole.[20] Other studies illuminate the ways in which black masculinity becomes hypervisible in popular culture and the limited subject positions available to African Americans within these discourses.[21]

The images of black women are similarly inflected with a series of cultural stereotypes that can be traced to the era of slavery. Then and now, African-American women's experiences of sexual violence are framed and informed by the myths of the promiscuous Jezebel and Sapphire. Evelynn Hammonds contends that black women's sexuality continues to be constructed in binary opposition to white womanhood. Black women's sexuality is rendered simultaneously invisible, visible (exposed), hypervisible, and pathologized in dominant discourses.[22] Consequently, in popular culture, representations of the black woman as "unrapable" dominate.

In general, critical race theorists agree that the complementary myths of black male bestiality and black female promiscuity shape the ways in which African Americans experience oppression. These studies reveal that the problematic images of racialized sexuality inevitably normalize white sexuality, particularly white masculinity. As the analysis in this chapter reveals, these images of black sexuality are not static. They are produced relationally with the subject positions available to whites. Often, though, in a tradition recurrent since the Scottsboro cases, news narratives enact a strategic separation of gender and race in their coverage of rape. Invariably, news coverage reiterates stereotypes of (racialized) sexuality.

In what follows, I examine the individual rape cases and the manner in which the white masculine gaze of the news shapes the characterization of these intersections of gender and race. I examine the interracial Central Park case and then two intraracial sexual assaults, the first a white-on-white case and the second involving African Americans. This foregrounds the different ways in which the white masculine gaze inflects news portrayals of sexual assault, the accuser, and the accused.

ANATOMY OF RACIAL ANXIETIES

On an April evening in 1989, a New York City woman jogging in Central Park was gang-raped and violently attacked. Her assailants beat her unconscious and left her for dead. The mauled woman, who was not expected to survive, was white, in her late twenties, wealthy, well educated, an investment banker, and a jogger. The accused were working-class African-American and Puerto Rican teenagers from Harlem. Originally, eight teenagers were arrested, but only six of them were brought to trial in three separate cases.

This sexual assault hewed closely to stereotypical understandings of "real" rape. It was a stranger, interracial gang rape, accompanied by brutal violence. Statistically, it was typical of gang rapes, which are overwhelmingly committed by teenage boys on a lone female who does not know the assailants. Gang rapes are likely to involve more sexual humiliation, beating, and torture than single-assailant rapes. Above all, victims are picked for their availability, not for their looks or personality.[23] The only abnormal element of this case was its interracial component; studies reveal that interracial rapes constitute the exception rather than the norm.

Network news coverage of the gang rape can best be described as spotty and sensational. Together, all three networks carried nine reports on the attack and six more on the ensuing trials. While these numbers may seem insignificant, the attention devoted to the case was substantial. Disregarding rape statistics, network news coverage focused primarily on the interracial component of the rape and secondarily on the physical violence committed on the victim. As the following analysis reveals, the white normativity of the news is brought out in sharp relief in the coverage of the accused. News narratives located the teenagers within a discourse of alterity that was informed by the historical myth of the black rapist.

To scrutinize the concerns developed in the news coverage, it is necessary to understand the racial anxieties that had surfaced at that historical moment in the country, particularly in New York City. At the time of the attack and during the trials, New York City residents were exposed to a series of incidents involving interracial violence. In the period 1986–1987, the local media focused on a case where several whites in Howard Beach beat to death a black man; in 1987, a black teenager, Tawana Brawley, accused six white men of raping her; in 1989, a black teenager was murdered by several whites in Bensonhurst. When the trials began, relations between the Korean-American and African-American communities had come to a head following the death of an African-American woman inside of a Korean-owned deli. Local media coverage of the St. John's University interracial gang rape and trial raised several stereotypes surrounding black female promiscuity. On a national level, the Willie Horton advertisement deployed by the Republican Party during the 1988 presidential election campaign resuscitated historical myths of the threat that black men posed to white society. Emerging at this historical moment, it is not surprising that the local news presented the Central Park case within the parameters of racial difference.

These circumstances cannot explain why the network news, which solicits a national audience, also framed the case within a similar racialized framework. Television news coverage was ostensibly spurred by the brutality of the rape, however, network narratives paid little attention to the issue of sexual violence. They focused incessantly on the teenagers, casting them as alien and incomprehensible. Network news narratives foregrounded dominant understandings of racialized sexuality and reiterated several myths about rapists.

Even before the networks aired their first report on the sexual assault, visually they presented the teenagers as cultural others. All three networks used an identical video clip of the arrested teenagers to advertise their coverage of the rape. It comprised a nighttime shot of the handcuffed teenagers being led out in pairs from a police station and into the waiting journalists' cameras.[24] This visual condensed many of the trends that were later developed in the verbal narratives. The accused teenagers tried to avert their faces from the cameras, but with little success; despite their juvenile status, the media surrendered their rights to privacy. The clips articulated the incongruence of youth with the familiar television news iconography of black male criminality.[25] These images foreclosed the possibility of other narratives of rape and presented the assault primarily as one that centered on issues of race and urban crime.

Even as the visual captured the cultural significance of racial difference, all three networks constructed narratives of shock and disbelief that foregrounded

the youth of the assailants and their violent behavior. The narratives constructed the teenagers as racial others through their focus on three aspects:
inner-city language, structural conditions of inequality, and the criminality of
African-American males.

CRIMINAL CULTURE

Despite minor variations, in their first reports on the case, all three networks
focused on the inner-city culture that had fostered the assailants. News workers focused on the word "wilding," which the teenagers are believed to have
used in their confessions to describe the assaults they perpetrated in Central
Park.[26] Introducing the report on *ABC World News Tonight*, anchor Peter Jennings explained that "wilding" is terror by *our* definition. *NBC Nightly News*
anchor Tom Brokaw broadened the definition, describing it as "a new teenage
slang term for rampaging in wolf packs, attacking people just for the fun of
it." These anchors' introductions encapsulated the process of othering, which
rendered the teenagers and their actions alien and incomprehensible.
Brokaw's use of terms such as *wolf pack* and the attention he brought to the
belief that the teenagers characterized violence as fun dehumanized the
assailants and emphasized their difference from the rest of society, an aspect
also highlighted by Jennings' "us-them" vocabulary. News workers failed to
interrogate the racist assumptions that framed their focus on the word *wilding* or how the repeated use of the term served to locate the teenagers within
the category of other. Similarly, in reports that constructed the events prior
to the rape, news workers repeatedly used animalistic metaphors of wolf
pack, herds, and mobs to describe these "children from Harlem" and their
activities.[27] The language deployed by news workers reveals the white normativity from which the networks constructed the rape narrative and solicited
their audience. According to Benedict, during initial coverage of the case, the
media adopted the "stance of respectable, out-of-touch whites learning to
their horror about this 'street' [i.e., black] term."[28] It must be noted that none
of the news workers specifically revealed the racial identity of the accused,
however, the focus on the alien language and the accompanying visuals clarified it. As Page argues, within a white public space, issues of racial significance appear "fair, just, legitimate, and simplistically obvious."[29] These trends
are apparent in network coverage of the accused teenagers.

The subsequent reports built on this fascination with a term only
"youngsters from the tougher neighborhoods" understood. In his role as
expert on both *ABC World News Tonight* and *CBS Evening News*, psycholo-

gist Alvin Poussaint suggested that wilding may be a "frightening," "ritual . . . of manhood."[30] The reports often concluded that once New Yorkers understood the alien language that "children of the city" spoke, they could "tame" them. These conclusions capture what Foucault identifies as the power-knowledge nexus—the manner in which knowledge is put to work to regulate social conduct. In the discourse constituted by the news, it was the arrested teenagers and, by extension, inner-city culture that needed regulation. The narrative focus on racial difference supplemented by familiar representations of racial subjects resuscitated myths of black male bestiality and also normalized whiteness.[31] The gendered nature of sexual violence is marginalized in these early reports.

When they did not discuss language, news workers turned their focus to the structural inequalities that mark inner-city culture. Reports emphasized the class difference between the victim and her assailants and suggested that the gang rape could be explained by race and socioeconomic inequalities. News workers turned to sociologists and Harlem teenagers to understand the inner-city culture that led the teenagers to gang rape. They isolated anomie as the primary cause for the violence. "There is no recreation, no activities, you know. The community services, the centers, the organizations that are supposed to supply some kind of recreation for the kids, they don't do it," several teenagers told news workers.[32] These reports present social location rather than social norms as the cause for rape. Within such a framework, sexual violence becomes an eruption of "pent-up energy," and such violence can be controlled by transforming the inner-city into structures resembling more affluent neighborhoods. Although these reports attempted a class-based understanding of the crime, they were structured by what Stuart Hall calls "inferential racism." The reports "naturalized representations of events and situations relating to race that have racist premises and propositions inscribed to them as a set of unquestioned assumptions."[33] In these reports, wilding, Harlem, and inner-city culture become code words for articulating racial difference. Paul Gilroy contends that in contemporary society, racial politics often are alluded to by code words. In this instance, the use of the words wilding, inner-city culture, Harlem, and so on allows news workers to speak about race without mentioning the word.[34]

Repeatedly, network texts exposed the inability of the white gaze to frame inner-city culture outside of the familiar matrices of racial animosity or the more material ailments of drugs and greed. Initially, news workers announced with amazement that the accused were "kids who come from quiet, respectable homes," who "suddenly went bad." In later reports, like the other media, network news workers interviewed neighbors and reconstructed the biographies of the accused as perennially bad teenagers.[35] Through these sound bites, the networks developed a profile of the rapist as "always-already other." The new evidence about the teenagers' pathologically violent nature complemented concerns about the word *wilding*. News workers consistently demonized the rapists as abnormal, brute monsters who remained throughout a nameless "mob." Network coverage constituted the otherness of the teenagers by repeatedly presenting black masculinity in a rhetoric of deviancy and criminality.[36]

A different set of narrative practices allowed news workers to present the inner-city male inhabitant as "always-already" criminal. Networks aired sound bites from prominent citizens that reinforced the image of the black man as criminal. Long before the trials, New York City Mayor Ed Koch presented the teenagers, presumably because of their race, as always-already criminal. "Don't you believe ever that it is ever the first time when they are caught." All three networks also aired the full-page advertisement that business tycoon Donald Trump issued in the *New York Times*, calling for the death penalty for the rapists.[37] While the focus on wilding and the visuals invoked the myth of the black male rapist, these statements advocating vigilante justice echoed the complementary rhetoric of the lynch law of the turn of the century. By unproblematically presenting these statements, the networks tacitly revealed the white gaze of the news. Only certain aspects of racial behavior were interrogated, whereas those of the mayor and Trump were not perceived as emerging from a position of whiteness.

WHITE VICTIMHOOD

The brief network coverage of the Central Park case offered multiple, shifting explanations for the gang rape: structural conditions of inequality, police negligence of the inner-city, and peer pressure. They argued ultimately that the teenagers' actions were derived directly from inner-city culture, a specific configuration of race and socioeconomic status. Effectively, network discourses presented rape as a manifestation of black male deviance. The absence of a monolithic explanation of rape is welcome, however, the one theme consistently absent from news reports was gender role socialization and the social structures of domination that make such violent behavior possible.[38]

In network narratives, the jogger and the teenagers occupied radically opposed discursive positions. Whereas the teenagers were consistently portrayed as abnormal and unambiguously as victimizers, network descriptions of the rape survivor amounted to an eulogy. She was twenty-eight years old, a Wall Street investment banker, young, and according to a schoolteacher, "a golden girl." News workers did not divulge the woman's name, nor did they discuss aspects of her life that may be characterized as private. Network news portrayal of the rape survivor was favorable but derived at the expense of the demonic vision of the accused teenagers. As Benedict points out, when the woman-victim is presented as a "good" woman, media coverage focuses on the culprit.[39] Significantly, only one report identified the woman as white. Most others marked her whiteness by not identifying it.

After the initial attempts to understand wilding and the lives of inner-city children, the case disappeared from network screens. The networks provided occasional on-screen updates on the trial process of "one of the most talked about crimes in the history of New York." These reports indicated that the six teenagers were to be tried in three different trials; they did not explain why all eight arrested teenagers were not indicted on charges of sexual assault and battery. An exploration of the racialized discourse of rape emerged briefly during trial coverage.

CBS Evening News covered the first trial in one report, where the news worker referred to the charges of racism and police incompetence that had surfaced. Reverend Calvin Butts argued in a sound bite that, "There is no evidence of any kind, no fingerprints from the rocks, no fingerprints from the brick, no blood on their clothing, the semen does not match, the DNA tests come back negative. There is nothing that links these boys to the crime." The news narrative failed to continue this thread and glossed over the absence of forensic evidence and the controversy surrounding the teenagers' taped confessions. Instead, the report focused on the jogger's "dramatic" testimony when she identified her "blood-soaked" shirt but had no memory of the incident, and the "chilling words" of the teenagers' videotaped confessions. This report, like the rest of network coverage, left viewers secure in the understanding that the accused teenagers were the monsters we had come to know.[40] They presented as well a sensational and sentimentalized account of rape and the rape victim.

In on-screen reports, the anchors on *ABC World News Tonight* and *CBS Evening News* presented the guilty verdict in the first trial as a boost to "law and order." *CBS News* quoted the presiding judge's characterization of the teenagers as "mindless marauders seeking a thrill who turned an oasis into a torture chamber."[41] Abruptly, news coverage of the Central Park case and the trials came to a halt. None of the networks covered the trials of the other accused teenagers, or the other verdicts, nor did viewers receive any follow-up report on how New Yorkers were controlling urban violence.[42]

As rape texts, network news narratives lacked a center. They elided the gendered aspect of the violence. Even the word rape was rare. Instead, news workers used the euphemism "brutal attack." Only one news worker mentioned that the gang rape highlighted "the vulnerability of women." The reports provided little information on rape: they did not reify cultural misunderstandings about the "good" and "bad" woman, but neither did they incorporate feminist understandings of the crime. The absence of feminist voices was glaring in this instance.

From network news reports, one would gather that the brutality of the crime was a racial issue. With their focus on the rapists, network news constructed narratives where the pathology of the teenagers, not gender-role socialization processes, led to the crime. These reports reiterated several myths about rapists and the singular nature of gang rape. Contradicting findings on rape, these narratives presented the rapists as cultural "others," abnormal and outside of the realm of humanity. Journalists, in their coverage of the rape, tapped into dominant stereotypes, recreating a historic "other": the black male aggressor.

Network narratives were informed by cultural and historical fears of the black rapist and residual memories of lynching and slavery. They valorized a unique discourse of rape, whereby issues of gender and race were central features, but only in one particular configuration. The gaze of the news could accommodate a coverage of race or gender but not the ways in which these intersect to constitute the social subject. In these narratives, white sexuality was the invisible referent, the norm against which black sexuality was measured. This becomes particularly obvious in the ways that news workers glossed over the lynch rhetoric that accompanied the demonization of nonwhite sexuality. In the William Kennedy Smith case that I analyze in the next section, the white masculine gaze of the news inflects definitions of private and public issues in a similar manner but along a different axis of difference, gender.

The sensational and breathless coverage of this interracial gang rape is in striking contrast to the erasure of black women's rapes. I alluded earlier to the Tawana Brawley and St. John's University rape cases, which did not generate the same level of national attention. While the Central Park coverage was suffused with references to the racial identity of the accused teenagers, in the St. John's University case, the local press referred rarely to the interracial nature of the gang rape. Instead, media coverage focused on the woman-accuser's behavior prior to and after the rape, her sexual habits and so on. The media covered all aspects of her life as though this microscopic attention to details could serve as an explanation for the crime.[43]

Similarly, in the Tawana Brawley case, news coverage gradually drew attention to the teenager's biography to discredit her account. From the beginning though, the focus was not on the rape charge but on the practices of her "flamboyant" attorneys. When news workers turned to the rape, they cast Brawley as an unreliable rape claimant by referring to her behavior at "wild parties," rumors of drug use, and so on.[44] The lack of representation of these two cases where black women filed interracial rape charges highlights the white male gaze of the news. One of the avenues available to resist such silence is to repeatedly inscribe these histories.[45] The anger directed at the teenagers in the Central Park case and the glowing terms in which the jogger was described by network news were in striking contrast to their silence on interracial rape cases involving black women. Perhaps this silence is the most evocative example of the ways in which status, power, and material inequality shape who can speak and whose voices are heard in the public sphere enabled by television news.

A POLITICAL SPECTACLE

On Easter weekend, 1991, William Smith was vacationing in Palm Beach, Florida, at the Kennedy family estate with his relatives. Late one evening, he accompanied his uncle, Senator Edward Kennedy, and his cousin, Rhode Island state legislator Patrick Kennedy, to a local bar, where he met a woman, Patricia Bowman.[46] From all accounts, Smith and Bowman danced, flirted, and then returned to the family compound late at night and took a walk on the beach. The woman filed charges that she was raped by Smith at the beach, while he claimed that they had consensual sex. Network news coverage drew an unprecedented amount of attention to a rape case; the 24-hour cable channels, Courtroom Television Network and CNN, aired gavel-to-gavel coverage of the trial (interrupted by advertisements on CNN).[47] The three national networks provided remarkably identical reports, and NBC's use of the accuser's name was the singular distinguishing feature. Since the coverage of this case was more extensive than in the previous case, one could expect to see a better development of issues pertaining to rape, but once again the news focused on the accused. The celebrity status accorded to Smith displaced concerns from sexual violence. The effects of the focus on the accused, however, were remarkably different from the Central Park case. In this instance, network coverage illuminated what was considered appropriate masculinity.

The William Kennedy Smith and Mike Tyson cases were celebrity rapes, gaining media attention because of the high-profile identity of the parties involved.[48] The networks devoted a substantial amount of airtime to the Smith rape case—seventy reports and over four hours of airtime—much of it devoted to critical analyses of media coverage, but this introspection did not affect or alter reporting styles.[49] The networks did not cover the charge of sexual assault any differently than other news reports. News workers relied on traditional news sources, the police and lawyers, for definitions of rape, and they defined objectivity in terms of balancing sources' opinions. This reliance on legitimated sources shaped the debates that were enabled by the news. Primarily, network coverage reproduced institutional definitions of rape, not those experienced by individuals.

This case has been characterized as a date rape, because the accuser and the accused were not strangers to each other. As recent studies have revealed, contrary to the definition of "real rape," the majority of sexual assaults fall into the category of acquaintance rape, where the perpetrators and victims are known to each other, even if only casually. It is the category of rape that is most underreported; it occurs often in safe spaces and does not involve the use of a weapon to coerce the victim into acquiescence. Definitions of consent and resistance are more contested in this form of sexual assault; these problematic aspects are heightened by identifying this category of non-stranger rape as *date rape*. Nancy Gibbs contends that the term date rape tends to imply an ugly end to "a raucous night on the town."[50] Such a term displaces concerns from the criminal aspects to the sexual aspects and brings the woman's behavior into scrutiny.[51] One reporter covering the Smith case encapsulated popular misgivings about this phenomenon. "If a woman consents to be alone with a man, where does consent end and rape begin."[52]

I have isolated three aspects of network coverage in this case—the portrayal of the accused, the presentation of rape as a phenomenon, and the depiction of the accuser. In each of these aspects, I highlight the manner in which the white masculine gaze of the news inflects portrayals.

REVISITING CAMELOT

Discussing the technological and cultural features of television, Raymond Williams identifies the flow of programs, the "relative unification of otherwise diverse or at best loosely related items," as a unique characteristic of the medium. Williams uses the word *flow* to refer to three distinct levels of unification in television: the smooth, unmarked transition between programs and advertisements; the seamless narrative constructed within programs, where "sometimes connections between several items are deliberately not made"; and certain words that are used to construct a particular worldview within these narratives. Williams argues that the flow both within and between programs reveals the preoccupations of society, predominant social values, and a "consistent set of cultural relationships."[53] The flow within news items helps constitute them; consequently, "questions about the nature of the news and the relevant area of information can only be answered in terms of flow," Tania Modleski elaborates.[54]

Other scholars examining television news have revealed how new events are introduced with unmarked transitions in an effort to produce a seamless text.[55] This concept of flow permits an understanding of the manner in which production practices privilege particular understandings of the rape charge. The "naturalized" juxtaposition of the Smith case with other reports provides clues about which elements within the event were articulated to construct a unique discourse, which connections were deliberately not made, and the cultural significance of the event itself.

The rape charges filed against Smith became a newsworthy event because of his family name and Senator Kennedy's presence at the family estate. During initial coverage, news discourses constituted Smith as a subject whose significance was derived only from his Kennedy connection. All three networks presented their initial reports in the political news segments. The flow of these texts, the physical location of the report, and their narrative structures presented the rape charge as a Kennedy political foible rather than as a criminal event. *NBC Nightly News* anchor Tom Brokaw described it as an extraordinary case because it involved "not one, but three Kennedys."[56] Other news workers emphasized visually and verbally Senator Kennedy's presence at the Palm Beach estate. They aired every avowal of innocence and denial of culpability that Senator Kennedy made. He was the narrative center of these early reports, which tried to rewrite the rape charge as a 1990s' version of Chappaquidick. News workers questioned the senator's probity, hinted at the possibility of a "cover-up," and asserted the power and influence that the Kennedy name wields.[57] The early reports on the case were not about rape but about politics. Significantly, most of these reports emanated from Washington, D.C., not from Palm Beach. Just as in the Central Park case, the networks failed to report on inconsistencies in police procedure, such as the delays in collecting evidence or questioning the Kennedys. The networks articulated a discourse that derived its significance from the political realm and occluded the gendered aspects of the rape charge.

As a result of this flow, cultural ambivalences and ambiguities about the Kennedy family were displaced onto Smith's persona. An *ABC World News Tonight* report exemplifies this trend; it attempted to understand the cultural fascination with the Kennedy name and served to locate Smith firmly within the family history. The report, describing "the spectacle that clings rightly or wrongly to the family name," was accompanied by archival footage of President Kennedy in the Oval Office, Senator Robert Kennedy announcing his candidacy for the Democratic presidential nomination, and a youthful Senator Edward Kennedy addressing the press after the Chappaquidick scandal. The visuals resuscitated cultural memories about sexual misconduct associated with the Kennedys. The verbal text meanwhile foregrounded the relevance of this visual reinscription of Kennedy history in current public discourse.[58] This report and others like it ensconced Smith's identity within an unruptured historical lineage of Kennedy notoriety.

NORMALIZED MASCULINITY

Despite the consistent focus on the accused, network news narratives did not present a monolithic image of Smith. The subject position offered to white men in the news is relationally determined, depending on the ways in which the woman in the rape case is portrayed. While initial reports pointed out that Smith, because of his Kennedy name, was heir to a legacy of sexual misconduct, later reports, where aspects of the woman's behavior were discussed, depicted him sympathetically. In striking contrast to the coverage of the accused teenagers in the Central Park case, news workers cautioned against casting a hasty judgment of Smith's guilt. *CBS Evening News* anchor Dan Rather clarified that the rape charge did not mean that he was "guilty of anything. It means he stands as an accused citizen."[59] Other reports revealed the "human side" of Smith. News workers included sound bites from friends, relatives, and acquaintances who described the accused as the archetypal boy-next-door: a "pleasant, considerate, hardworking, diligent individual."[60] Even as reports asserted that Smith was a member of the Kennedy family, thereby establishing the newsworthiness of the event, they pointed out that the accused did not really belong to the Kennedy clan. He was "something of an outsider," "a gentle person," who collected antiques and worked in "philanthropy."[61] During the trial coverage, news workers often referred to the accused as "Willie." They showed him playing touch football, photographed him with his puppy, discussed his "preppie" clothes, and showed him attending church.

These narratives presenting a Janus-faced Smith, the boy-next-door and inheritor of sexual misconduct, did not collapse under the strain of internal inconsistencies. They gained coherence instead from dominant definitions of (white) rapists, who are seen primarily as abnormal, pathologically sick men. And Smith, notwithstanding his Kennedy name, did not fit this definition. Unlike the accused in the Central Park case who were characterized primarily as bestial and sexually rapacious, despite the early focus on Kennedy misdemeanors, network narratives overwhelmingly presented Smith as occupying a position of normalcy. Here the white normativity of the news was obvious. In

White Women, Race Matters, Ruth Frankenberg points out that whiteness is a location of structural advantage, "a place from which white people look at ourselves, at others, and at society." Here we see the networks resort to universal claims about what *we* understand and accept as normal.[62] Significantly, these "human" elements of Smith emerged as the news started to pay more attention to the accuser. In the gender identities the networks constructed relationally, the white masculine gaze of the news allowed Smith to occupy the position of normalcy and, as I show below, the accuser presented as abnormal.

Network coverage of the case effectively shifted attention from the charge of rape to enunciate what is culturally and historically accepted as normal masculinity. This emphasis on masculinity is nowhere more obvious than in network portrayals of rape qua rape. The early coverage contained little information about the rape charge, the injuries that the accuser sustained, or the delay in reporting the crime. Many reports promised to delve into the issue of rape, but few ventured beyond the political ramifications of the Smith case. Only one report briefly presented rape as a social phenomenon; a *CBS Evening News* report on the charges filed against Smith included a Florida prosecutor's remark that "rape . . . is the most underreported crime," but failed to expand on it.[63] News workers did not offer specific information on the prevalence of rape in the United States. They did not generate an understanding and did not clarify misunderstandings about the phenomenon.

Nightline provided the single text that attempted to situate the charges against Smith within larger social structures. Anchor Ted Koppel introduced the program with police statistics on sexual assault, cautioning that since "nine out of ten rapes are never reported" the numbers cited underestimated the prevalence of the crime. He critiqued as well the media focus on unnecessary details. "Is it relevant that they were drinking in a bar together?" After providing this possibility of a broad-based discussion on sexual violence, the program returned to the familiar terrain of the effect of rape charges on "young Mr. Smith."[64] Repeatedly, network news coverage failed to inscribe the violence committed on the female body. She is left out of a story that purportedly centers on her physical violation. As Nancy Fraser has cautioned, the public sphere is underpinned by issues of power and inequality.[65] In the public sphere enabled by news narratives, feminist voices were absent. There was no woman-centered definition of sexual assaults. Instead, one report described the rape charge as a "whiff of sexual misconduct."[66] The notion about who could speak in the public sphere enabled by the news became more problematic when the coverage turned to the trial.

As the *Nightline* episode I have just cited attests, network coverage of the case was characterized by detailed descriptions of events immediately prior to and after the rape: the bar where the two met, what they ate and drank, and so on. By ignoring broader understandings of rape, the systemic and cultural features that permit such assaults, in network news narratives these superficial details assumed the significance of causal factors. Sylvia Walby and others have identified a similar trend in the British press coverage of rape cases and have called this a "novelette" style of reporting.[67] This was highlighted during the coverage of the trial.

Two months after networks began covering the event, the case had established a media significance of its own. Reports were now juxtaposed with other crime stories, such as the Bank of Credit and Commerce International (BCCI) scandal and Jeffrey Dahmer cases. Once the focus of news coverage shifted from the charges to the trial, news workers repeated legal practices of defining rape, foregrounding issues of resistance and intentionality.

During coverage of the trial, network narratives presented Smith as the victim by focusing on the effects of rape accusations on men, and they unconsciously presented his accuser as "crying rape." Examining the rhetoric of rape trials, Gregory Matoesian points out that they reify patriarchal understandings of rape. While prosecution lawyers tend to emphasize the "good" reputation of the accuser, defense lawyers rely on definitions of "real" rape to acquit their clients. Often defense lawyers try to rewrite the rape charge as consensual sex, pointing out that the woman wanted violent sex and so shares responsibility for the act. When news workers cover trials, they tend to reproduce the opposing lawyers' arguments and thereby reiterate patriarchal definitions of rape, Matoesian contends.[68]

Network coverage of the Smith case followed this pattern. The narratives repeated unproblematically defense arguments casting the accuser as the person who provoked the assault and/or as crying rape. In the absence of any information that these portrayals of women were routine courtroom strategy, network narratives reiterated understandings of the "good" woman who could be raped and the "bad" woman who by definition could not be raped. They reinforced the belief that a woman's lack of consent must be physically inscribed on her body. This tendency was encapsulated in a statement that lawyer F. Lee Bailey made on *Nightline*, where he argued that the Palm Beach case did not fit the legal definition of rape.

> There are no bruises. There was no violence. Apparently the clothing wasn't shredded. There is no clear-cut indicator. It may be the classic non-case, that is, where the woman feels she was raped and the man doesn't. . . . Rape can only occur in the mind of a man and nowhere else.[69]

This definition, which none of the other guests on the show challenged, erased feminist efforts to focus on the sexual violence inherent in rape. Bailey provided the archetypal patriarchal definition of rape, which depends entirely on the intention of the assailant and deprives the woman of the ability to apprehend her own lack of consent. The woman's body is expected to reveal her lack of consent as well as the perpetrator's ability to override that refusal.

Smith's testimony during the trial provides another instance where network coverage sustained patriarchal definitions of rape. "How do you defend yourself when somebody over and over again says the word rape?" he cried out in the lead story of all three networks. In the absence of any contextualizing information that this was normal courtroom strategy, network news revived the centuries' old bias against rape victims: the male fear of false accusations. Within the patriarchal definition of rape as a charge easily made, the question that Smith posed appeared natural and legitimate. News narratives did not contain any information on how the rape charge or the assault may have affected Smith's accuser; instead, she was cast as the victimizer.

The masculine perspective of the news is evident as well in network coverage of the verdict. *ABC World News Tonight* was alone in trying to contextualize this rape trial within the larger social context. Anchor Peter Jennings described the rape trial as involving a "subject of pain for millions of women," but he did not elaborate on it. He also emphasized the significance of the verdict, pointing out that Smith's lawyer argued for acquittal on grounds of "reasonable doubt," and that half of the jurors agreed.[70] The *NBC Nightly News* report, on the other hand, aligned itself with Smith and declared that "it was over swiftly, this long ordeal." Further, it interpreted the verdict as a declaration that "Smith is not a rapist," since the jury had no doubt about who was telling the "truth in this case." An expert-analyst on the newscast went on to redefine the trial as a case of misplaced jealousy and vengeance, with people screaming to "bring the rich guy to trial." In the absence of any rebuttal, this statement recast the charge as one of "crying rape" and falsely accusing an "innocent" man.[71]

APPROPRIATING FEMINISM

Like the trial coverage that reiterated patriarchal definitions of rape, network news narratives presented the accuser in very narrow and limited terms. While for the most part network coverage ignored feminist understandings of sexual assaults, there was one instance where a rhetoric emphasizing "sexist stereotypes" entered the public sphere enabled by the news.

During initial coverage, network narratives laudably referred to the accuser simply as a woman, with no other descriptors. This tendency changed though when a week after networks picked up the case *NBC Nightly News* revealed the accuser's identity, defying conventional journalistic practices. NBC News President Michael Gartner justified this decision by referring to a London-based tabloid, the *Sunday Mirror*, and the Florida-based *Globe*, which had already revealed the accuser's identity; he claimed that the question of anonymity was pointless now. In a domino effect, the *New York Times* and several other "elite" newspapers used a similar rationale to publish the woman's name. *NBC Nightly News* and some newspapers thus became part of the event that they were covering.

The decision to reveal the accuser's identity resulted in a debate that alluded to feminist understandings of rape. Reports covering this decision included many female sources, rape counselors, feminist scholars, and activists. This dominance of women's voices, however, did not enable a feminist understanding of rape. In the archetypal strategy of objective reporting, the reports balanced arguments for victim anonymity with comments from those who opposed it. Those who heralded NBC's decision argued that there should be "no shame in being a victim of rape." They appropriated feminist rhetoric to argue that granting anonymity allowed society to frame victims as "damaged goods." They contended that rape should not be "mythologized" as being different from other crimes. Feminist redefinitions of rape have emphasized the need to destigmatize victims, but they have repeatedly pointed out the specificity of sexual assault as being different from other violent acts. The *NBC Nightly News* report's assertion that rape should not be characterized as a unique crime, however, relied on a misreading of an early strand of feminism.[72] These reports revealed the convoluted manner in which even pseudo-feminist understandings of rape enter the public sphere and who can utter them. Inadvertently, these reports reiterated the ideological nature of the public-private division that feminists have repeatedly contested. The reports pointed out that publicity and privacy are arbitrarily defined terms, that the lines separating them are blurred and often defined by powerful institutions. This, in turn, shapes the voices that are heard in the public sphere enabled by the news.

The absence of feminist understandings of sexual assault was nowhere more apparent than in network portrayals of the accuser. Even as the *NBC Nightly News* report, cited above, co-opted feminist rhetoric, it continued to describe the accuser within the limited social roles that patriarchy offers women: as a "full-time mother of a two-year-old" and as a stepdaughter of the General Tire Company founder. *NBC Nightly News* proceeded to name the accuser in its coverage, however, the other two networks refused to reveal her identity. During the court trial, all three networks hid the accuser's face behind a blue electronic blob. Examining the implications of this practice, Jann Matlock points out that despite the intentions of the news to render her anonymous, in practice, media coverage fixed the accuser's identity inflexibly as gendered. While the accuser attempted to present her body as violated by nonconsensual sex, news coverage and the trial process projected a series of identities on her that stripped her of the ability to voice her experience of violation.[73]

As I have already stated, network coverage of the court trial relied primarily on lawyers' arguments and thereby reiterated patriarchal definitions of rape. Echoing defense arguments that positioned the "29–year-old accuser" as promiscuous, news narratives pointed out that the rape charge was made "after a night of drinking in several Palm Beach bars."[74] In airing this particular detail from the eight-page affidavit, news workers attributed the rape charge to alcohol-induced loss of control. Other reports during the trial coverage aired sound bites from Palm Beach residents that cast the woman as an incredible victim. Surely the woman did not go to the Kennedy estate at 3 A.M. "for high tea." These statements imply that the assumption of risk constitutes consent. The reports transformed associational details into causal factors and did not focus on the social relations between the sexes or on the way "men view women as sexual objects."[75] Ironically, in the absence of eye-catching visuals, all three networks used a stock visual of the bar where Smith and Bowman first met. The camera work solicited the viewer as a voyeur to examine the various women who were dancing and drinking at the bar. Even as the verbal texts recounted the developments in the rape case, the cameras slowly panned down women's bodies, re-producing them as sexual objects.

The accuser's testimony offered the only instance when news narratives presented a female-centered understanding of rape. All three networks used long excerpts that allowed her to define the event. All of them clarified for us that the woman behind the electronic blob remained calm for the most part but broke down when describing the assault. Media coverage of rape trials, Benedict argues, is governed by a paradox: if the woman is calm in court, the media portray her as not having suffered long enough, signifying that she is not a genuine claimant of rape; if the woman is sobbing and frightened, the media portray her as hysterical, unstable, and thus unreliable.

Network narratives also provided extended excerpts of defense lawyer Roy Black's cross-examination of the accuser, which attempted to redefine rape "as an act of love."[76] Summarizing the cross-examination, reports pointed out that the woman did not remember details about the attack, but "she recalled perfectly what she had for dinner that night." In the absence of any contextual information that memory lapses often accompany traumatic experiences, there was no other option than to agree both with the reporter and, by extension, with Smith's team that the accuser was lying. Other sound bites pointed out that the accuser "was capable of putting up a fight."[77] Defense arguments portraying the accuser as "mentally unstable" and as an incredible victim also were repeated verbatim. News narratives did not contextualize these arguments as routine courtroom strategy. Further, network experts did not focus on the content of her testimony but on her performance. Significantly, none of the networks included the voices of rape counselors or feminist scholars as experts on their programs. It is news workers' reliance on legitimated sources of information that reifies the masculine gaze of the news.

In *Virgin or Vamp*, Benedict isolates several factors that result in the portrayal of the accuser as a vamp. These factors repeatedly occur in the Smith case and can account for the defense and, by extension, network portrayal of the accuser: she knew her assailant; no weapon was used; it was an intraracial case; and she was young, "pretty," and had deviated from the traditional female sex role of being at home with family or children. In this instance, network coverage pointed out the accuser's unwed-mother status, her clothes, and her alcohol consumption. This novelette style of reporting that foregrounds associational factors allowed the networks to present the accuser as an inappropriate claimant of rape.

Apart from her testimony, the networks ignored the accuser and her attorney's attempts to define the event as rape. Once the rape charges were dismissed, networks returned to the case when the newsmagazine *Prime Time Live* interviewed the accuser. In the program, she repeatedly asserted that the interview was meant to clarify issues that had been raised by the media coverage but that had remained unanswered by the trial.[78] Networks covered this explanation with skepticism and disdain. Questioning "Patty" Bowman's decision to become a "cover girl," *CBS Evening News* pointed out that during the trial she had demanded privacy. "Now she doesn't want it, why?" By ignoring the fact that some of the media had already surrendered her identity, these post-trial reports once again questioned her credibility as a witness. They infantilized her, cast her as a capricious woman given to changing her mind, and thereby cast her rape charge as incredible.

In this case, news coverage declared certain areas as being off-limits (accusations of sexual assault against Smith cast by three other women), however, the accuser was unable to establish a similar strategy. Her motives and character were the subject of intense scrutiny and intrusive speculation, since her credibility was to be evaluated in a conceptual vacuum (one that was not informed by a nonmasculine perspective of rape). Comparing media coverage of the women in the Central Park and Smith cases, Katha Pollitt argues that the "jogger could have been the daughter of the men who kept her name out of the news (the media). But William Smith could have been their son."[79] The white masculine gaze resulted in a patriarchal definition of rape. Contradicting feminist redefinitions, news narratives focused on the accused rapist and the ill-effects of the rape charge leveled against him, and presented the accuser as an incredible witness; she had to prove her resistance and chastity. The white masculine gaze shaped the kinds of information that were discussed and the people who were allowed to speak. Nevertheless, it remains an elusive gaze, because it speaks from a position of universal experience, as rational, legitimate, and normal. These elements though become more apparent in the coverage of black sexuality, as we will see in the Mike Tyson case.

COLLAPSE OF AN AMERICAN DREAM

If news coverage of an intraracial rape among whites ended up presenting the accused as victim, in this instance of intraracial rape among blacks news coverage presented the accused as unequivocally bestial. As with the accused in the Central Park case, network news cast Mike Tyson as a bestial and rapacious black male; the stories coalesced around issues of violence and criminal deviance. The accuser though was not presented as sympathetically as was the jogger. Cultural stereotypes that have coalesced around the images of black women informed the complicated network portrayals of the woman. News coverage revealed the different valences that black sexuality takes on in an instance of intraracial rape and brought to the forefront dominant myths that prevail in our society about African-American male and female sexuality.

Long before this case, Tyson had gained notoriety for his proficiency inside of the boxing ring and his violence outside of the ring. His boxing skills had made him one of the most popular and recognized athletes in the United States. He had become the youngest heavyweight champion in 1988 and had already earned over $100 million. The over half-dozen biographies on him point out that the boxing world anticipated that he would mature into the greatest heavyweight, but his skills in the ring had already begun to deteriorate by 1991.[80] Outside of the ring, his first wife accused him of beating her; several women sued him for fondling them, and he had settled out of court with one of them; he was involved in street brawls; he had rammed his car into a tree; and he was once convicted of battery and ordered to pay a fine of $100.

Organizers of Black Expo 1991 invited Tyson to Indianapolis to generate publicity for their events, particularly the Miss Black America beauty pageant. In July 1991, the former heavyweight champion was charged with sexually assaulting a beauty pageant contestant. Tyson met his accuser, Desirée Washington, during a rehearsal for a promotional video, and later that same evening he went out with her.[81] The boxer took her to his hotel room, where he claimed that they had consensual sex, while Washington filed charges of rape. The charges were typical of those in other acquaintance rape cases. In this instance, the rape charges gained newsworthiness because of the stature of the accused. As in the Smith case, *NBC Nightly News* was once again the only network to reveal the identity of the accuser. Tyson was convicted on one count of rape and two counts of "criminal sexual deviate" conduct.[82] He was sentenced to a six-year prison term and was fined $30,000. He was released in March 1995 after serving three years in jail.

Primarily, network narratives of the trial were characterized by themes of loss and lamentation over the collapse of the Horatio Alger myth. All three networks presented the rape charges filed against the boxer as a betrayal of the American dream. This was a "heartbreaking, . . . mesmerizing" fairy tale gone bad,[83] the quintessential American rags-to-riches dream that had "self-destructed."[84] Network narratives presented the rape as a fall from grace as well as a betrayal (presumably to the white people who had supported Tyson and shaped his winning career). Reports lamented the boy who fought his "way out of the slums to become a champion and a role model" and had turned out not only to be bad but also exposed "the dark side of the American psyche."[85]

"ALWAYS-ALREADY" CRIMINAL

On all three networks, the announcements of the rape charge and other pre-trial developments were brief. While the print media hovered uncertainly between locating this event as a sports or as a criminal event, the networks located it in the criminal realm, along with reports on the Jeffrey Dahmer trial. The flow of the news positioned this rape charge unequivocally as a crime, a gesture that reflected some feminist demands but probably was a product of the absence of sports coverage on national news. The pre-trial reports were brief, on-screen announcements of the charges and its effect on the world of boxing. This event was overshadowed by developments in the Smith case, but no report made any connection between the two rape charges. By presenting these as individual, unrelated cases rather than as instances revealing the gendered nature of sexual violence and the power structures that enable such acts, the news depoliticized the issue of rape.

The analysis presented here is derived primarily from network coverage of the trial process. Unlike the other two cases examined in this chapter, network news coverage did not end with the trial verdict but included reports on Tyson's life in prison, the impact of the verdict on the boxing community, the rape survivor's response, and reactions within the African-American community. Once again, I examine the portrayals of the accused, the accuser, and rape qua rape and the manner in which the white masculine gaze inflected coverage. I argue here primarily that the white masculine gaze becomes tangible by the hypervisibility accorded to African-American sexuality, initially male sexuality and later female sexuality. As numerous scholars have pointed out, and as I have argued in this chapter, gender is always constructed relationally. In the coverage of the trial, network reports were framed by stereotypes of black male deviance and criminality. In this context, Tyson's accuser appeared as a "good" victim. Once Tyson was deemed guilty, network coverage shifted focus to his accuser, and now her identity was constructed by tapping into stereotypes of African-American female promiscuity. While Tyson's image remained fairly stable, in this case it was the portrayal of the accuser that shifted.

In her analysis of *L.A. Law*, Judith Mayne contends that the program engages with feminism as though it were a door that can swing both ways. The narrative offers multiple points of identification, both celebrating and criticizing feminism.[86] The door that swings both ways is an appropriate metaphor to address the manner in which Tyson's background and his race functioned in network news narratives. For the most part, network narratives tapped into the boxer's ghetto youth to construct an unchanging historical lineage of violence. Using the testimony of sports writers and biographical details already available to news workers, these narratives cast Tyson as an "always-already" other. He "was a teenage mugger and has always had a violent, uncontrollable, undisciplined side to his nature, ever since he got arrested the first time at age ten."[87] The twelve-year-old Tyson would "stand outside the supermarket and pretend to be a sweet, nice kid and offer to carry packages for old ladies back to the projects. And once he got them alone in the elevator, he would knock them out and steal their pocketbook." By age twelve, Tyson was in reform school and "seemed headed for a life of crime, but his marvelous boxing skills gave him a way out."[88]

After he became the youngest heavyweight champion, his marriage "fizzled" in public, he rammed his car into a tree in what was believed to have been a suicide attempt, and he beat up a man in a Harlem fistfight. These violent acts, along with his term in reform school, informed network depictions of Tyson as an abnormal, aggressive, animal-like character who "belongs in a cage."[89] Tyson's race and his athletic socialization were key to understanding his conduct, news narratives contended.

The boxer's physical attributes, particularly his height and weight, were transformed into menacing characteristics in network narratives. His strengths as a boxer were recast as features that were a threat to women. Examining the O. J. Simpson trial, the authors in *Birth of a Nation'hood* conclude that before the murder trial, the football star was proclaimed a race-neutral celebrity. Once the trials began, though, characteristics that were once celebrated were recast as embodying African-American criminality and irresponsibility.[90] Tyson was presented as an athlete who partially transcended his race before the rape charges were filed, but once the court trial was underway, news workers emphasized his racial identity. His alleged sexual violence was linked to his past, "to what black men to the ghetto born are destined to do by nature."[91] Sound bites remarking on Tyson's past behavior helped construct him as the embodiment of criminality and black male bestiality. "If I wasn't in boxing, I'd be breaking the law; that's my nature." He was "trained" to hurt people and "could be violent in a hotel bedroom as well as a boxing ring."[92] An ex-manager described the boxer as someone who "loves to make women bleed . . . he likes to see them in pain when he makes love to them."[93] There was no aspect of Tyson's life that remained unexamined. News workers scrutinized even his vocabulary and declared it unusual, "lewd and suggestive."[94] These descriptions of the boxer's violent nature were accompanied by archival shots of Tyson in the ring bringing down an opponent or shots of him practicing in a gym.

The verbal and visual texts combined to produce a biography of violence that resonates with Norman Mailer's definition of the psychopath:

> He is a rebel without a cause. His rebelliousness is aimed to achieve goals satisfactory to himself alone. . . . All his efforts, hidden under no matter what disguise, represent investments designed to satisfy his immediate wishes and desires.[95]

These narratives outlining the "dark side of Mike Tyson" reified the myth of the rapist as abnormal and pathologically sick, "a thug and a wolf in sheep's clothing."[96] By casting his athletic training and inner-city culture as the reason for his violent behavior, these reports recast rape into an individual problem that had little to do with contemporary social relations between men and women.

The door of Tyson's past though swung the other way to present him as a victim of unfortunate circumstances. His managers' greed had helped create the atmosphere where the boxer's violent behavior continued unchecked. They "impaired his ability to make the appropriate judgments that he would have to make," and we should not "blame the victim" [Tyson], these reports argued. They included sound bites from his Brooklyn neighbors, who testified that the boxer was a "lovable" person who had not allowed his wealth to alter his lifestyle. He was "thoughtful, sensitive, but deprived of nurturing as a young man."[97] In these sound bites, Tyson emerged as a good person lacking the will to act in his own best interest. Once again, the "inferential racism" here implied that African Americans, despite their best efforts, cannot effect successfully the rags-to-riches dream. In these reports, the boxer was recast as a victim of circumstances.

Jack Lule arrived at a similar conclusion in his examination of press coverage of the case. He concluded that reporters presented an image of the boxer that was entrenched in racist imagery. The press offered two visions of Tyson, both informed by stereotypes of African Americans. He was a crude, sex-obsessed, violent savage who could barely control his animal instincts, or he was a victim of terrible social circumstances, almost saved from the streets by a kindly overseer, who finally faltered and fell to the connivance of others.[98]

It could be argued that the causal connections that news workers drew between athletic socialization and Tyson's violent behavior outside of the boxing ring were informed by feminist scholarship. Michael Awkward argues against such a reading, contending that a feminist perspective of the Tyson trial would have highlighted that the boxer "employed techniques he learned not via an educational curriculum restricted to male athletes and celebrities but from the larger culture" in which he resided.[99] It is possible that news workers tapped into the connections enabled by feminist scholarship but, like Awkward, I contend that these themes of learned brutality emerge more as a result of the white masculine gaze of the news, where all aspects of African-American life become hypervisible. This is particularly apparent in the biographies that news workers constructed, where Tyson appears as a hapless victim of circumstances, unable to transcend his ghetto childhood. Judith Butler has characterized such knowledge formation as the ritualistic production of blackness.[100] The black body is circumscribed as dangerous, and (white) society is presented as helpless against it.

THE TRIAL AS SPORTING EVENT

In their coverage of the trial, network narratives were replete with analogies between the court proceedings and boxing matches. "Michael Gerard Tyson is once again about to step into an arena. The outcome of this contest appears far less certain than any of his heavyweight bouts," curtain-raisers to the trial intoned. In keeping with this metaphor, different developments were cast as individual rounds, and jury deliberations became the "final round." During his testimony, Tyson "came out swinging but quietly," the guilty verdict was a "knockout punch," and, stretching the metaphor to its limits, Tyson's lawyers were a "heavyweight team." These metaphors transformed the rape trial into a sporting event and trivialized the issue of sexual violence.

Observers of the Tyson trial have pointed out that his lawyers decided against casting his accuser as a "disreputable sex-seeking groupie," a strategy popularly adopted in acquaintance rape cases involving athletes.[101] They opted instead to portray the boxer as a sex fiend whose reputation should have been enough of a deterrent to the accuser. While the defense arguments were constructed to present the accuser as crying rape, by repeating these arguments without offering contextual information, network news narratives developed further the stereotype of black male sexual rapacity.[102] In network news coverage, Tyson emerges as the buck figure: brutal, violent, virile, tough, and strong.[103] The defendant, a "hulking client in nifty suits, was a kind of caveman: depraved, for whom women were simply meat." Since the boxer had delivered "sexual come-ons" to many of the pageant contestants, the accuser should have known his intentions.[104]

These characterizations of the black male rapist did not ensure against stereotypes of rape. Quoting verbatim from Tyson's testimony that he had participated in consensual sex, which the woman initiated, these reports reproduced a range of patriarchal definitions of rape and female sexuality. These sound bites recast rape as an act of vengeance, undertaken to redress the boxer's cavalier attitude toward his accuser. Other sound bites from experts echoed patriarchal definitions of rape that were aired by the defense. "When a man asks you to accompany him into his bedroom, wouldn't you take that as an invitation to engage in sexual activity?"[105] These statements were invariably accompanied on screen by two stock visuals. The first was a videotape of the pageant contestants in a dance routine. It showed various contestants in bathing suits dancing, while Tyson, in a pair of shorts, sang to them. The women in this video were present as sexual objects to service Tyson, and the lyrics of the song gave voice to this objectification. None of the reports interrogated this visual or its relevance to the trial process, or pointed out how by repeatedly airing it, the news narratives themselves re-produced these women as objects. The woman-victim remained unidentified in these visuals; nevertheless, this imagery of women as sexual objects pro-vided viewers with another opportunity to question the credibility of the rape charge. The second visual transported viewers to the hotel room where the rape was said to have occurred. This visual consisted of a shot of the hotel door and then a tight close-up of the bed dominating the room. By using the bed as a condensation symbol for the hotel room, the imagery casts doubt on the woman-victim's credibility. Within definitions of "real rape," the bed signifies a site of consensual, rather than nonconsensual, sex. Specifically, the camera taps into the popular belief that if a woman goes to a man's house or room it implies that she is willing to have sex. The bed becomes representative of this particular (mis)understanding of rape. Together, these stock visuals raised the specter of rape myths by questioning the woman-victim's location in an "unsuitable" public place.

Network coverage of the trial enabled several other misunderstandings about rape. During his sentencing, Tyson reified traditional understandings of "real rape." He pleaded that he was not guilty and redefined the rape as a situation that "went out of hand . . . I didn't hurt anyone. There were no black eyes, no broken ribs."[106] Airing this statement without any rebuttal, the networks reified the conception that a woman's nonconsent must be physically inscribed on her body, even as they reinscribed the image of black male bestiality.

(E)RACED FEMALE SEXUALITY

With the guilty verdict, network portrayals of the boxer altered marginally. News workers grieved over the "tragic" end of a glorious boxing career and constructed a fall-from-grace text. Tyson's plight became representative of the growing social crisis in America and revealed how "a plotline of struggle, redemption, and triumph" was derailed.[107] Tyson, who was once thought of as the archetypal American hero, whose "incredible promise" allowed him to "overcome an incredibly troubled background," now embodied the culture's loss of innocence. The American dream lay shattered, and Tyson was now simply another "disappointment." He was no longer "Iron Mike," and his walk was no longer characterized as "jaunty."[108]

These post-trial reports also became a site where Tyson's supporters recast the guilty verdict as the product of a racist judicial process designed to punish black males. "No matter how wealthy he is, he is regarded as an uneducated, young black man who uses his fists in a violent way to earn his fame and fortune," a sound bite intoned.[109] In these texts, Tyson was transformed into a "black male that has never really been given a chance," who, during the trial, in the words of business tycoon Donald Trump, was "railroaded."[110]

Observers have attributed Trump's statements to his business interests; Tyson's matches often were held in one of Trump's concerns and garnered him profits. The networks did not reveal this information. Uncontextualized, Trump's statements could tap into the belief that, as in the days of lynch law, an innocent Tyson was convicted by a woman who cried rape. Trump's response in this case is in striking contrast to his espousal of vigilante justice in the Central Park case.

Other fans defended the boxer by pointing out the racial biases of the judicial system and invoked the imagery of black male persecution. Their statements, however, marginalized black women's struggle against violence, intraracial and interracial. By articulating these statements and in the absence of any historical information contextualizing such concerns, networks recast these expressions of racial solidarity as an inability to identify criminality. Simultaneously, these statements presented the accuser as an incredible victim. Unlike the earlier reports that were juxtaposed with criminal stories, the flow of these reaction reports constituted them as racialized narratives. The post-verdict reports were juxtaposed with stories on trends within the African-American community, for example, Afrocentric education or re-migration to the South.

While the white masculine gaze of the news, informed by stereotypes of African-American sexuality, resulted in the portrayal of Tyson as irredeemably bestial, it constituted the accuser differently. For most of the coverage the accuser was constructed as functionally white, in contrast to the boxer's racialized identity.[111] MacKinnon contends that the "law of rape divides women into spheres of consent according to indices of relationship to men. Which category of presumed consent the woman is in depends upon who she is relative to a man who wants her, not what she says or does. . . . The paradigm categories are the virginal daughters and other young girls, with whom all sex is proscribed, and the whorelike wives and prostitutes, with whom no sex is proscribed."[112] The subject position of white womanhood bestowed on Tyson's accuser was relationally developed, and the coverage contained features characteristic of interracial rape. Until the guilty verdict, the network narratives cast the accuser in the role of "virgin," a woman who seemed pure and innocent and was attacked by a monster. Listing her achievements, the narratives repeatedly described the woman-victim as "a model citizen."[113] She was a poised, eighteen-year-old scholarship "honors student at a Catholic university, who teaches Sunday School, and does volunteer work for the mentally handicapped."[114] The networks even provided information about her physical attributes; at 5'4" and 108 pounds, she was half Tyson's size. In all respects, these network narratives told us that this "all-American girl" was the antithesis of the violence-prone boxer and was easily cast into the role of the victim as virgin; in this reinvigorated black rapist myth, the accuser was cast in the role of the helpless white victim. Together these reports reify, rather than dismantle, understandings about the "good" (white) woman who can be raped and the "bad" woman who, by definition, cannot be raped. Considering that historically black women's sexuality has been rendered hypervisible as promiscuous, network news characterization of Tyson's accuser as the All-American girl positions her as the "white," virginal woman.

The majority of reports presented the accuser in glowing terms, which outweighed stories that revealed defense arguments that attempted to cast her in the "vamp" role. News narratives included sound bites that the "accuser was far from Miss Goody Two Shoes" but was a "smart, money-hungry" woman, a "gold digger," "worldly wise," and aware of "what was coming to her." The majority of these characterizations emerged from uncontextualized statements from defense lawyers and other Tyson supporters, but news workers did not dwell upon them.

Despite these sympathetic portrayals during trial coverage, the accuser was depicted in a different manner in the post-trial reports. Once Tyson's guilt had been established, network narratives recast his accuser as a "vamp." Most post-trial reports did not focus on the boxer but instead aired comments from his supporters that tapped into myths of black female sexuality and of rape as a false accusation. In an interview that was aired on all three networks, Trump displaced the rape verdict from Tyson's behavior to the woman-victim's conduct. "You have a young woman that was in his hotel room late in the evening of her own will. You have a young woman who was seen dancing for the beauty contest, dancing with a big smile on her face, looked as happy as could be."[115] So how could she have been raped, he demanded by implication. Similarly, another report argued, "She didn't go to Tyson's room to look at his etchings." A female fan of the self-proclaimed "baddest dude on the planet" questioned the woman-victim's credibility, saying, "At 1:30 in the morning, I think she knows what she is going there for."[116] These narratives engendered sympathies for Tyson by recasting the woman-victim as an unmistakably "bad," conniving woman. Sexual politics had undermined the happy ending of the rags-to-riches myth in this text.

In Chapter 2, I outlined black women's engagement with the anti-rape movement and the conflicts that they experience in trying to hierarchize race- and gender-based oppressions. In the absence of this contextual information, African-American women's support for the boxer helps draw support for the incredibility of the rape charge.

During trial coverage, news workers deployed the myth of the black rapist, and within such a narrative structure, his accuser was presented as functionally white; she was effectively cast in the role of the white woman who needed to be protected from the sexual rapacity of the black male. Once the trial ended, news narratives foregrounded the problematic characterization of African-American female sexuality. News workers and their sources described the accuser by drawing upon a limited repertoire of images available to portray black female sexuality. Network narratives tapped into historical myths of black female sexuality and cast the rape survivor as the seductive temptress Jezebel or the evil manipulative Sapphire. Consequently, it seemed normal to portray her as a "spiteful young woman who willingly had sex with Tyson and then concocted the rape story" without offering any further explanation.[117] These portrayals emphasize that network news narratives can focus on either race or gender issues, but never the two together. In initial coverage, race occupied the narrative center, while in later reporting, gender became the focus. It is clear here that "the mythology of black sexuality is related to the mutually reinforcing ideologies and systems of white supremacy and patriarchy."[118]

In this case, as in the other two cases, the woman-victim's body became an empty signifier on which several different male figures imposed a series of shifting identities. Her body was spoken for, by, and about as a virginal "school girl" and later also as a money-grasping, oversexed Jezebel. Evelynn Hammonds has argued that in the United States, black women's sexuality is rendered simultaneously invisible, visible (exposed), hypervisible, and pathologized.[119] All of these aspects are present in network coverage of Tyson's accuser. If post-trial news reports had continued to present the victim as virgin, they would have had to confront the myth of the black male rapist and reveal that black women, not white women, are statistically the most likely victims of black rapists. By recasting her as Jezebel, news narratives blamed the woman for her victimization, suggesting that her behavior caused the assault. As Frankenberg has argued in another context, these images reveal that the "strategies for thinking through race were learned, drawn upon, and enacted repetitively but not automatically or by rote, chosen but by no means freely so."[120]

The post-trial coverage reveals the continued hold of patriarchal definitions of female sexuality in news narratives. This tendency is exemplified in a series of CBS Evening News reports that covered the "pattern" of rape victims relinquishing their identity: "It happened in the Anita Hill case. It happened after the William Kennedy Smith rape trial. And it happened again today."[121] All three women cited in the report were portrayed as trading in their anonymity for the public limelight, and the reporter implied monetary motives for these self-disclosures. The report ignored that, as in the Smith case, the accuser's anonymity had long before been surrendered by the media. *NBC Nightly News* had consistently identified her by name, and courtroom sketches revealed her face as well.

In this series of reports, while the reporter talked about the "eighteen-year-old honors student," the visuals on screen underscored her physical appearance, showing her in the different outfits required to participate in the various segments of the beauty pageant. "Until now we couldn't show her dancing at the Miss Black America pageant," the reporter announced. The juxtaposition of these images with the verbal text implied that these visuals contributed meaningfully to our understandings of rape. The use of the beauty pageant visuals suggests that she precipitated the rape through her inappropriate dress and behavior; the fact that she danced in a bathing suit a day after her assault is presented as a measure of her (in)credibility. One of the reports included a sound bite from a feminist scholar, who explained "going public" as an attempt to "take some control of the definition of who they [rape victims] were," but this remained a marginalized thread. The reports ignored as well the victim's definition of the interview, to clarify "unanswered questions, so many things that weren't covered." Instead, by constantly returning to images from the beauty pageant, the text questioned the woman's version of the events. This series of reports undermined any feminist impulse within network coverage, reifying myths about female behavior and redefining rape as a stigmatizing event.

I have been arguing in this chapter that news images of the accused and the accuser in intraracial rape cases have been complex and shifting. In the Smith case, the accused was allowed to occupy multiple and often contradictory subject positions. Similarly, in the Tyson case, his accuser was allocated the role of both virgin and vamp.

Foucault has argued that, within the discourse of sexuality, power is "essentially what dictates its laws to sex. Which means first of all that sex is placed by power in a binary system: licit and illicit, permitted and forbidden."[122] We see these distinctions at work in network representations of rape. In network news practices, the black body, particularly the male, becomes the site where forces of containment converge; it is the locus of domination. Black sexuality, male and female, emerges in these narratives as unruly and in need of policing. The imaging and rhetorical practices in this case reveal that the field of visibility made available by the news is saturated with whiteness.

REWRITING RAPE AS PRIVATE TEXT

In all three cases examined in this chapter, rape entered the public arena of news discourse through the back door as a sensational phenomenon. Network coverage unproblematically focused on the unique aspects that endowed a particular incident of rape with media significance. In the Central Park case, the coverage centered on the spectacular elements of violence, while in the Smith and Tyson cases, it focused on the celebrity status of the accused men. The primary result of such a focus on newsworthy elements was that news narratives portrayed rape cases as isolated, individual, monstrous crimes. The focus on the sensational emphasized the brutality of the crime and inferentially cast doubt on its pervasiveness. Reports rarely situated the phenomenon of sexual violence as a manifestation of the gendered structures of domination that prevail in society.

As I have enumerated in the three cases, network narratives of rape can be described as adhering to a "novelette style" of reporting: reports concentrated on minute details about the incident. They provided unnecessarily detailed description of events immediately prior to and after the rape, the scene of the assault, the circumstances leading the participants to the location of the assault, and the sequence of events. As a result, the networks constructed texts whereby these superficial details and associational factors assumed the significance of causal factors.

Stuart Hall has expanded on theories of articulation to help explain the repeated inscription of hegemonic ideology in everyday cultural practices. Articulation, he suggests, provides a way of describing the continual severing, realignment, and recombination of discourses, social groups, political interests, and structures of power in society.[123] It refers to the ways in which two or more different elements are united; this link can be broken, and since the different elements have no essential sense of belongingness, it is not absolute and essential. This unity, however, is not formed randomly; it is created under specific historical or social circumstances. The theory of articulation provides a way of describing the process by which objects and identities are formed or given meaning. It helps uncover the ways in which ideological elements cohere under certain conditions to become a discourse, and how this discourse is in turn articulated to social subjects. In this analysis, the theory of articulation can help explain why hegemonic understandings of rape appear as common sense.

In the 150 reports analyzed in this chapter, the white masculine gaze of the news articulated only certain aspects to create a discourse of rape. Not one explained or addressed an individual case within the context of the general phenomenon of rape or of contemporary sexual politics. All three networks consistently presented the specific instance of rape within a dramatic form, a narrative structure that depoliticized the phenomenon. The narratives reiterated the belief that rape is an isolated event, having no structural relationship to other social practices or phenomena. Further, these reports tended to erase the sexual violence of rape; in the Tyson and Central Park cases, the network discourses presented rape as a manifestation of black male bestiality, while in the Smith case, uncontextualized sound bites allowed networks to present it as consensual, violent sex.

These erasures of sexual violence were accompanied by radically different portrayals of white and black masculinity. When the cases involved men of color, news discourses characterized them as predatory and rapacious, their sexuality being criminal and out of control. In these instances, network coverage focused on the violent nature of the black men. In the William Smith case, though, the accused was depicted in a more complex manner—initially as a sexual predator, but later as the boy-next-door. These portrayals reveal that whiteness itself is a practice rather than an object; it emerges in relation to racial formations. In the discussions enabled by the news, black masculinity is a "key site of ideological representation, a site upon which the nation's crisis comes to be dramatized, demonized, and dealt with."[124]

From network portrayals, one could conclude that a rapist is an abnormal person, different from the man next door, yet is himself a victim of unfortunate circumstances, so he is not to be blamed for the sexual violence. These descriptions of the rapist as abnormal served to reify rape as the impulsive eruption of male sexual desire.

The woman-accuser part of the rape equation remained consistently marginalized, and when she became the focus of coverage (during trial reports), she was cast in the role of agent provocateur: she initiated the sexual assault by her "provocative" dress, her behavior, her location in an "unsuitable" public space, or her sexual history. This tendency to focus on women's behavior implies that consent could be gained inferentially through their behavior prior to the attack. Such a focus on associational details is not innocent; it directs attention toward female responsibility for constraining male desire; not toward the social relations between the sexes that enable sexual violence.

The intersections of race and class with gender played an important role in the portrayals of the individual women. It is important to remember though that these characterizations are not formulaic but evolve in relational practices. The specific characterization of the women depended on the way in which the accused was depicted. Or, as Helen Benedict contends, "how thoughtfully the press will embrace rape myths and blame the victim depends on the circumstances of the crime."[125] In the Tyson case, the woman accuser was initially located as an exemplary citizen and presented as functionally white. By highlighting the criminal and sexual deviancy of Tyson's persona, I argue that network coverage initially presented the accuser as though she were a white woman involved in an interracial rape, a subject who needed protection from predatory black males. Stereotypes of black female sexuality, however, informed news portrayals of her constantly but became more pronounced once Tyson was convicted of the rape charge. Similarly, in the Smith case, the accuser was initially enshrouded in silence, while Smith was presented within a lineage of Kennedy male sexual misdemeanors. As the networks began to portray him more sympathetically, his accuser was characterized more negatively. Smith's accuser was not presented in a manner analogous to Tyson's accuser, as a woman who needed protection from the sexual rapacity of men. Charles Lawrence has argued that by emphasizing the accuser's promiscuity, Smith's lawyers presented her in a manner akin to the "unrapable" black woman. I argue that by highlighting inconsistencies in her account of events, her clothes, and her activities before and after the rape, television narratives presented her as a "fallen woman." In this instance, network news workers tapped into persistent myths of the "unrapable" woman. Historically, nonvirgin women, irrespective of race, have been cast in the same way, as unrapable. Television narratives ensconced Smith's accuser within this lineage. Television narratives of Tyson's accuser, following the guilty verdict, and of Smith's accuser were similar.

The absence of a monolithic image of the woman accuser is welcome. Nevertheless, it is problematic and necessarily shaped the nature of debate enabled by the news. Network narratives functioned like colonizing discourses—the female experience was spoken for and spoken about by others. Despite the networks' different portrayals of the women, the accuser rarely emerged outside of the peripheries. News narratives thus effect a paradox of the raped subject—she is constantly spoken of but herself remains inaudible or inexpressible; she is displayed as a spectacle but remains unrepresentable. In network narratives, she is a being whose existence and specificity are asserted and denied, negated and controlled.[126]

Some of this can be accounted for by the absence of feminist voices, particularly black feminists, in the public sphere constituted by the news. There was no position to speak of women's vulnerability to rape or the use of misogynist stereotypes to justify such abuse. The voices represented reflected the asymmetry of power relations along gender and racial lines, and also testified to the gendered character of the public sphere.

The accused men and their actions were the central discursive axis of the news accounts. Their understanding of the event and their lawyers' definitions of consent and love making or bestiality and illogical violence were endowed with a significance that contradicted feminist understandings of rape. Individuals, rather than systems of law, gender, class, or race, became responsible for the crimes covered. The news provided limited avenues to debate the issue of rape outside of these parameters.

Rather than function as a public sphere for a wide-ranging debate of rape, network news coverage provided a very limited understanding of the issue, one framed by institutional voices. Over and over again, the texts revealed cultural anxieties about female sexuality and the transgression of racial boundaries. The fear of the black male rapist prevented networks from providing the human side of the accused black men. In the post-trial reports, network narratives tapped into historical stereotypes about black female sexuality to portray Tyson's accuser as a Jezebel. These images of African-American male and female sexuality were complementary. Indeed, I contend that these images of African-American sexuality were the invisible referents against which the networks produced identities of the accused and the accuser in all of the cases.

News narratives framed sexual assault as a contest of credibility. Did the accuser cry rape? Was the rape charge an act of vengeance? Network coverage revealed the hold that patriarchal definitions of female sexuality have on our collective imagination. The reports reified the myth of real rape and failed to point out the structural and systemic features in society that countenance rape. The networks articulated discourses of celebrity rape, whereby sexual assault could only be read as depoliticized, individual crimes of passion, with no structural relation to gender politics or other social phenomena. The network reports did not give women any agency. Like rape, the accusers remained on the margins as subjects whose identities were constructed by the accused and various lawyers. The violence committed on the female body was sublimated and displaced by male anxieties about false accusations. These texts fostered a debate about rape and rapists that valorized a semiotics of violent masculine desire.

In this chapter I have exposed how the white masculine gaze of the news regulated and contained the debate and discussion of rape. Specifically, I argue that news narratives either focused on race or gender, but rarely both. The legacies of the Scottsboro cases continue to shape news practices, revealing the enduring hold of myths of (racialized) sexuality and the inertia to integrate feminist understandings. The coverage of these three cases highlighted how gender and race intersected to create multivalent, shifting definitions of the public and private. The recurrent stereotypes of African Americans and the absence of feminist voices in the news underscored the issues of power and inequality constitutive of the public sphere and shaped whose voices were heard. The absence of coverage of interracial rape cases involving black women underscored the white masculine gaze of the news and how it shaped whose voices were heard and which meanings of sexual violence were valorized.

4

White Men Do Feminism

Multiple Narratives of Prime-Time Rape

Rapists rape. You sure as hell wouldn't ask . . . What did you do to make that guy rob you?[1]

> —police officer, from *In the Heat of the Night*

This statement in the popular 1980s cop show has an officer explaining the phenomenon of sexual violence to a male colleague who is unable to comprehend that a "fine lady" could be a rape victim. This conversation is emblematic of the majority of prime-time fictional narratives about rape that I analyze in this chapter. The writers of the program have incorporated into their story line a key feminist criticism of police investigations of sexual assault. In this episode, however, as in all of the other prime-time narratives I examine, patriarchal understandings of rape and female sexuality are imbricated inescapably with feminist redefinitions of sexual violence. The programs I analyze in this chapter repeatedly thematize the contestation and negotiation between these polarized discourses of rape; they hover uncertainly between these two ideologies and cannot be valorized as constituting feminist texts. Unlike news narratives, many of the programs foreground women's experiences of sexual violence, particularly the obstacles they face in obtaining justice. Nevertheless, these are primarily stories about the individual and rarely engage with the broader social issues concerning sexual violence that feminists have emphasized. I argue in this chapter that prime-time rape narratives contain rather than enlarge discussions about power and violence.

While the title for this chapter draws attention to the roles assigned to white men, in what follows I emphasize the variability that exists within the genres of prime-time programming. My analysis highlights that prime-time's engagement with the topic of rape is neither uniform nor simplistic. Many scholars, such as Todd Gitlin, David Buxton and Lisa Cuklanz, have argued that prime-time programs work within limited narrative strategies. The novelty of each episode is leavened with a degree of sameness.[2] In the rape narratives that I examine, the striking feature is the different and complex ways in which prime-time programs mobilize sexual violence to generate story lines. Rape is sometimes an allegory to address a broad range of social concerns, such as urban alienation. In some cases, sexual violence becomes the flashpoint to draw attention to racism and the resilience of stereotypes of racialized sexuality, particularly those of the promiscuous black woman and the criminal black male. In still others, rape is the fulcrum around which differences between women and men are rendered concrete. Examining these episodes together allows us to see the differences that mark prime-time's deployment of rape, they highlight as well the ways in which television fiction engages with the social.

To return to the epigraph that opens this chapter, it is significant that a male character utters the polemic about sexual double standards in police procedures. As this chapter reveals, prime-time rape narratives have incorporated and sometimes appropriated the rhetoric of feminism. Like the consciousness-raising groups of the 1970s, the programs emphasize the trauma and aftermath of sexual violence. These fictional rape narratives, however, undertake a gender inversion with female characters serving as the mouthpieces for patriarchal, nonfeminist interpretations of rape. The women resurrect several rape myths, primarily blaming the victims for their victimization. In these narratives, sexual assault does not serve as a catalyst for the formation of a collective gendered identity based upon a shared oppression. Rather, it serves only to alienate women from feminism. In contrast, the majority of men in these shows respond with a unified spirit that actively promotes female-centered definitions of rape. The male characters have arrogated to themselves the right to instruct women on feminism and the appropriate responses to sexual assault. In prime-time entertainment, father still knows best, even if he is only a symbolic father figure. Through these male and female characters, who espouse polarized understandings of rape, prime-time episodes highlight the contested terrain between the dominant ideology (i.e., patriarchy) and a counter-hegemonic discourse.

The epigraph is drawn from an episode on interracial rape. When dealing with issues of race, once again fictional programming undertakes an inversion: rather than address the myth of the black rapist, the episode presents the rape of a black woman by a Caucasian man. Traditionally, the rape of black women has been invisible, so these narratives provide a refreshing end to the silence. As the following analysis reveals, cultural stereotypes about race and gender provide the dramatic structure and propel the plots of prime-time rape narratives. The episodes, however, interrogate hegemonic understandings rarely; they fail to examine how rape is differently experienced by racialized and gendered subjects. One could easily substitute a Caucasian woman for the African-American woman who experiences sexual violence. In what follows, I argue that these narrative inversions reveal the limits of critiquing patriarchal ideology within a commercial medium. The nature of the debate and discussion promoted by prime-time entertainment that seeks to appeal to a wide audience is limited, contained both by production codes and economic needs.[3]

FICTIONAL REALISM

Rape as portrayed and discussed on television entertainment programs repeats many of the themes touched upon by the news and talk shows (see Chapters 3 and 5). Despite their fictional status, many of the story lines borrow elements from the news, especially from "celebrity" rape cases. During the period analyzed in this book, prime-time entertainment programs thematized instances of rape that were debated vigorously in the national news media: the issue of gang rape, cases of interracial rape, and cases involving athletes. In some instances, viewers need to be familiar with the news to fill in the gaps and construct a coherent story line.[4] Often, though, there is a slippage between the "true story" and its fictionalized account. This slippage reveals how prime-time entertainment relies on actual events for legitimacy but reshapes the narrative in significant ways to address sexual violence in novel ways. The intertextuality between news and entertainment programming also provides the possibility for television to elaborate on news discourses and to make available other ways to understand rape. In terms of media scholarship, the intertextuality between genres emphasizes the need to examine the flow of television, a concept that I developed in the previous chapter, rather than a focus on an individual genre or program.

Entertainment programs, with their focus on dramatic storytelling, provide an understanding about events that leads to a particular incident of rape, show how the victim is affected, and explain the legal processes that follow a rape.[5] Here the characters are fleshed out, and we learn about the rape from the perspectives of several characters. This provides an opportunity for a more in-depth, albeit fictionalized, exploration of the phenomenon of rape. Like most fictional texts, the episodes I analyze here are partially open-ended, and viewers have a degree of latitude in interpreting the narrative. In theory, viewers could debate the various understandings of rape that are put forward, agree or disagree with some aspects, and arrive at individual definitions of sexual violence. Yet the narrative closure that is enforced on the text directs our attention toward a particularized understanding of rape, while marginalizing other interpretations.[6] In the process of narrating rape, these fictional texts enable specific definitions of sexuality, gender, and race. It is this double movement of opening up multiple understandings of rape and simultaneously closing down certain avenues of discussion that makes entertainment programs such a compelling, complicated genre of television.

Between April 1989 and March 1992, twenty episodes of prime-time programs thematized rape. These programs were identified using the Television Script Archives at the University of Pennsylvania, which houses scripts for all prime-time programs aired since 1968.[7] The collection included the different versions (editions) of the script, including the final one, for each episode. These documents reveal changes that were incorporated at different stages of production and how the story line was altered prior to final taping.

DISCOURSES OF CRIME AND PUNISHMENT

All but one of the narratives I examine in this chapter can be characterized as belonging to the law and order genre: cop shows, legal dramas, or some combination of the two. All have a central cast of characters that appears in almost every episode, and the story lines lack narrative closure. These shows function like melodramas, thematizing the restoration of moral order out of chaos, and they repeatedly enact the contestation between good and evil. These discourses of crime and punishment come fully equipped with heroes and villains, conflict and resolution.[8]

In the shows I examine, *In the Heat of the Night* and *21 Jump Street* adhere closely to the cop show genre. Blending elements of the family melodrama with the detective show, cop shows are propelled by a single plotline and follow a linear narrative: the enactment of the crime, often off camera, and the apprehension of the criminal. The central cast of characters works en masse to unravel the crime, while interactions within the workplace family provide tangential commentary on the narrative.[9] In an analysis of the acclaimed 1980s series *Hill Street Blues*, Carol Deming points out that cop shows thematize the conflict between good and evil at three levels: the societal level, where the evil is presented as violent crime or corruption; the interpersonal level, where the evil is behavior that undermines the goals of the group; and the personal level where the evil is presented as insanity or an inability to cope with circumstances.[10] The cop shows I examine here contain story lines that represent all three levels of contestations. Unlike *Hill Street Blues*, though, they tend to follow a single narrative in an episode.

The cop show genre, with its focus on social crises, has the potential to offer a radical critique of society. Jane Feuer and Todd Gitlin concur that they fail in this enterprise.[11] The shows promote an ideology that indicts the state and public institutions for their inability to fulfill their assigned tasks. The criticism they offer is a populist view of bureaucracy. "People suffer and institutions authorized to redress that suffering fail in their stated purposes. What is left is a creative coping that honors both the suffering and the failure of a society now seemingly beyond remedy, one in which a change in the social structure seems out of the question."[12] The narratives rarely offer a sociological explanation for crime, and serve ultimately to secure consent for the operations of a repressive state apparatus. Cop shows often align the interests of the "local police state with the needs of ordinary citizens, in common alliance against the political bungling of the federal state."[13] The story lines present all moral victories in personal terms and offer only tenuous solutions. All social phenomena are reduced to the possession of certain human qualities, or lack of them. All manner of crime, according to David Buxton, is reduced to "a private sport between humanised cops and dehumanised psychopaths."[14] These generic conventions shape the rape narratives that I analyze below.[15]

In legal dramas, the narrative focus is on the practice of law, and the courtroom becomes the site for highly charged public discursive contestations. In their effort to pin down the responsibility for a crime they engender a conclusion similar to that of cop shows: they identify guilt and innocence but are unable to provide resolution. The justice enacted in these shows is partial and tentative. In their exploration of individual guilt, these legal dramas tend to promote a liberal attitude toward most issues. According to John Brigham, the story lines present a worldview that asserts, "Racial tolerance is good, racism is bad. Gender equality is good, old inequalities are bad."[16]

The legal dramas I analyze, *L.A. Law* and *Reasonable Doubts,* have multiple, overlapping story lines. Only some of these plotlines are resolved during the hour-long episodes, while others arc across multiple episodes. *Law & Order* is slightly different than these melodramatic legal dramas; I enumerate its characteristics later in the chapter. In the rape plotlines undertaken by

legal dramas, the regular cast is not central to the action but it is the bit players, who walk into a show for a single story line to propel the plot. This static and formulaic representation of good and bad characters is integral to the
formal structure of the genre. Recurring (and often "good") characters are not
easily transformed. Their moral determinations are immediately visible. Conflict within this form is catalyzed by adaptable "bad" guest characters inter-
vening from the outside.

During the time period examined in this study, *Knots Landing* was the
only show outside of the law and order genre to address sexual assault.[17]
Knots Landing can best be characterized as a prime-time soap opera. It
focuses on the relations between family members and scrutinizes the private
lives of individuals. As with other prime-time soap operas, rape here functions to highlight the (in)stability of an existing family order. The specific
characteristics of these genres have important consequences concerning the
nature of rape narratives produced and the debates that they enable. Most
importantly, the crime and punishment framework suggests the inevitability
of sexual violence. Rape can either be feared or legally repaired, it can rarely
be fought or resisted.

In what follows I do not describe exhaustively the individual rape narratives. Instead, I highlight the dominant themes that recur. There are three
predominant trends in prime-time rape narratives. In the first section of
this chapter, I outline the manner in which several episodes use rape as an
allegory to address other social issues. Even though rape propels the story
line, in these episodes sexual violence functions only to illuminate some
other issue, such as police corruption. This absent presence of rape shapes
the public sphere of debate and discussion enabled by fictional programming, marginalizing the violence committed on the female body. In the
second section, I isolate programs that deal with interracial rape but with
crucial inversions.[18] I argue that in these programs, race and racial difference become dramatic devices to mobilize the story line—the narratives fail
to explore the manner in which racialized subjects experience rape differently. These narratives address only issues of racism or oppression structured along gendered lines, not the two simultaneously. They fail to examine how the discourses of crime and punishment evaluate and solicit
racialized masculinity and femininity differently. In the third section, I
focus on the portrayal of women and their responses to rape. As mentioned
earlier, many of the female characters in these episodes espouse an anti-feminist understanding of sexual violence, while the men's engagement with
feminism is more complicated. I explore the nature of debate and discussion engendered when symbolic patriarchs instruct women on the appro-

priate feminist response to rape and the responsibilities of sisterhood. Before I analyze the individual episodes, I situate my work within the scholarship already conducted on this topic.

PRIME TIME RECONFIGURES THE HOME

Unlike news-based programming, which remains resistant to issues raised by feminism, entertainment programming, since the early 1970s, has been receptive to a limited number of issues raised by the women's movement. As several scholars have pointed out, entertainment programming has been a fertile site for the integration of *some* feminist ideas.[19] The emergence of the single-woman situation comedy, particularly the *Mary Tyler Moore* show, is usually identified as marking mainstream programming's incorporation of key concepts of liberal feminism.[20] The working woman sitcom shifted the site of action from the home to the work arena and opened up the roles that female protagonists could play. The "new woman" was expected, however, to fulfill the traditional female roles of caretaker and nurturer of the workplace family. According to Serafina Bathrick, the new woman narratives affirm female friendships. Nevertheless, within the workplace, woman's position can only be inscribed narratively in relationship to male prerogatives.[21] Because these programs continued to rely on the family as the central site of action, they were unable to transcend the gender-based expectations that pervade the private sphere. Most story lines acknowledged gender politics but rarely confronted them.

In the "new woman" programs of the 1970s, feminism itself was presented as a lifestyle choice rather than as an ideology. In Chapter 2 of this book, I outlined aspects of feminism that the U.S. media appropriated. In the realm of prime-time programming, feminist influences have resulted in a role-reversal strategy that showcases women in traditionally male roles. In the limited vision of feminism these programs promote, self-improvement and transformation of the self are the preferred responses to gender-based oppression. Power issues are ignored, and the need for social transformation is rarely acknowledged. Instead, the programs present the individual as being in need of change. Despite these limitations, most scholars concur that the "new woman" sitcoms often played the key role of raising consciousness about the different ways in which women are excluded from the public arena.

Beginning in the late 1980s, this limited vision of feminism began to disappear. Scholars contend that the prime-time programs of this time period were more likely to espouse a postfeminist ideology with story lines that insisted that women could seek happiness and fulfillment only through their achievements in the domestic sphere.[22] Specifically, in *Seeing Through the Eighties* Jane Feuer argues that the postfeminist story lines developed during the 1980s reproduced the structure of feeling that dominated the era of Reaganomics and the conservative ideology characteristic of that period. The shows hark back to a "new traditionalism": the successful women in these shows want something more than professional success, and they invariably find this fulfillment in the domestic arena. Prime-time entertainment's portrayal of women reflects a backlash against contemporary feminism, she contends. Effectively, postfeminist television reconfigures the home as the site for women's activities. Concurring with this analysis, Elspeth Probyn adds that television portrayals present the home as the natural and fundamental site of love and fulfillment.[23]

In tandem with these shifts in prime-time programming's engagement with feminism, rape has become a fertile site for story lines. These fictional accounts of sexual violence highlight certain aspects of feminist reinterpretations of rape and marginalize others. According to Claudia Dreifus, television programming in the late 1980s dramatically increased the number of rape narratives. Sexual assault became a staple fare, resulting in a subgenre characterized as women in jeopardy, a form of programming that shares features with the "bodice rippers" of pulp fiction. In these story lines, the female protagonist is violated, she turns to authorities, who are indifferent to her plight, and then through her own efforts she is rehabilitated to society after some act of enlightenment and/or revenge. In these programs women's lot is just one horror after another.[24] In Chapter 6 of this book, I develop how this formulaic story line shapes made-for-TV movies. Despite the proliferation of rape imageries, scholarly analyses of these representations have been uneven.

A substantial part of the literature on media analysis of rape falls under the larger category of analysis of crime. These studies primarily explore media effects. Influenced by behavioral science theories, they posit a cause-and-effect relationship between media images and the behavior of viewers. These studies do not offer an analysis of media representations. For instance, Barbara Wilson and others examine the impact of television programming on people's attitudes about rape. Through a field experiment, they concluded that people exposed to a television movie on acquaintance rape were more aware of the phenomenon as a social problem than those who had not seen it. They contended, however, that watching the movie tended to reinforce rape myths among older men.[25] In similar studies that attempted to correlate media depictions with social violence, Daniel Linz and others and David Phillips and John Hensley showed men movies and television programs that depicted violence against women. Watching violence on the screen tended to make men less sympathetic toward rape victims, and often enabled male violence against women, these studies concluded.[26]

TIRED THEMES

Interpretive analyses of television programs on rape are limited but quite expansive in film. These studies are radically different in their aims than those I have just cited. They focus on the regimes of representation that dominate popular culture. I have included some analyses of films that are illustrative of the issues that feminist cultural studies scholars have developed. I do not offer an exhaustive overview of these analyses but have culled those most relevant to television's representational grammar—how sexual violence and the female subject are portrayed visually and verbally in popular culture.

The sexual assault of women has been a recurring theme in U.S. commercial cinema; one in every eight films produced in Hollywood contains a scene depicting violence against women.[27] Susan Faludi, in *Backlash*, argues that the rise of the women's movement was followed by a backlash against women. In the Hollywood films of the 1980s, this backlash was translated as violence against female characters. Moving away from the complex positions occupied by female characters in the 1970s, women in rape narratives were once again depicted in a binarized manner: as virgin or whore. The independent, career-minded woman tended to be characterized as evil and eventually met her just and often violent reward, while the passive homebody was the "good" woman who was rewarded with the affections of the hero. This trend, Faludi argues, reinstated the view that women were responsible for the violence they encountered.[28]

Earlier, Molly Haskell, in her thought-provoking book *From Reverence to Rape*, examined the historical portrayal of women in Hollywood films and arrived at a conclusion similar to Faludi's: the female protagonist as a sexual being historically has been cast typically in an either/or role; either a "sexpot" or a "nice girl." The sexpot or whore is incapable of intelligent thought or a lapse of sexual appetite. The virgin, on the other hand, is incapable of a base instinct or a hint of sexual appetite. She is a primal, positive figure, honored and exalted beyond any merits she possesses as a woman, while the whore is publicly castigated and cautioned against, and privately sought by men. Haskell contends that this unrealistic portrayal of women has reinforced prevalent myths about women and rape. Not surprisingly these tendencies continue to prevail in television representations of sexual violence, as my analysis reveals.[29]

Analyzing the portrayal of women in war films during the 1980s, Tania Modleski argues that representations of sexuality and aggression are inextricably intertwined. In these films, sexual and military conquest are portrayed as intimately related. Sexuality is manifested in violence, and violence carries an explosion of sexual charge. This portrayal justifies the hero's primary task of breaking hearts and taking lives. Inevitably, in these films, the female characters emerge primarily as victims of sexual violence.[30]

In a similar manner, bell hooks has examined the portrayal of rape in *She's Gotta Have It*, a film by Spike Lee. She argues that the movie begins with the portrayal of an independent woman clearly aware of her sexuality. During the course of the movie, the woman is raped by her lover and is finally portrayed as capitulating to his need for violent sexuality, thus hooks concludes that this depiction not only condones the action of the rapist, it also ends up portraying women as passive, as secretly desiring rape, and it reiterates popular perceptions that only "bad" women are raped.[31] Revisiting this film, Michael Awkward concludes similarly that despite Lee's intentions of producing an affirming narrative, the film reifies the sexual fundamentals of male dominance.[32]

In contrast to the cinematic representations that these studies reveal, television images of rape and of women in general are far more complex and complicated. They appear less resistant than films in incorporating feminist ideas. On shows such as *L.A. Law* and *Law & Order*, the virgin/whore dichotomy does not shape the presentation of raped women. Similarly, although television representations are flawed, unlike in Lee's film, rape narratives deploy rape myths self-consciously to draw attention to their prevalence. These trends indicate the dynamic ways in which television can respond to social change. One would expect that the discussions about sexual violence in prime-time programs would be significantly different than the cinematic imaging practices I have just outlined.

Scholars who have examined the regimes of representation in television's fictional rape accounts point out the startling ways in which the medium's portrayal of sexual violence has changed. Susan Brinson has isolated one *Cagney and Lacey* episode on acquaintance rape as unique. One of the protagonists, Christine Cagney, is raped on her first date with an executive. Through an exploration of Cagney's response to the assault and the investigation that follows, the episode foregrounds the victim's perspective of sexual violence, social attitudes, including those of police officers, toward acquaintance rape, and the ways in which women cope with the aftermath of rape. While the assailant tries to reframe the charge to claim that Cagney was drunk and attacked him, the investigating officers (her colleagues) remain skeptical of her version of events. Cagney herself is shown initially as feeling responsible for the assault, but by the end of the episode, through her participation in a support group, she is able to transform her response into one of anger. As a female police officer, Cagney's character becomes the site where the roles of victim and rescuer converge. It is this aspect that makes this episode unique.[33] Expanding her analysis to other prime-time programs, in her dissertation Brinson argues that television depictions of rape communicate the conflicting cultural attitudes about sexual violence. Her content analysis reveals that while a few portrayals support feminist tenets, others may depict rape accurately but continue to serve patriarchal interests. Brinson concludes that television programming's inclusion of rape narratives, even though problematic, represents a "positive" change.

In a less optimistic analysis, Lisa Cuklanz's *Rape on Trial* examines television's ability to incorporate the rape reforms mobilized by the women's movement. She concludes that "feminine" genres of entertainment, such as the TV movie of the week, are more receptive to airing victims' experiences of rape than other programming. While welcoming the presence of programming that enables women-centered knowledges, Cuklanz points out that such meanings are isolated to these devalued genres. Through this process of isolation, television contains and resists oppositional meanings of rape, she contends.[34] Although Cuklanz examines only news coverage of three cases and their fictional representation, her conclusions could be extended to other prime-time entertainment.

Developing the theme of rape representations in prime-time episodic television between 1976 and 1990, Cuklanz argues in *Rape on Prime Time* that sexual violence serves primarily as an arena for the demonstration of ideal masculinity. Depictions of rape altered significantly during the period of her study, from a predominance of stranger rapes to ones where acquaintance rape became the norm. These changes were influenced by the demands of the women's movement, she argues. Nevertheless, the emphasis on masculinity has remained consistent.

These studies illustrate the specific ways in which prime-time programming has responded to feminist redefinitions of sexual violence. The emergence of acquaintance rape rather than stranger rape, which these studies document, has become commonplace in the programs I examine.[35] By interrogating the specific ways in which race and gender intersect in television portrayals of rape, my analysis complicates this narrative of seeming progress.

In more recent years, prime-time entertainment's treatment of rape has sometimes interrogated and teased the intersection of race and gender. *L.A. Law*, during its eight-year tenure, consistently engaged with issues of gender and sexual politics. In her analysis of the first two years of this program, Judith Mayne contends that the series identified feminism as an explicit or implicit protagonist. Its story lines repeatedly returned to the issue of rape as the ultimate test of whether the law was patriarchal or not. She concludes that while *L.A. Law* might have dealt with issues central to a feminist analysis of rape, the narratives also reintroduced consistently patriarchal visions of gender relations.[36]

Developing this argument, Sarah Projansky provides an excellent analysis of the manner in which *L.A. Law*'s tendency to "have it both ways" with feminism inflected its portrayal of rape. The series did not simply appropriate feminist rhetoric. Its narratives emerged from a postfeminist space that rendered the treatment of rape very problematic. Specifically, Projansky points out that in a prime-time world saturated with postfeminist ideology, race and rape are carefully separated. Episodes may deal with a number of key issues pertaining to rape, but the way in which racial identity shapes the experience of sexual violence is kept at bay. I develop this concept later in this chapter.[37]

From these different studies and my examination of the early program scripts, it is clear that there has been a remarkable shift in television images of sexual violence, a directional shift informed by feminist debates and discussions of rape. Until the early 1980s, fictional programming adhered to the definition of "real rape": sexual violence occurred in dark, isolated public places, and the rapist was invariably a stranger jumping out of a bush. In these programs, rape was inscribed unerringly and uncomplicatedly on the victim's body with visible signs of injuries. Sexual violence, however, often was a peripheral development in the plotline. For instance, a 1976 episode of *Starsky and Hutch*, "A Slow Case of Rape," fails to live up to its title. The episode employs the rape of a "mentally retarded" teenager as a vehicle to showcase the talents of its two male protagonists and their unorthodox methods of ensuring justice. Cuklanz concludes similarly that sexual violence in these programs served to reify concepts of hegemonic masculinity as representing good values. Prime-time episodes tend to focus on the individual "bad" male rather than on social structures of domination.[38]

The studies I have highlighted have explored the ways in which television representational practices have accommodated feminist demands. My analysis alters this framework by specifically articulating these representational practices with the project of democratic community formation. I do not only examine the feminist communities that these prime-time narratives make possible, I interrogate the kinds of debates and discussions such story lines promote and the consequences for the formation of democratic public spheres.

PATRIARCHAL ALLEGORIES

In this section I explore prime-time story lines that deploy sexual violence as an allegory to describe other social issues, and I evaluate the kinds of discursive spaces that such narrative strategies enable. In its simplest form, allegory is the representation of abstract ideas as concrete images; it is the use of language to say one thing and mean another. Walter Benjamin has argued that the use of allegory can destabilize commonsensical understandings; it has the potential to restore and destroy, to redeem and undermine.[39] Television's allegorical deployment of rape is not productive in the ways that Benjamin postulates. Allegories of rape function instead to refer to other social problems. In the process, sexual violence itself disappears from the narrative landscape.[40]

A *21 Jump Street* episode, "Blackout," exemplifies this problematic presentation of rape and resembles aspects of the media coverage of the Central Park jogger's case.[41] As I elucidated in Chapter 3 of this book, network news coverage of the Central Park rape was marked for its demonization of racial difference. In the fictional account I analyze here, sexual assault functions similarly as a trope to explore youth alienation and inner-city anomie.[42] Racist stereotypes that prevailed in news portrayals of the African-American and Hispanic teenagers were unproblematically transported to characterize Caucasian teenagers in this episode. While the allegorical use of rape directs attention away from sexual violence, the use of terms such as *wilding* to refer to the Caucasian teenagers' behavior also bleaches out the issues pertaining to racism that were central to the "true story."[43]

21 Jump Street, which aired from 1988 to 1993, was a cop show where the protagonists were so young that they went undercover in high schools and other centers of youth activity to solve crimes. The program tended to focus on the detection of crime rather than its cause. Cuklanz praises *21 Jump Street* for its treatment of rape. In the six episodes that featured the phenomenon, she found its narratives "complex, sensitive, and progressive . . . granting more legitimacy to feminist or victim-centered views."[44] The episode I analyze here is not marked by these features. Indeed, the rape itself is physically and temporally isolated from the rest of the narrative. In an extended pre-credits segment that runs for over five minutes, viewers witness the gang rape that the police officers have to uncover during the rest of the episode. Being made witness to the crime ensures that the audience is convinced of the brutality of the assault and foreshadows the bestiality of the assailants.[45]

The episode, "Blackout," begins with a white woman in an expensive car preparing to go jogging in a park. The camera cuts to a group of predominantly Caucasian teenagers that arrives at the same park, carrying beer.[46] Subsequently, the camera alternates between the jogger and the rambunctious teenagers, until the moment of the assault. As the story line goes step-by-step through the activities that lead up to the rape, every action is overdetermined and loaded with significance. The lighting, the camera work, and the background music reproduce the threat of sexual assault; the jogging woman is shown in tight shots that exaggerate the darkness of the park, and the sound of baying wolves adds to the menacing atmosphere. The teenagers' actions are shown, however, as being unpremeditated. "There was an opportunity [and] we grabbed it." As the teenagers begin to chase the jogger around the dark park, the camera aligns the viewer with the victim; unlike the police officers, the audience is convinced from the beginning that these teenagers are not "normal kids." In this respect, "Blackout" is representative of a number of cop shows where the theme of capture rather than the unmasking of crime forwards the narrative. The viewer is rarely kept in the dark for long about the identity of the criminals, but it often takes the police longer to arrive at the same conclusion.

The "wilding" itself is presented from the victim's point of view; the pre-credits segment ends as the woman loses consciousness when a stone smashes into her face. After this moment, the story line does not return to the victim, and the viewer's point of identification shifts to the undercover cops. Above all, the issue of rape disappears from the narrative, and the gendered aspect of sexual violence is replaced by a sociological explanation for youth crime. The story line leads the viewer to a very pointed, unavoidable conclusion about right and wrong, justice and injustice; there is a narrative and ideological closure. The rest of the episode is devoted to apprehending the assailants; the site of action also shifts from the park to the teenagers' high school. The rape becomes the site from which the narrative showcases the talents of the undercover police officers.

The resemblances between this episode and the Central Park case are both overt—the nature of the attack, its location, the rhetoric used to describe it—and covert—the hip-hop music in the background from which the term "wilding" is believed to have originated as well as the sound of baying wolves to represent the bestiality of the teenagers. The images of untamed brutishness that characterized news coverage of the Central Park assailants are replicated here. The script specifies that the teenagers should be presented like a wolf pack. The scriptwriters have undertaken significant alterations, though; most notably the assailants are presented as predominantly white. This shift in the racial composition of the assailants does not in any way alter the story line's depiction of the assailants. The bestial imagery that marked news narratives is replicated here giving the impression that the charges of racism leveled against news coverage of the Central Park case are baseless. The story line presents all the teenagers consistently as cultural others; characters in the show describe them as restless "natives" and as incomprehensible. This unproblematic transposition of media images specific to black teenagers to a multicultural cast allows prime-time entertainment to present a "color-blind" view of the ways in which people experience rape. As the police officers uncover the crime, the story line replicates key themes enacted in the pre-credits segment as well as in its camera work.[47] The teenagers are repeatedly presented as a marauding mob, vandalizing their school premises with the same indifference that they exhibited in the park. The demonization process here is quite explicit—the rapist is not/cannot be domesticated. Paradoxically, the undercover police officers refer to the teenagers as corralled animals, suggesting that they can be controlled even if they cannot be tamed.

By erasing the specificity of sexual assault, eliding the racial identity of the assailants that led to the extensive coverage of the Central Park case, and examining instead the criminal proclivities of deracinated teenagers, the episode reiterates many rape myths. Primarily it promotes the view that rape is an act of defiance, a release of pent-up energy. Consequently, the program indicts the lack of recreational facilities for inner-city youth and the inability of school systems to channel teenagers' energies gainfully. Further, it describes sexual assault as the natural consequence of individual problems; the assailant is a weak individual, unable to resist peer pressure. The narrative elides the cultural and gendered norms that permit such brutality.

Such allegorical use of rape is not unique to television programming. Literary scholars have repeatedly isolated the use of sexual assault in various "master" works. For instance, the seventeenth-century classic *Clarissa* by Samuel Richardson deploys rape as an allegory for the social instability in England following the political decline of the aristocracy and the concomitant economic and social rise of the bourgeoisie. While Clarissa's rape is central to the narrative movement, it has to remain unrepresented, Terry Eagleton contends.[48] In an analogous textual strategy, E. M. Forster's *Passage to India* uses rape to explore the interaction between the colonizer and the colonized, the British and the Indians, respectively. Rape becomes the site from which to examine incommensurable social and cultural differences, Brenda Silver argues.[49] Illuminating the central problematic of these "master" narratives, Rajeswari Sunder Rajan points out that in each of the novels mentioned above, the rape victim is the scapegoat in a larger struggle of social forces. The narratives thereby elide the impact of the crime on women.[50]

In an analogous manner, in a couple of episodes *L.A. Law* deploys rape allegorically.[51] The rape trial becomes the site for dramatic action and a location where key characters are able to resolve personal problems. In "Guess Who's Coming to Murder," the trial of a serial rapist-murderer and the issue of rape per se serve only as pivotal moments for a narrative that focuses on two recurring characters, Mullaney and Clemmons, as they come to terms with their recent divorce. Sexual assault is an elusive subject and appears only as a plotline that presents all of the female characters as being always vulnerable to the threat of rape. Not only does the law fail to punish the rapist, the prosecutor, Clemmons, has to be rescued from the rapist by her ex-husband, Mullaney, an action that restores his hurt pride. This episode ignores the specificity of rape and presents women as subjects who need the protection of good men.[52]

In a different but equally troubling manner, "Dances with Sharks" deploys rape as a trope to address police corruption. During the pre-credits segment of this episode, the police arrest Jonathan Rollins, the only recurring African-American cast in *L.A. Law*, because he is jogging in a white neighborhood where a rape has been committed.[53] Rollins resists the arrest, and through the use of legal terminology, he attempts to convince the police of their mistake. The viewer is assured that, as a recurring character on the show, he is innocent. After an altercation, during which one of the officers holds Rollins in a choke-hold, the lawyer is arrested on suspicion of rape and assault. As Sarah Projansky points out, the pre-credits segment draws attention to the fact that the myth of the black rapist continues to threaten African-American men's everyday lives.[54] The rest of the episode explores, however, the issue of police corruption. It ignores both rape and the theme of how racialized subjects experience social institutions such as the police. Nevertheless, restoring an enduring cavil, the episode hints at the ease with which a rape charge can be leveled against an innocent man.[55] As the story line progresses, a corrupt district attorney threatens Rollins with a rape trial unless he pleads guilty to a lesser charge. The false rape charge is leveled by a white man raising the specter of lynch laws. The story line does not address, however, any of these issues.

As Jacquelyn D. Hall and Angela Davis have pointed out, in the United States, the black rapist myth has been invoked repeatedly in moments of crises, uniting whites across class divides.[56] However, this phenomenon is not unique to the United States and has been used elsewhere to ensure the maintenance of power. Jenny Sharpe, in her analysis of Anglo-Indian fiction, points out that the rape trope is repeatedly used to manage crises in British colonial authority. The imagery of the violated body of the English woman surfaced at strategic moments to manage rebellion and permitted the British to record any counterinsurgency as the restoration of moral order in a society that viewed the natives as barbaric and in need of civilizing, she contends.[57] In the *L.A. Law* episode cited above, the producers derive their dramatic momentum by tapping into this myth, but they fail to examine it at any great length. It is the failure to explore this myth that allows the episode to ignore as well the sexual violation of women. Rape functions instead as a barometer of social lawlessness, and the protection of woman becomes a signifier for the maintenance of a good society.

This allegorical use of rape as representative of different forms of aggression shapes the nature of debate and discussion enabled. These episodes reify numerous rape myths, particularly about the nature of sexual violence, rapists, and the male fear of false accusations. They present women (and African-American men) as subjects of violation, but they do not offer them any agency. In these allegorical tales, women and racialized subjects are the backdrop (and props) against which other issues are addressed. Such narratives of rape prevent the possibility of offering ways in which sexual violence could be prevented. Further, they do not provide a female-centered understanding of rape.

COLOR-BLIND ENTERTAINMENT?

The racialized aspects of rape myths are invoked more productively in some other story lines. These fictional narratives address directly some of the historical and cultural stereotypes of racialized sexuality, most frequently by depicting interracial rapes. They invert, however, some of the essential elements of the stereotypes. This narrative strategy defamiliarizes the stereotypes at the same time it dilutes the critique offered. Scholars such as Gitlin have recorded networks' reluctance to alienate any segment of their audience. Since most stereotypes about interracial rape center on negative, bestial images of the nonwhite assailant, television programs avoid and simultaneously address the issue through their inversions. Consequently, the story lines I analyze below engage with racial myths sedimented around rape but in a manner that redirects attention away from nonwhite populations to the behavior of Caucasian characters. The only subject position offered to nonwhite characters in such story lines is as victims; nonwhite men are falsely charged with rape while nonwhite women suffer violation by white men.

Unlike the stranger rape episodes analyzed above, the rest of the story lines depict acquaintance rape—the rapist and the rape victim know each other, the assault occurs in a safe space, and there are few physical signs testifying to the woman's resistance. The rapist often looks like the boy-next-door, a clean-cut, handsome figure, and he does not fit the stereotype of the pathologically abnormal rapist. The woman's account of sexual assault is considered incredible by the institutions of law and order as well as by individual characters. In the fictional narratives analyzed below, the focus remains on the woman and on proving her lack of consent.

One of the most evocative and sensitive portrayals of rape examined in this study was depicted in "Rape," an *In the Heat of the Night* episode. Derived from the 1967 Academy Award-winning movie, the series elucidates the various cases undertaken by the police force in the white supremacist town of Sparta. While the show adheres closely to the cop show genre, the episodes repeatedly thematize issues of racism.[58] The depiction of rape in this particular episode underscores the racial undercurrents that structure white and black lives in the United States; it references a series of stereotypes about racialized sexuality. The story line centers on the rape of a recurring character, Althea Tibbs, the wife of black detective Virgil Tibbs. A white colleague, Steven Ainslea, brutally assaults her at home.[59]

The story line inverts the myth of the black rapist to depict the white male entitlement to black women's bodies that dominated the history of slavery; the historical antecedents are not explored though.[60] The inversion could permit an exploration of the cultural stereotypes (within the black and white communities) of black women's promiscuity and "unrapability." This narrative strategy opens up the possibility of a new avenue of debate on rape, one that underscores how women's lives are shaped by the intersections of race and gender. The story line, however, effects a closure of this avenue of debate by distancing the audience from race-based understandings of rape.

The episode establishes the racial hostility that marks Althea's relationship with Ainslea in the opening shots. He dislikes being a subordinate to a black woman and accuses, "You just love cracking the whip, don't you?" Through this statement and others similar in tone, the story line introduces the myth of the black matriarch, the powerful dominatrix female figure whose presence emasculates the men around her. The episode, though, encourages identification with Althea as a recurring character rather than with her assailant. Viewers' intertextual memory will not allow them to cast her as the black matriarch. In this episode as in many other story lines, stereotypes are introduced as a substitute for character development. The story line introduces the subject of the black matriarch and other stereotypes but glosses over the consequences of these myths. Through a narrative strategy that distances viewers from such sentiments, the episode avoids engaging with racist stereotypes and the processes through which individuals are racialized. In this instance, racial difference functions as a transparent phenomenon and precludes any development of race-based issues. Further, by mouthing racist sentiments, Ainslea is alienated from the viewers.

As is characteristic of most television sexual assaults, in this episode viewers see the brutal violence that precedes a rape. Returning from a trip to the grocery store, Althea is assaulted in her kitchen by a man wielding a knife. Although the assailant remains unseen, viewers hear his disembodied voice bark out instructions. Ainslea and Althea may be colleagues, but the depiction of rape in this episode contains all of the hallmarks of "real" rape.

A Caucasian police officer, Bubba, finds a brutalized Althea and takes her to the hospital for an examination. The nurse, however, insists that there are other hospitals available for "her kind." The force of Bubba's anger overrides the nurse's racism, but he is unable to change her attitude or pursue the matter. In a narrative trajectory characteristic of cop shows, this episode inscribes an ideology that privileges the individual over the social. In several instances, the episode reveals the inability of social structures, primarily the law and order system, to punish the bad, protect the good, and maintain the moral order.

The Sparta police force is vocal in expressing its anger and outrage over Althea's rape. The white male district attorney refuses, however, to pursue rape charges against Ainslea for lack of evidence, noting that, "The rape kit only proves that Mrs. Tibbs had intercourse with somebody other than her husband that day. It does not prove she was raped."[61] This statement introduces the cultural myth of black women being promiscuous and untrustworthy, "their honesty questioned and their word discounted."[62] Feminist scholars such as Hazel Carby and Adele Alexander explore the persistence of this myth and its consequences since the era of slavery. Cultural stereotypes assert that, "Sex between a black woman and white man is almost always prompted by her insatiable sexuality . . . her erotic proclivities" corrupted the innocent man, Alexander contends.[63] This episode taps into these myths but presents Althea Tibbs ultimately as a deracinated woman. Although the characters express racist sentiments, the narrative fails to present how a black woman's experience of rape is shaped by these myths of black female sexuality.

The specificity of the black female experience of rape is glossed over as well in a *21 Jump Street* episode, "Stand By Your Man." Judy Hoffs, an African-American protagonist, is raped by an acquaintance while on an undercover assignment. Despite her professional status as a decorated police officer, on technical grounds the authorities refuse to file the rape charge. The assailant denies the charge and because of the enduring myth of the "unrapable" black woman is effectively able to cast doubt on Hoffs's version of the events. Most women's accounts of rape are discredited, but my argument here is that the aspersions cast against a black woman gain coherence from cultural myths about the "unrapable" black woman. Unlike the police officers, through a series of flashbacks, viewers witness the rape. This strategic use of the flashback allows the audience to empathize with a recurring character, confirms her credibility, and marginalizes narrative threads that could explore the specificity of the African-American female experience of rape.[64]

Racial difference is the generative moment of the *In the Heat of the Night* episode analyzed here. The police chief raises it as a specific cause for the rape when he interrogates Ainslea, "You got a problem with all women or just black women?" His line of questioning points out that in some instances rape is not just an assertion of male power but becomes a mode of inscribing racial and sexual authority. These statements rupture the myth of a racially harmonious U.S. society, but the cracks are quickly papered over as the narrative redirects its attention to the dominant discourse of the cop show, the apprehension of the criminal. The eruptions of racist sentiments are enacted in counterpoint to the harmonious interracial friendships established by the regular cast of characters that comprises the workplace family.[65] They offer audiences a view of "positive" race relations. Despite the repeated references to racial difference and racism, the episode might as well have been about an intraracial rape.

As for rape per se, the episode reveals graphically the violent nature of the assault, the shame and trauma the victim experiences, and above all the inability of institutions to deal humanely with victims. Repeatedly the story line provides information made available by feminist scholarship. The narrative reveals the painstaking medical examination undertaken after an attack. Through the figure of the police chief, the story line reveals the prevalence of acquaintance rape. "[M]ost women are raped by men they know. Men who present themselves as friends." He discredits several rape myths and asserts the tendency of unapprehended rapists to be multiple offenders. The insertion of factual information in a fictional narrative transforms the nature of debate enabled by the program. Even as it dramatizes the ways in which individuals experience rape, the narrative provides information crucial to conducting a rational-critical debate about the topic.

Despite the many positive aspects of this fictional account of rape, there are several problematic areas. Unlike the police officers, viewers witness the assault that occurs in the Tibbs home. This scene establishes Althea's unequivocal innocence, but the rape itself is presented from a male point of view, that of the assailant. During the assault scene, the camera does not reveal the person inflicting the violence, nor does it reveal the rape. The viewer sees only

Althea as the object under attack. Later, the camera reveals the aftermath of sexual assault as well through male eyes—this time that of a police officer, Bubba, who has come to visit Althea. As Lauren Rabinovitz has argued in another context, in this episode, male characters possess the power of vision, whereas Althea is figured primarily as the object of male sight.[66]

Until the last scene of the episode, Althea is shown as having little agency; it is the men around her who take actions on her behalf. The only exception to this is Althea's outburst of anger in the district attorney's office when he decides not to file charges against Ainslea. While the police chief and her husband protest the decision, Althea voices her anger and echoes the frustrations that feminists have pointed out that women experience in the legal system. When asked if she concurs with the district attorney's decision not to pursue the case, she expostulates, "I think you don't need me here. I think the three zippers in this room (the police chief, the district attorney, and her husband) and all the zippers in all the courtrooms everywhere are making the decision for me about my experience, my choices, my future, my justice. But hey, boys will be boys."

While Althea struggles to cope with the aftermath of her assault, the white men, particularly the police chief, espouse feminist understandings of rape and instruct her on the appropriate response to sexual violence. The police chief also monitors her husband's response to the assault—these scenes reassure the audience of the merits of the benign patriarch.[67] Susan Jeffords contends, in her analysis of the television movie *Opposing Force*, that prime-time narratives rewrite sexual assault as a battle between men. Rape becomes an occasion for the critique of "bad" masculinity and the reproduction of hegemonic masculinity.[68] In an analogous manner, this episode separates clearly good masculinity from bad masculinity. While Ainslea represents "bad" masculinity, all of the male police officers of the series are cast as representing "good" masculinity. They are willing to restore the moral order, even willing to take extra-legal steps against Ainslea, and have to be physically restrained by the police chief. All of the men, except the assailant, believe that they are duty-bound to protect women and that the rape is emblematic of their failure. This story line presents rape as the excess of "bad" masculinity; hegemonic masculinity is presented as upholding the moral order.[69] The repeated allusions to racism in this episode open up the possibility of discussing the systemic and social structures that enable male sexual rapacity. Simultaneously, the reassertion of "good" masculinity closes such a discussion; it legitimizes the belief that "bad" individuals are to blame for rape.

Apart from Althea Tibbs, the only other woman in the show is the rapist's wife, who provides him with an alibi. It is left to the police chief to teach Ainslea's wife how sisterhood operates and the ground rules for female solidarity. The feminism espoused here valorizes a tenuous agency permitted through male protection. Victimhood does not provide Althea access to a collective gendered identity; she does not turn to other women for support, or seek protective measures or assistance from rape counselors. The episode ends when Althea manages to successfully avoid a second attack by Ainslea and he is apprehended. In the last scene, after defending herself successfully, Althea agrees to attend a rape counseling group. In this instance, she gains catharsis through her individual actions, and not through collective action undertaken to overcome a gendered oppression. The story line thus privileges a feminist individualism over a collective gendered sense of oppression. The story line appropriates feminist rhetoric to point out the specificity of rape, yet the debate it enables about gender and race is very limited—it allows a discussion of either gender-based oppression or racism and forecloses any discussion of the specificity of a racialized subject's experience of rape. Significantly, the myth of the black male rapist is a topic that remains unexplored.

BROADENING THE SPECTRUM

A 1990 three-episode arc story on *L.A. Law* confronts the myth of the black rapist more pointedly, but again with an inversion. A white woman, Allison Gottlieb, is raped by a Hispanic man, Henrico Mores. Unlike in the black rapist myth, where the white woman is cast as victim, here she has to prove her lack of consent. In this story line the nonwhite rapist is not cast as a threat to white women. Instead, it is the victim who is viewed as promiscuous, a sexually desiring subject who is responsible for the rape. The story line traces how racial difference inflects the trial process and explores the subjective experience of sexual assault.[70] The narrative derives its drama from the court process and illuminates the unique nature of interracial rape trials, particularly the difficulty in asserting the coercive nature of sexual assault when racial boundaries are transgressed.

Allison is the companion of one of the regular cast members, Hispanic lawyer Victor Sifuentes. The story line explores the issue of interracial sexuality on two levels: the consensual interracial relation between Victor and Allison, and the nonconsensual charges that Allison files against Henrico. In the courtroom, both are recast as analogous situations. Allison tries to prove that one relationship was nonconsensual, hence illegal. By recasting the consensual relationship between Victor and Allison as culturally illicit, however, the defense attorney attempts to present this as a false accusation of rape.

Oscillating between these two modes of characterizing interracial relationships, one legally illicit and the other culturally illicit, *L.A. Law* makes available the space to discuss the legal system's inability to account for the intersections of race and gender in rape and the cultural anxieties that surround the transgression of racial boundaries. It draws attention to the discourses of nonwhite sexuality that shape issues of volition, choice, and agency. The story line reveals that race and gender do shape the ways in which individuals can participate in the public arena. It reveals as well that institutional discourses locate racial and gendered subjects differently. This narrative exemplifies what Abdul JanMohamed has characterized as a discourse of racialized sexuality. This concept highlights the sexual transgression of racial boundaries— in this story line Victor, Allison, and Henrico are all accused of transgressing racial boundaries, but only the woman is expected to explain her complicity and participation in this transgression.[71]

Neither Allison nor Henrico is a recurring character, and this narrative does not allow the viewer to witness the rape. Viewers, like the courtroom jury, have to determine the truth based on the two accounts of the event. During the preliminary hearings, the focus is not on the assailant's actions but whether the unsupported word of a woman can represent rape. It is Allison and her actions that come under scrutiny, and she has to prove that, despite her interracial relationship with Victor, she does not desire all nonwhite men. The narrative reveals how easily rape myths are sustained when resistance and consent have to be asserted legally; rape shield laws can easily be bypassed, and lawyers can make a woman's sexual history the locus of determining consent and resistance. Feminist scholarship has focused on the skewed nature of rape trials and has pointed out that the accuser and the accused are treated unequally in the process. (See Chapter 2 of this book for a discussion of this issue.) The differential treatment manifests itself in the accuser being questioned about her sexual history and other details of her past conduct, while the accused is not subject to the same questions. In this fictional instance, the defense attorney questions Allison's sexual history in an attempt to suggest that she was not a chaste woman, therefore, the legitimacy of her rape charge is suspect. Under such questioning, Allison's attorney persuades her to settle for a plea bargain. The legal system, this story line asserts, will not accept one woman's account unless it can be supplemented. The story line ends when the district attorney finds another woman who was raped by Henrico Mores, ensuring that Allison will be vindicated. Only through such an assertion of Henrico's past conduct can the story line effectively silence the argument that Allison is attracted to all nonwhite men.

In this story line the opposing attorneys are women and espouse both feminist and nonfeminist understandings of rape. Victor is a feminist character who challenges rape myths others may espouse. He believes Allison is not responsible for the rape, however, he feels beholden to physically attack her assailant as Henrico is taken into custody. Allison herself is shown as feeling guilty and responsible, yet insistent on prosecuting her assailant. Henrico's attorney offers the most compelling arguments as she invokes familiar rape myths that focus on the woman's activities prior to the rape. The defense lawyer makes available a patriarchal definition of rape that centers on the woman's behavior rather than on her experience of violence. The show promotes multivocal understandings of rape and reveals the subjective experience of the different characters involved in the story line. Unable to accommodate the issue of racial transgression or how discourses of sexuality hail a racialized subject, the story line erases Allison from the series without explanation at the end of the three episodes. She is written out of her guest role when she ends her relationship with Victor; the two cannot seem to move beyond the rape.

Unlike news narratives, in the two episodes that I have analyzed in this section understandings of rape cannot be abstracted from the operations of race. While problematic, these story lines provoke a debate and discussion of sexual violence that also confront women's subordinated location. In formal legal structures and in the practice of everyday life, the story lines reveal that women are positioned differently than men. These narratives open up a discursive space that goes beyond presenting the aftermath of rape to interrogating the institutional options available to raped and racialized women.

POSTFEMINIST WOMEN/FEMINIST MEN

The presentation of women in the *L.A. Law* story line, as raped subject and as lawyer, encapsulates the argument I present in the following section about the representations of women. In prime-time fictions, the victims are rarely believed—their private violation is followed by a traumatic public ordeal. The story lines present at least two understandings of rape, one of them the victim's perspective. The women attorneys often are presented as postfeminist: they may individually espouse feminism, but in their presentation of the cases, they are less vocal about, if they do not eschew completely, feminist understandings of rape.[72] Most often the assailant is represented legally by a nonrecurring character (male or female) who enunciates a nonfeminist understanding of rape. The regular characters, on the other hand, elucidate a feminist rhetoric about rape, challenging their coworkers, juries, and judges to reconsider their understandings of sexual violence. With the female characters cast as postfeminist, the feminist perspective of rape is presented most often through a male character. These narratives acknowledge that rape is a feminist concern, but in the world they construct, feminism is so accepted that it is redundant for women to focus on it.

Invariably all of the narratives present the victims as unequivocally innocent. The viewers are made aware of their probity either by witnessing the assault (often through flashbacks) or through an insider's look, where the accused makes clear his guilt. For instance, a *L.A. Law* story line in "The Gods Must Be Lawyers" opens with the man accused of statutory rape and his lawyer in a plea bargain session.[73] The accused expostulates, "She got what she was looking for," aware that this admission cannot be used in court. This narrative strategy allows the viewer to identify with the victim rather than the accused. It indicates as well how lawyers can deliberately misread women's actions to fit into particular definitions of female sexuality and rape.

Although the women are presented as innocent victims, guilty at the most of poor judgment, the narratives hold them responsible for making themselves available to the male gaze. In "The Gods Must Be Lawyers" episode, the defense lawyer proclaims that his client's response is that of "any red-blooded American" male. The fault lies not with the male but with the woman for making a spectacle of herself. In the majority of these episodes, the women's clothes are scrutinized, their behavior immediately prior to the assault is examined, and their resistance is measured by these factors.

As I have indicated already, the majority of the accounts analyzed here are postrape narratives that focus on the aftermath of sexual violence. The victims' response to sexual assault corresponds to research findings on rape trauma: they express feelings of guilt and shame. Irrespective of their social location, all measure themselves against a socially defined female code of conduct that they have internalized. None matches this social norm, and each feels partly responsible for the assault, a perspective augmented by defense arguments. They are rarely capable of even defining the situation as rape and are assisted in this task through paternal figures.

The only agency these women seem to have is their ability to file charges and/or prosecute their assailants. Feeling partially responsible for their victimization, they do not seek to forge a collective identity with other women; in fact, most have no female allies. None takes the steps to defend themselves against (additional) sexual violence. In these narratives, the logical conclusion of a scenario where the woman is subject to physical subjugation, coercion of will, and psychological humiliation is self-extinction.

The woman may successfully prosecute her assailant, but volition, choice, and agency remain in abeyance. The theme of annihilation is enacted in some narratives by writing out a recurring character, as we have already seen in the case of *L.A. Law*'s Allison.

In a four-episode narrative arc, *Reasonable Doubts* explores the issue of acquaintance rape in a complicated manner.[74] The extended coverage of this narrative allowed script writers to develop a nuanced discourse of rape: one that explores how the victim, the accused, and those surrounding them are affected by the event. *Reasonable Doubts* combined elements of both the cop and legal shows; it depicted cases that were pursued by the district attorney's office. The acquaintance rape episode centers on Kay Lockman, a recurring character who is the owner of a local pub. She is assaulted by Andrew Cromyer, a decorated police officer she had dated. At the conclusion of a dinner date, Cromyer attacks Lockman, and viewers witness the violence that precedes the sexual assault. The police initially refuse to file charges against a fellow officer, but faced with overwhelming evidence, they accede. Similarly, the district attorney's office is reluctant to undertake the case, as Lockman could easily be portrayed as "the whore of Babylon." While Lockman wins a difficult case, she dies a couple of episodes later. Lockman is depicted as being incapable of coping with the emotional aftermath of sexual violence.

Apart from the victims who, as I have elucidated, have very little agency, the only other women in these story lines are often lawyers. In striking contrast to the victim's inability to claim an assertive self, the women lawyers often are presented as postfeminist. In popular culture, postfeminism references a linear historical moment after feminism. And, postfeminists are those who refer to their own status to assert that women have already acquired equality in all of the arenas singled out by the 1970s' women's movement. Feminism itself thus becomes redundant. According to Sarah Projansky, postfeminism is a nostalgic return to a mythical point in time prior to feminism's realization that there is something wrong with patriarchy and a blasé acceptance of feminism that makes it passé.[75]

Whether they represent the state or the accused, these postfeminist women do not deploy feminist understandings of rape in their courtroom presentations. Often the accused men deliberately seek these postfeminist women lawyers to represent them. The women lawyers who refuse to espouse feminism overtly often are the only allies of the accused, and they present the most coherent arguments about rape forwarded in the story line. The lawyers often are unconvinced of their client's innocence, but to secure their professional interests, they willingly explore the loopholes in the law. These women are not immoral: they are aware of feminist arguments about rape and may deploy them in private, but in the courtroom they are willing to deploy patriarchal definitions of female sexuality to win their cases. Their tactics foreground a familiar feminist criticism: in the political economy of the rape trial, the very content of the victim's speech provides the means by which to discredit her. The women lawyers operate from a discursive site that allows them to ignore gender as the vector along which a collective identity formation could be organized. They have transcended the feminist tendency to cohere around a shared gendered oppression. They construct a semiotics of credibility that is constituted exclusively within patriarchal understandings of female chastity and sexual purity. Paradoxically, the arguments they forward in the courtroom reveal that men and women are positioned differently vis-à-vis the law, and that rape laws continue to center on the male fear of false accusations.

In these story lines, the courtroom arguments focus on the difficulty of distinguishing resistance from consent. For instance, in the *L.A. Law* episode I cited earlier, Allison has to prove that her relationship with Victor and the fact that she had a drink with her assailant do not constitute consent. The female defense lawyer, however, insists that her charge was incredible, because "this is a woman who was known to be sexually aggressive. She was known to have affairs, she customarily dresses very provocatively. She says she resisted, and that this was violence, but there were no bruises, no property damage." The defense lawyers twist the feminist slogan "no means no" to support their attempts to redefine lack of consent to mean "passionate sex." To discredit the accuser, the lawyers repeatedly present her as a "bad" woman: she has a sexual history, she wears provocative attire, she consumes alcohol, and so on. The episodes rarely present an articulated rebuttal to this account of "consensual sex," so the viewer does not receive a feminist account of sexual relations. Few lawyers present the feminist argument that associational factors and poor judgment do not constitute consent. Instead, the story lines dissuade the logic of consensual sex by presenting the mouthpieces of this account as reprehensible. The characters, rather than their message, prevent the viewer from recasting the rape as consensual sex. *L.A. Law*'s "The Gods Must Be Lawyers" episode exemplifies this trend. The defense lawyer describes the teenage victim as a "little tramp," while his client declares that she "got what she was looking for." Long before viewers see the victim, they witness instead the legal maneuvers through which the lawyers shape the trial process. These story lines offer little space for debate about feminist reconceptualizations of sexual violence. Instead, they seek identification with these arguments through sympathy. The episodes rarely develop the ways in which cultural norms and social acculturation processes could account for both men's and women's behaviors.

In addition to these postfeminist women who occupy a masculine social space in the courtroom, these episodes enact a crucial gender inversion. With the exception of the assailant, the majority of male characters are represented as champions of feminist understandings (at least by the end of the episode). If the defense lawyer is male, the camera shows him looking repulsed by the arguments he forwards in the courtroom. The viewer is aware that the male is deploying the "crying rape" theory strategically, not because he believes in the woman's culpability. The male characters in these story lines often are critical of female postfeminist lawyers and are vocal in enunciating a feminist rhetoric of rape. Unlike the victims, male characters know how to characterize and label sexual violence: as an act that has little to do with the victim's character. The male characters become repositories of a feminist politics that foregrounds a collective identity based on gender oppression. They gently instruct the victim on the appropriate response to sexual violence, motivate her to take action, and point out the merits of female solidarity. As we saw in the *In the Heat of the Night* episode, the police chief urges Althea to attend a counseling group. He also instructs the assailant's wife on where her allegiances should be—with her sisters, who share a gender-based oppression, and not her husband, who inflicts pain. Similarly, in *L.A. Law*, Victor instructs Allison on the appropriate response to sexual violence—to prosecute her assailant.

If the victims have any agency in these story lines, it is enabled by the protection of these benign men. These story lines effect a masculinization of feminism: a politics opposing gender oppression can be articulated only by men. Even as the women shun feminism, the men's espousal of its politics serves to shore their authority. The men are aligned proactively with the forces attempting to restore the moral order, and they are presented as the experts on feminism. While women represent the voice of white male authority, the men in these shows "do" feminism. Through such a maneuver, the narrative contains the feminist discourse that it introduces.

Although these men are heroically feminist in a postfeminist landscape, they continue to operate within the male roles ascribed to them by patriarchy. Their visceral response to rape is a physically violent one—at any opportunity, they attack the assailant and seek to avenge the rape. The narratives paper over these contradictory impulses and instead present the masculinity represented by these men as sustaining the moral order. Reifying the value of hegemonic masculinity, these story lines underscore the fragility of feminism. Even if women advocate a feminist politics, they cannot espouse it in public—only men, and not just those who occupy a masculine discursive space, can do so. These representations underscore a crucial point about who has the authority to address and identify themselves with controversial topics such as feminism in the public sphere.

The second-wave women's movement in the United States gained social currency by focusing on the nature of sexual violence. In the prime-time narratives of the late 1980s and early 1990s, female characters rejected or at least distanced themselves from a central plank of liberal feminism. As I have pointed out, the majority of defense lawyers are women who, during the trial process, espouse a consciously anti-feminist stance. We see this in the *Reasonable Doubts* story line as well as in a number of episodes of *L.A. Law*. The presence of these female lawyers in the once-male-dominated world of the courtroom is testimony to one of the central demands of liberal feminism, gender equity. In their arguments, these women lawyers rarely acknowledge the ways in which the legal process can facilitate casting doubt on a woman's account of rape. Instead, they deliberately seek loopholes to the rape shield laws and other reforms that feminists initiated to secure their client's innocence. The story lines argue implicitly that feminism as rhetoric and as politics has become redundant to those subjects who were supposed to benefit from it. The episodes foreclose the debate about feminism and alternative conceptualizations of sexual violence. The male characters who espouse a feminist politics rarely interrogate the structures that facilitate male domination. The feminism they advocate is skin-deep.

REVALORIZING NO

An *L.A. Law* episode, "From Here to Paternity," which aired on the day Mike Tyson began serving his prison term, deviates from some of the aspects outlined above.[76] It provides a site from which to observe how news events are reworked in the arena of prime-time fiction. In particular, this episode reveals how commonsense discourses of rape paper over the specificity of racialized sexuality. The narrative presents a discourse centered on women as victims of male sexual rapacity and the male inability to acknowledge abuse of power. It resonates with features of the Mike Tyson and William Kennedy Smith cases, as I explain below. The narrative elides the differences that mark the ways in which Tyson, Smith, and their accusers experienced the rape charge. It ignores that the gender, race, and class of the individuals shaped the ways in which society understands their role in the rape cases. This racial erasure is particularly striking, as this episode of *L.A. Law* was followed by local news programs that showed Tyson being frisked and patted down as he began his jail term.

In this episode, Tara McDermott, a white woman, accuses white baseball superstar Robbie Richards of raping her at the beach. The two had met earlier in the evening at a bar and later took a walk on the beach, where the woman says the assault occurred. Apart from the obvious similarities to the Smith case, the episode resembles the media coverage of the Tyson case, which focused on athletic socialization and the perils of celebrity culture. Like the majority of episodes examined here, this story line hinges upon the feminist slogan "no means no" and distinguishing consent from resistance. "From Here to Paternity" begins with a subplot of an interoffice romance between two recurring characters. Roxanne, a secretary, pursues her boss, Arnie Becker, a philanderer and divorce lawyer. Here a woman is the aggressor in a consensual relationship. The episode then cuts to the rape subplot, where most of the recurring characters read Tara's charge of rape as an aggressive pursuit of a celebrity. The juxtaposition of these subplots that pivot on female consent foregrounds the dynamics of contemporary sexual politics. They allow *L.A. Law* to undertake a complex engagement with rape, revealing that representational practices shape social understandings of sexual violence.[77]

Relying on a positive polygraph test where Robbie asserts "no," he did not rape Tara, recurring character Grace Van Owen decides to represent the baseball superstar.[78] While Grace presented herself in other episodes as a feminist, in this story line she finds herself having to explain her decision to her colleagues. In a discussion polarized along gender lines, all of the women lawyers in the firm object to Grace's decision to represent the baseball star. Enunciating feminist arguments about the nature of sexual violence, they point out that false rape rates are minuscule. In this story line, Grace is the only one who transgresses the gender divide and dismisses feminism as a "politically correct" stance. The male lawyers in the firm echo her perspective; they are convinced that the charges against Robbie stem from his celebrity status. "He's a guy who was dumb enough to take the fall," one lawyer expostulates. Another exclaims, "What do you think, he's got to be guilty just cause a woman yells rape?" These and other statements echo the rhetoric that surrounded the Smith and Tyson cases.

During the trial, Grace repeatedly tries to cast the accuser as a scorned woman who seeks revenge by crying rape. She points out the gaps and inconsistencies in Tara's account and resurrects many rape myths. Here the similarities to the Smith case are striking. Smith's attorney cast doubt on the accuser's testimony by highlighting lapses in her memory and her past sexual history.

The crucial moment in this story line occurs outside of the courtroom. With the help of her colleague, Jonathan Rollins, Grace decides to coach

Robbie for his appearance on the witness stand. As Rollins questions the superstar about his behavior at the beach, Robbie describes a classic acquaintance rape scenario. Unable to decode the signs of nonconsent, the male overrides a resisting woman. Robbie recognizes that Tara struggled, resisted, and cried out, but he does not see his actions as those of a rapist. Coercion and female resistance, he believes, are an integral part of consensual sex. Similarly, Tyson, in his defense, repeatedly asserted on the witness stand that, "I did not hurt anyone. There were no black eyes, no broken ribs." For him, as is the case for the fictional Robbie, only "real" rape counts as sexual assault.

While earlier in the courtroom Grace attempted to recast the victim's no into a yes, she now realizes that the superstar's no in the polygraph test really referenced a yes. Despite his protestations of innocence, Robbie had raped Tara. Both Jonathan and Grace are capable of naming the problem, and they help the athlete realize that he is a rapist. The narrative effectively foregrounds the fragility of the feminist assertion that "no means no." As Michael Awkward has pointed out, this scene that reveals the complex dynamics of acquaintance rape could serve as an exemplary educational narrative. It does not, however, serve to raise Robbie's consciousness; he can name his actions, but he is not motivated to alter his behavior.

Once cognizant of her client's guilt, Grace refuses to let Robbie take the witness stand. She limits her courtroom arguments to discredit Tara's no. She forces a doctor at the witness stand to admit that the injuries could have been sustained during "passionate sex." Grace also discredits the testimony of her client's teammate by characterizing him as an orthodox Christian. She effectively rewrites the rape charge as an act of vengeance on the part of both Robbie's teammate and the woman-victim.

In a rare occurrence, this story line provides a well-defined feminist rebuttal to this interpretation. The narrative does not promote a feminist reading of rape by engendering sympathy for the victim. Tara is marginalized and does not serve as a point of identification for viewers. A feminist understanding of rape is clearly articulated here, both inside and outside of the courtroom. The prosecutor, a white male, focuses on the theme of athletic socialization. The thrust of his argument is that athletes are socialized to be aggressive, and that they do not take no for an answer. "From early on, their world is defined in terms of winning and losing. We ask them to perform spectacular feats and to ignore their own pain. But if they can't feel their own pain, how can they possibly sense or respect it in others? . . . Robbie Richards did not see Tara McDermott as a sexual partner. He saw her as an opponent to be conquered."[79] This episode, unlike the others, attempts to explain why the rape occurred; social norms and acculturation are cited as the causes for the rape. The story line does not cast the rapist as an abnormal person; indeed, the prosecutor calls him an "all-American boy" with a winning personality.

As in most legal dramas, the system once again fails innocent victims. The episode points out the inconsequentiality of feminist interpretations in the courtroom. The baseball star is acquitted, and Grace seeks to redress the situation by ensuring that he will seek help. Even this individual effort at offering salvation fails, thereby, the narrative hints at the intransigence of the problem. The story line ends with a scene that highlights the unrepentant rapist continuing his behavior. Grace meets him at a bar and provides him with a list of therapists who could assist him.[80] The athlete sets aside the list to pursue an adoring female fan. As it began, this episode concludes with a female who desires male attention, thus actively pursues the athlete. Sandwiched between two nos that are discredited—Tara's by the legal system and Robbie's by his own cognition—these images of desiring women suggest that female sexuality is mysterious and unknowable.

By asserting the male athlete's inability to apprehend the criminality of his actions, the narrative echoes Catharine MacKinnon's analysis of the origins and manifestations of male domination. "The power inequities that determine crucial aspects of the social construction of gender and sexuality are so pervasive for both men and women that to escape from their efforts is virtually impossible."[81]

Similarly, an episode of *Law & Order*, "Out of Control," underscores the legal flaws that permit the unpunished exercise of male sexual power. This story line raises issues pertaining to fraternities and gang rape, gender role socialization, and the inability of the legal system to respond to systemic flaws. *Law & Order* combines elements of the cop show with the legal drama. Its narrative is evenly divided between these two genres. The first half follows a linear structure where the criminal is apprehended, and the second half follows a different trajectory, in the words of producer Dick Wolf, it explores a "moral mystery."[82] The latter part of the show explores who is responsible for the crime. In the process, the story line tends to move away from individual culpability to identifying the complex and institutional roots of crime. "Out of Control" pinpoints the systemic roots of rape and highlights the limits of the legal system.

Unlike the other shows that explore the private lives of individuals, *Law & Order* is an issue-based show. According to Dawn Keetley, the law, not individual characters, is the central protagonist of the show.[83] Its story lines deliberately rework events in the news.[84] This particular episode shares features with the St. John's University case, where a Jamaican immigrant unsuccessfully tried to prosecute several Caucasian members of a fraternity with gang rape. As is the case with the *L.A. Law* episode I analyzed above, the racialized aspects of the "true story" are bleached out, and all references to interracial rapes are erased—the primary characters are all Caucasian. "Out of Control" devotes the first half hour to tracing the difficulties that investigators encounter when trying to build rape charges against a group of fraternity members. Even though the investigators possess the forensic evidence that the men raped a drunk Andrea Fermi, they are hard pressed to file charges, since rape cases have a very high standard of evidentiary requirements. In the second half, the episode explores the rape trial process and outlines the manner in which defense lawyers try to ensure that their clients' lives "are not ruined."

The story line explores men's inability to recognize when or how violence and coercion enter into sexual relations, and the systemic roots of rape culture, particularly male socialization. Simultaneously, it points out individual guilt and does not absolve the men for their actions. As is true in the *L.A. Law* episode, here too the rapists are acquitted. This show, however, does not even offer the solace of an individual gesture toward ensuring justice. The lawyers and detectives have no response to the victim's charge that she has to live with the consequences of a flawed legal system. This narrative highlights the difficulty in prosecuting an acquaintance rape case, notwithstanding recent rape law reform. It is the only story line that draws attention specifically to feminist rape law reform efforts; one of the prosecutors refers to rape shield laws and also seeks specifically to be briefed on feminist interpretations of acquaintance rape. The story line pointedly calls for a radical restructuring of the law, to "rewrite the entire sexual history of women in the courtroom."

Both of these episodes reveal a familiar feminist argument: the law's inability to accommodate feminist reinterpretations of rape. As MacKinnon points out, these two narratives assert that the law is indeed male. By dramatically presenting the ways in which the accused and the accuser are treated in the courtroom, these narratives assert that men's and women's experiences with the law are different. To this extent, the narratives replicate an important aspect of feminist discourses of rape. Whereas a feminist politics would use this realization to forge collective action, these narratives offer tenuous and individual responses. Their focus on individual criminals and individual solutions forecloses the possibility of enabling a feminist public sphere.

SPACE FOR DEBATE

As I have elucidated above, most prime-time narratives oscillate between patriarchal and proto-feminist understandings of rape. Most of the narratives present these two understandings of rape in a familiar "he said, she said" format. While the accuser seeks to assert resistance and lack of consent, the accused man foregrounds associational aspects that could contribute toward consent. These narratives depict rape primarily as a heinous, though logical, conclusion of a communication breakdown between the sexes. Sexual violence is the consequence of the irreconcilable differences between male and female ways of seeing.

By repeatedly presenting feminist interpretations in contestation with patriarchal definitions, the narratives enable a liberal conceptualization of the public sphere, as though the two perspectives are able to enter the arena of debate as equally valid explanations. The shows do not take into account that feminist redefinitions still constitute counter-hegemonic discourses and are not perceived as legitimate as patriarchal definitions of sexual violence. However, even in these narratives, only the male characters can comfortably espouse a feminist understanding. The women, on the other hand, speak in the voice of the white male authority figure. This is an aspect that Habermas does not account for in his conceptualization of the public sphere. He assumes that all citizens can participate as though they are equal, but even on prime-time narratives, men can present themselves as feminist with greater ease (and authority) than women.

In the fictional narratives analyzed here, feminism and feminist critiques function as backdrops against which well-rehearsed arguments about the bureaucratic nature of social institutions are played out. Contrary to the spirit of the epigraph, in most of these shows, one could easily substitute rape with any other crime and not have a very different narrative. The public sphere enabled by these programs allows for a debate about the nature of the crime and its effects. These debates do not offer any avenues for action; most of them even undermine the possibility of isolating gender as a common terrain for identity formation. As Gayatri Spivak points out in another context, the figure of the woman disappears from these narratives not into pristine nothingness but into a violent shuttling between patriarchy and a liberal feminist conception of equality.[85] Feminism itself functions only as a narrative strategy that disrupts and upsets categories integral to legal and crime dramas.

Feminist theories of rape have isolated the systemic nature of sexual violence: while individuals may commit the crime, feminists have pointed out that social structures create the climate that enables rape. They have isolated gender role socialization and the gender-based hierarchies sustained by patriarchal institutions as the central factors that allow men to not understand when and how coercion and violence enter sexual relations. In contrast, these fictional accounts construct sexual violence as arbitrary and isolated eruptions of a pathologically sick male desire. These narratives, except for the last two episodes I analyze here, do not raise the possibility that rape is the excessive logic of the privileges accrued to males in a patriarchal system. Cultural norms and social acculturation processes have little bearing on the acts of violence fictionalized here.

Prime-time rape narratives facilitate complex ways of understanding rape. The striking feature here is the variability of entertainment genres, with each of the episodes enabling new discussions of sexual violence.

As I have already elucidated, many of these accounts present sympathetic portrayals of the ways in which victims are treated by public institutions. Indeed, in these shows the victims are the only sympathetic female characters. Consistently, all story lines present state institutions, particularly the legal system and the police, as sustaining patriarchal definitions of female sexuality. Through such a critique, these narratives reveal the underbelly of news discourses. The official voices of the police and the legal system are the primary framers of news discourses of rape. Prime-time entertainment may air many of the arguments forwarded in the news, but it casts doubt on the validity of these hegemonic discourses. Through their narratives, prime-time fiction enables debates and discussions that have the potential to be radically different from that offered by news programming.

The narratives repeatedly present the victim as unequivocally innocent; this depiction is counterproductive to a feminist perspective that would seek to eliminate the distinction between "good" and "bad" women as the criterion for evaluating the credibility of a rape charge. Hayden White argues that all narratives inscribe a moralizing impulse.[86] The dominance of patriarchal discourses ensures that the moralizing impulse of these narratives is that women who do not fit the mold of the virginal figure will be cast as incredible victims.

When the issue is race, the shows are unable to reveal that nonwhites experience rape differently. When prime-time fiction deploys rape allegorically to address issues of racial difference, sexual violence slides out of view, permitting only an exploration of racism. On the rare occasion when they represent interracial rape, the narratives either undertake a problematic inversion or focus on the male experience of oppression. *L.A. Law* was the only show to directly engage with the myth of the black rapist and its effects on nonwhite males; but such an understanding is eked out at the expense of the female experience of rape. When the narratives foreground how discourses of racialized sexuality affect individuals, the focus is exclusively on males; the narratives elide the nonwhite female experience of rape. Further, when the black rapist myth is deployed, the narratives cast the white woman accuser as a malingerer who is responsible for the persecution of oppressed males; the ghosts of Scottsboro continue to haunt popular imaginings of this particular configuration of interracial rape. Both of these strategies of dealing with race indicate that the public sphere constituted by prime-time fiction can engage most easily with white-on-white rape, and in this case the influence of feminist discourse is tangible in the sympathetic portrayals of the female experience. When racial difference is introduced or the narratives attempt to chart the operations of racialized sexuality, it is revealed unambiguously that it is the racialized male who is admitted into the public sphere—the women are left out.

What we see repeatedly is that the various prime-time narratives attempt to negotiate between discourses of race and gender in their rape narratives. The privileging of one category over the other is a strategic choice made to ensure a dramatic narrative that can easily identify the villain from the hero. Such choices, however, shape the nature of public debate facilitated by these programs. The universal subject of the public sphere constituted by these narratives is multivalent. Nevertheless, nonwhite women's experiences and voices are muted.

5

Testifying in the
Court of Talk Shows

Recently the university where I teach decided to undertake a series of initiatives to facilitate diversity in the classroom. The first session replicated the structure of the daytime talk show. Students, university administrators, and faculty comprised the panelists who were placed on a stage. All of them narrated their personal experiences with issues of diversity, primarily those pertaining to racial difference. The organizer then proclaimed mockingly that she would be Oprah Winfrey for the hour and proceeded to thrust a microphone at audience members to develop the conversation. As is common in talk shows, the results of the session were mixed: the audience and the guests provided empathetic, moving accounts of their experiences. The topic was discussed from multiple perspectives, but the session offered little resolution. The only thing effectively communicated was the existence of a problem.

What is striking about this event is that discussion of issues in academe, the hothouse of expert knowledge, is usually characterized by expositional discourses. The decision to resort to the talk show model, where the storied voices explain the difficulty of ensuring diversity in classrooms, reveals the extent to which the experiential and conversational aspects of talk shows have seeped into everyday culture.[1] Was it the topic that led to this format? Would the organizers have used a similar format if the topic were the honor system or student enrollment policies? Can topics dealing with race, gender, or identity issues, still characterized largely as private, be discussed productively only in the conversational format? When addressing public issues the traditional form of debate, using empirically verifiable evidence to marshal one's arguments, is preferred. An exploration of the dynamics of gender and race hierarchies appears to be more productively conducted in a format that replicates the intimacy of conversations associated with the domestic sphere.

In this chapter I explore the contributions the "intimate," emotional, and sometimes raucous conversations of daytime talk shows make toward the democratic public sphere. Critical responses to the genre have either celebrated the energy and vitality that characterize the multiple, ordinary voices that prevail on the shows or have been dismissive of the sensational and spectacular topics they address. Eschewing these two positions, I both validate the progressive impulse of the genre and point out its limits. This double focus characterizes the structure of this chapter.

A central argument I put forth in the following analysis is that while daytime talk shows do not facilitate the rational-critical debate that Habermas defines as being integral to the public sphere, they offer the first steps toward the formation of a counter-public sphere. Indeed, I contend that the daytime talk show makes possible an affective public sphere, one where discussion of issues pertaining to the body and emotions become central to democratic community formations. As I pointed out in Chapter 1 of this book, many scholars, notably feminists, have argued against the construction of a monolithic public sphere, especially one that brackets out issues pertaining to identity. They suggest that multiple, overlapping, and competing public spheres, counter-public spheres, more accurately account for the processes through which individuals participate in society. A counter-public sphere does not claim a representative universality. Instead, through a recognition of differences, it affirms the formation of identities specific to gender, race, class, and so on. A counter-public sphere is one of many public spheres enabling democratic community formation, particularly by giving voice to marginalized subjects. The majority of this chapter outlines the modalities through which talk shows could facilitate the formation of a counter-public sphere, an affective public sphere, that coalesces around the topic of sexual violence experienced by women. In the final section, I critically scrutinize the validity of this counter-public sphere—which aspects of rape, gender, and race are highlighted in the shared identities encouraged by these conversations.

I analyze only two venues of the daytime talk show: *Oprah: The Oprah Winfrey* show and *Donahue*. (Hereafter, I address the former as *Oprah*.) Since the dynamics of the host-guest interactions shape the conversations developed, the arguments I make in this chapter are specific to these two shows and should not be extended to the genre as a whole. Even these two shows, as I illustrate below, are marked by tremendous differences in the nature of the debate they promote. Nevertheless, these two shows are often used as the prototype for contemporary daytime talk shows. The analysis that follows reveals the possibilities and limits of the genre, even as it underscores the complex ways in which individual episodes represent and talk about rape.

The ability to discuss personal experiences within the public domain has been valorized primarily by the women's movement of the 1970s. It was an integral part of consciousness-raising sessions and feminist confessional literature, two central modes of disseminating feminist ideology. Typically, in consciousness-raising sessions, speakers make public that which has been kept private, displacing the traditional opposition between public and private. For the most part, participants confront the effects of sexism in personal terms; collectively, the voices of individual women permit a political analysis of gender-based oppression, which in turn leads to the formulation of a response. The unique aspects of these two feminist fora is that they provide women with a voice to narrate their experiences, serve as sites for self-definition, and present women as the ultimate authority in speaking of the effects of gender oppression. In consciousness-raising sessions and confessional literature, individual accounts are seen as authentic and representative of a larger gender hierarchy that binds women together; they emphasize the typicality of individual women's experiences in relation to a notion of communal identity.[2] The experiential voice helps women renarrate the experience of being female in a patriarchal society, and it moves the speaker from object to subject status.

As I outlined in Chapter 2 of this book, these mobilizing strategies of the women's movement were encapsulated in the slogan, "The personal is the political," which attempted to capture the ways in which the domestic sphere is politicized. Testimony, self-disclosure, and the experiential voice also were key to raising public awareness about violence against women. These discussions helped generate a gender-specific identity grounded in a consciousness of a shared problem and produced solidarity among women. Further, it made possible a response to this realization of a shared problem—a rousing into action.

The structure and format of the daytime talk shows I examine in this chapter replicate many of these features, especially when they address issues pertaining to violence committed against women. Both Donahue and Winfrey have acknowledged the influence of the women's movement on the structure and content of their shows.[3] Of the various genres analyzed in this book, daytime talk shows most thoroughly engage with issues raised by the women's movement. Even though they thematize only some aspects of liberal feminism, by including "ordinary" voices that have traditionally been marginalized on television daytime talk shows offer one of the most productive sites for a discussion of the sexual politics that structure cultural understandings of rape.

Daytime talk shows privilege subjective experience over objective knowledge, blur the lines between the public and private, and above all are directed primarily at a female audience. On these shows the guests and the audience debate aspects of everyday culture with energy and urgency. Through the articulation of affective relations, they constitute, at least for the space of the hour, a shared community. With an examination of the discussions of rape on *Oprah* and *Donahue*, I explore the specific ways in which feminism functions as an explicit and implicit referent of talk shows and shapes the debates that they enable. I examine as well the strategies through which talk show discussions are able to forge a collective identity among guests, the invited experts, as well as the studio and at-home audiences.

My analysis reveals that in *Oprah* discussions, gender is the central plank around which participants forge a collective identity. The conversations, where guests and audience members bare open intimate details of their lives for public discussion, move beyond an exploration of individual cases to create a proto-feminist discursive space: they foreground the pain and violence that result from sexual violence. The act of giving a voice to pain permits rape victims and the women in the audience to forge a connection across this shared recognition of potential violence. However, the show never directly addresses the issue of race when discussing sexual violence. It could be argued that Winfrey's embodied presence as a black woman and her self-disclosures underscore the differences in black women's experiences of sexual violence. Even as I highlight the marginalization of this discourse on *Oprah*, I argue that Winfrey's communicative style produces an intimacy that permits gender to serve as a bridge across racial difference. *Donahue* tends to rely more on expert opinion and does not offer the same potential for women's voices. On this show, the discussions permit the formation of a collective identity around race or class rather than gender. This show provides more of the empirically verifiable data that characterize traditional debates in the public arena.

In what follows, I outline the characteristic features of daytime talk shows. Next I examine discussions of rape on *Oprah* and then outline the ways in which *Donahue* provides a different space for debate about sexual violence. I conclude with an evaluation of the counter-public sphere that daytime talk shows could facilitate.

A DOMESTIC TECHNOLOGY

Examining social and institutional histories, scholars have identified television as an exemplary domestic cultural apparatus, anchored in the family and the home. It is intimately linked to the sphere of privacy and sexuality.[4] Lynn Spigel points out that in the 1950s, television became the site where anxieties over sexual politics and domestic ideals were played out. Contradictory responses marked the installation of the medium. Some hailed it as a democratic medium that would link the suburban family to the larger public arena. Others found that by directing its programming at women, television could disturb the normative ways of seeing in patriarchal cultures. Since its inception, television has been linked to consumerism and marked as a gendered cultural product. These concerns and trends come into sharp focus in discussions of the 1980s' daytime talk show.

Daytime talk shows have been a staple of television programming since the 1950s and have been geared primarily at a female audience. Historically, women have hosted the majority of these daytime programs and have adopted a homey, folksy, friendly tone.[5] The programs either dealt with topics considered feminine, such as cooking and fashion, or they consisted of "celebrity" guests sitting around a coffee table and sharing "secrets" relating to the domestic sphere of activities. Virginia Graham's *Girl Talk* and Dinah Shore's *Dinah's Place* usually are identified as the antecedents of *Oprah* and *Donahue*. Firmly located within the domestic arena, Shore's program provided household and cooking tips from a studio set made to resemble a kitchenette and living room. *Girl Talk* was developed in the 1960s and was modeled on women's magazines, featuring celebrities who clarified the notion of femininity. It brought together women in public life; not the political woman, but the mass culture woman—movie stars, TV stars, female personalities—to chat about things, not issues.

The issue-oriented talk show format analyzed in this chapter originated in the late 1960s, and Donahue is credited with its formation. In 1967, he organized his hour-long show around a single controversial topic and focused on "ordinary" people rather than on celebrities. Furthermore, he was the first television host to integrate the studio audience into the program. He abandoned his place on the stage and positioned himself with the predominantly female audience, whose comments and questions he actively incorporated into the program. With this strategy, the show effectively blurred the lines between the guests and the audience. The audience, with its everyday knowledge, became central to the program. According to Laurie Haag, *Donahue* was "the first talk show to concede the importance of the female voice."[6]

Donahue altered the content of daytime talk shows as well. The focus was no longer on recipes, dress patterns, or so-called girl talk. Instead, his show, which has been characterized as an "exercise in sociopolitical discourse," tackled a range of issues dealing with serious national concerns,

such as presidential elections, war, poverty, and AIDS, and sensational topics, such as female impersonators and lesbian mud wrestlers.[7] This new talk
show gained fame not for its discussion of serious topics but for discussing
issues that were considered taboo.

Since the formation of Donahue's audience-driven program, the structure and content of daytime talk shows have altered considerably. Despite the
success and popularity of the show, *Donahue* remained unchallenged until
1984, when Sally Jessy Raphael's show was nationally syndicated. Winfrey's
show was syndicated nationally in 1986 and soon overtook *Donahue* in the
ratings war. Following the success of Winfrey's show, the daytime talk show
arena became very crowded. In an effort to distinguish their shows from competitors, hosts turned to salacious topics and encouraged more confrontational and violent interaction among guests.[8] Politicians and cultural critics
condemned this trend and characterized talk shows as "trash television."
Partly responding to these criticisms, Donahue aired his last show in September 1996.

Earlier in 1994, Winfrey renounced her successful format to adopt a
"more responsible" talk show. She abandoned the single-issue show and
shifted the focus away from so-called female topics to issues of spirituality.
Winfrey's new format resembles the daytime talk show of the 1950s and has
reduced sharply audience participation. Now Winfrey sits with her guests
separated from the studio audience, whose role is reduced to applauding
celebrities and occasionally voicing their appreciation for guests' achievements. In other efforts to distinguish her show from competitors, Winfrey
introduced an on-air book club and Oprah's Angel Network in 1997 to promote philanthropy. These gestures allow the *Oprah* show to appeal to an
audience broader than the stay-at-home female viewer and recast the host as
a popular intellectual. In this chapter, however, I focus on the earlier single-
issue, participatory audience format.

The popularity of talk shows has receded since their peak during the
1990–1991 season, but they continue to draw a large audience.[9] While viewers may find talk show content compelling and pleasurable, it is the economics of production that ensures the genre's enduring success. Each show
costs between $25,000 and $50,000 for an hour, in contrast to the $1 mil-
lion for each episode of a successful sitcom.[10] Further, according to Vicki Abt
and Leonard Mastazza, Federal Communications Commission (FCC) rules
do not permit networks to air shows during some daytime hours for their
affiliates. Local stations have turned to the syndication market to fill these
hours and have found that talk shows are not only cheaper, they allow greater
time for local advertisers as well.[11]

"Tabloid" Television

Discussions on daytime talk shows oscillate between "serious" topics such as gun control and typically female issues such as the "other woman." Focusing on the female topics undertaken, scholars, cultural critics, and journalists have derided the content of daytime talk shows. They argue that the programs appeal to the prurient interests of the largely female audience and do not serve the "public good." For instance, Abt and Mastazza believe that daytime talk shows are harmful to civil culture; their focus on deviance allows people "to brag about their irresponsible behaviors." Further, they showcase dysfunctional behaviors primarily for consumer gain.[12] Similarly, *New York Times* television critic Walter Goodman characterizes talk show debates on sexuality as "soft porn with redeeming content, a peep show in the interests of sensitivity training."[13] Such descriptions of talk shows are commonplace among cultural critics who rely on modes of theorizing, where any "public articulation of sexual difference and gender conflict renders the entire discourse . . . overblown, unreliable, and unbelievable."[14]

Some, though, have praised these programs for thematizing feminist concerns and providing marginalized people with a forum to express their ideas.[15] By foregrounding issues pertaining to women, these shows contain the capacity to empower and inform women. Scholars such as Elayne Rapping, Jane Shattuc, and Janice Peck point out that talk shows may not be taken seriously by those in power; their status as syndicated products contributes to this disdain. Paradoxically, this dismissive attitude—combined with low production costs, high profit margins, and daytime placement—permits the genre to tackle previously marginalized topics such as domestic violence and child abuse. Those who praise the potential of talk shows also point out that the genre provides new avenues for knowledge construction.[16] My analysis in this chapter is informed by these studies that are critical of talk shows but also single out aspects that permit them to serve as a forum for marginalized voices, particularly women.[17]

Hybrid Genre

Each talk show has developed signature features that distinguish them from their competitors, but there are still some generic conventions that one can identify. Jane Shattuc offers the most comprehensive examination of the genre in *The Talking Cure*. She has isolated five characteristic features that distinguish daytime talk shows from other programming: (1) they are issue oriented;

(2) audience participation is central to the show; (3) discussions are structured around the guests and host; (4) they are constructed for a female audience; and (5) they are produced by non-network companies for broadcast on network affiliated stations.[18] Each of these features requires some elaboration. As I have indicated already, unlike the girl talk shows of the past or their late-night counterparts, the daytime talk shows of the 1980s derived their content from current social problems. By highlighting individual narratives and placing the issues within a domestic context, they fleshed out the personal ramifications of a news story.[19] On talk shows, the personal is at the very least public, if not political.

Since *Donahue*, daytime talk shows have incorporated audience participation within the structure of their programs. While most critics have classified these as peep shows or charged them with encouraging voyeurism, Shattuc argues persuasively against such readings. These programs are predicated on an active and a vociferous studio audience that asks "guests the type of questions we would ask if we were there."[20] The technological apparatus of television visually identifies audience members, while the narrative structure gives them voice, transforming them from spectators into participants.[21] This is the only genre that actively produces the public as a protagonist. Scholars such as Wayne Munson and Donal Carbaugh have identified it as the archetypal site of the contemporary public sphere, a forum where people can come together to debate issues of concern. Carbaugh suggests that the genre exemplifies America talking to itself. Talk shows function as an alternative space from which dominant values can be questioned. They are the social equivalent of Greek agoras, where people verbalize their cultural beliefs and discuss problems.[22] While registering the problematics of the genre, these scholars point out that talk shows allow us to make a link between community and politics, social change and television programming.

Despite the centrality of audience voices and the seemingly unscripted nature of the conversations, talk shows are sharply regulated and structured.[23] The discussions center on the authority and knowledge of the host and the experts; together they shape which stories are told and how they are told. Notwithstanding the appearance of an extravagantly participatory conversation, what viewers witness is a controlled discussion. Typically, *Oprah* and *Donahue* open with the host introducing the issue and guests and setting out the parameters for the conversation. In brief segments, the guests, who become representative of social problems, narrate their stories, experts provide commentary, and the audience participates in the discussion of the topic as well as with the guests.[24] As Janice Peck describes it, after the introduction, the host's job is to draw out stories from the "ordinary" guests, to encourage and regulate feedback from the audience, to solicit advice from the experts, and to make sure that advertisers receive their allotted time.[25]

Many of the criticisms of talk shows seem to emanate from their degraded status as a female genre. Women are perceived to be the primary audience, and the "feminine" nature of the shows is produced through a battery of intentional and unintentional devices.[26] Marilyn Matelski points out that broadcasting executives target most of their daytime programming to eighteen- to forty-nine-year-old women, because they constitute the largest percentage of habitual viewers and are the primary purchasers of household items.[27] These structural features indicate the ways in which daytime talk shows are interpellated in television culture. I now highlight briefly those characteristics that could permit talk shows to facilitate a counter-public sphere that affirms a shared gender identity for women.

FEMININE DISCOURSES

Talk shows have been characterized as "feminine" programs. They typically lack closure, they emphasize process, dialogue, and intimate conversation, and they focus on relational issues, all aspects that Mary Ellen Brown and John Fiske characterize as constituting a feminine discursive space.[28] Irrespective of the topic scrutinized, daytime talk shows promote a mode of discussion that emphasizes the emotional over the analytical and foregrounds individual experience and interpersonal dimensions of issues. Conflicts and crises, which are the staples of the genre, are presented invariably as individual issues. All discussions are cast in everyday "plain folks" language. Peck points out that talk shows cast their topics in language that seems open and accessible, which producers believe is appealing to women.[29] The use of everyday language helps talk shows develop the intimacy characteristic of the domestic sphere, a space where private issues can be discussed safely. Even the labels assigned to the participants reflect this sensibility; the facilitator of the conversation is called the host, and the invited participants are the guests. In addition to this language of hospitality, most talk shows use the first name of the host as the name of the program. For instance, Winfrey's program is called *Oprah*. The choice of this first name identification marks the paradoxical notion of intimacy with a mass audience that talk shows build. The host, Oprah, is presented as a friendly, "regular" person, thus audiences can address her by her first name.

In addition, studios are made to resemble living rooms, disguising further the public nature of these discussions. On most talk shows, the panel of guests is seated up front on a podium that is disguised as a central sitting area. The host is not seated with the guests but instead wanders between them and the studio audience, thrusting a microphone at audience members. Effectively, the geography of the talk show studio and the nature of discussion collapse the categories of host, studio, and home audience into television's fictive "we." *Oprah* adds a further twist, since the host often participates in emotional self-confessions of childhood sexual abuse, weight loss, and other personal details relevant to the topic at hand. Gloria-Jean Masciarotte contends that Winfrey is always one of her own guests. She reveals aspects of her everyday life: Winfrey refers to her best friend, her battle to control her weight, and her partner repeatedly.[30]

Within the constructed privacy of this public-domestic arena, primarily women talk about painful experiences and ill-defined struggles. Both guests and audience members provide personal accounts about private topics, and the discussions center on personal experiences. Normally, by the end of the hour-long program, the studio and home viewing audiences become eyewitnesses to a personal confession or self-disclosure. Apart from contesting the distinction between the public and private spheres, talk shows obscure as well the distinction between experts and laypersons. They privilege the storytelling of personal struggles over the knowledge provided by experts. Often, the studio audience members challenge the experts and position their individual experiences as possessing greater validity and moral authority. In these programs, the real expert is considered the storytelling voice of the layperson. This focus on individual stories allows talk shows to highlight the familiar and the domestic over characteristics traditionally associated with the rational-critical debate of the public sphere. Additionally, the experts, who are predominantly women, are expected to exhibit their knowledge through the "feminine" characteristics of nurturance, interpersonal skills, and the ability to solve dilemmas with commonsensical solutions.[31]

Through these devices, talk shows "confound our coordinates, the lines of our cognitive maps, our familiar distinctions and stabilities," Wayne Munson contends.[32] They blur our understandings of public and private issues, public and private spaces, and the characteristics differentiating the guests from the host and the participants from the audience. They realign the various oppositions of fact/fiction, information/entertainment, expert/layperson, and objectivity/subjectivity. Primarily, they reconstitute the public/private divide; they tend to present private acts as socially relevant and the social as personal. Masciarotte believes that daytime talk shows also displace the opposition between story and issue. "Talk shows have renegotiated the kind of information that constitutes issues and have reconstructed the way those issues are represented for resolution."[33] Each of these reconfigurations echoes themes undertaken by feminism and the women's movement. One could expect that, like the women's movement, these features would permit talk shows to facilitate the formation of a counter-public sphere, a discursive space that affirms a collective identity around a shared experience and unites people beyond their differences. In the analysis that follows, I underscore the ability of *Oprah* and *Donahue* to undertake this task when dealing with the topic of rape.

CATHARTIC CONFESSIONS

Entertainment is the last thing I am looking for. . . . My goal is to try to uplift, encourage and enlighten you in some way. I'm looking for the moment that makes you say, "Ah ha, I didn't know that."
—Oprah Winfrey

Like Donahue, Winfrey started her television career in the newsroom but gave it up to become a nationally syndicated talk show host in 1986. In its first five months, *Oprah* became the leading daytime talk show and the third highest rated syndicated show, behind *Wheel of Fortune* and *Jeopardy!*.[34] By 1988, Winfrey's salary and the profits she earned from *Oprah* allowed her to buy the production rights to the program. She created Harpo Production, Inc.—the first African-American-owned film and television production studio—to produce her show. *Oprah* is currently distributed to 204 markets in the United States and to 113 other countries through King World Productions, a syndication company. In 1996, *Oprah* represented about half of King World's profits; the show had generated $180 million in revenues, and *Forbes* magazine named Winfrey the highest paid entertainer in the United States.

Several factors facilitated the success of this black woman in a medium dominated by white men. Most critics point out that Winfrey and the star texts that created her biography have authored a reassuring Horatio Alger legend: she is a working-class person who has overcome numerous obstacles to achieve success through her individual efforts. As Dana Cloud points out, both the Winfrey biography and her show interpret success and failure as a matter of individual responsibility, regardless of the person's location in systems of power and privilege. These ideas echo key themes of dominant liberal ideology and make Winfrey acceptable to her white viewers.[35]

The star texts emphasize her "feminine" qualities; they point out that she is soft, empathetic, emotional, instinctive, mystical, and sensuous, rather than a smart and shrewd businesswoman, qualities associated with masculinity.[36]

Primarily, Winfrey's star personality is constructed along two axes—as a black woman and as a person of working-class origins. By emphasizing these aspects, the star texts create a tokenist biography, Cloud contends, a narrative that assures viewers of the fairness and justice inherent in U.S. society.

Although most star texts refer only fleetingly to Winfrey's race, they invariably describe her in language that evokes the caring, nurturing, and empathetic "mammy" figure. Winfrey herself works very hard to e-race herself. "Race is not an issue with me," she has said in numerous interviews. *Wall Street Journal* reviewer Martha Bayles writes approvingly that while Donahue harps about the issue of racism, the black woman ignores it. Winfrey's refusal to engage with the topic reflects her emphasis on individual responsibility; she has a realistic assessment of her own cultural and religious roots, Bayles contends.[37] Others believe that Winfrey's success can be attributed to her refusal to overtly engage with the topic of race, and yet not become a "white" black person, someone who emulates white America's ideas of dress and decorum.[38]

In addition, the star texts focus on Winfrey's working-class origins. They point out in detail her various childhood travails. The authors of these texts perform acrobatic feats, recognizing her working-class origins but not drawing attention to the specific nature of black working-class living conditions in mid-twentieth century America. As the following analysis reveals, these aspects are repeated in her show as well—it is hard to ignore race, and yet the participants rarely address it.

In the time period of this study, Winfrey's show covered the topic of rape on three occasions, and she eschewed any discussion of "celebrity rape."[39] The shows foregrounded everyday women's experiences of rape instead. In all three instances, the discussions centered on cases of acquaintance rape and individual women's accounts of the trauma they experienced. *Oprah* tends to follow a problem-solution narrative structure, which facilitates a focus on the experiential voice of individuals. In the first quarter-hour, Winfrey and her guests identify the problem, establishing the parameters for the ensuing conversation. The guests present their experiences of sexual assault individually, often following a repetitive, fragmented narrative structure. In the second quarter-hour, the audience begins to address and confront the guests' inconsistencies, as the host plays moderator; at this stage, the personal experience of sexual assault is generalized to a larger social issue of collective gendered identity. In the final half hour, the "experts" are drawn into the conversation, and along with the audience they start to offer solutions.[40]

By allowing individuals to articulate ill-defined, ongoing struggles, the episodes facilitate social understandings about sexual violence rather than institutional definitions. During the hour-long show, viewers encounter rape victims who repeatedly articulate their experiences of sexual assault, and the guests and the women in the audience narrate their life stories, understandings of sexual violence, and bewilderment. Many of the rape survivors are emotional and defiant as they justify their behavior preceding the sexual assault. The survivors explain how they were affected by the rape, the trauma they suffered, and the guilt and shame they experienced.[41] "What did I do to provoke this?" one woman asked, while another explained, "I just could not go on with my life. I just wasn't concentrating. I gained a large amount of weight." These storied voices of rape victims call into question prevailing stereotypes of rape and female sexuality and clarify a survivor-centered understanding of sexual assault. They explain that, contradicting definitions of "real" rape, most of these women were raped by friends, ex-husbands, and acquaintances; they were attacked in "safe" spaces, and they rarely bore the physical marks of their resistance.

The discussions of sexual violence draw attention as well to the subjective pain of the women. By allowing women to speak about their experiences of victimization, *Oprah* focuses on the unspeakable reality of pain and its investment in the individual body. Elaine Scarry has pointed out the difficulties involved in expressing physical pain and its resistance to objectification in language.[42] *Oprah*, with its insistence on detailed descriptions of sexual assaults, transports the issue of individual, private pain into the arena of shared public discourse. By narrating sexual violence, the discussions on *Oprah* affirm a female experience that often has been repressed and rendered invisible. These storied voices seek explicitly to disclose the most intimate and often traumatic details of an individual's life to elucidate their broader implications. The debate engendered by these individual experiences transmutes the personal into the collective.

COMING IN TO VOICE

As in the consciousness-raising sessions of the 1970s, the panelists on *Oprah* did not define their assaults as rape initially; however, soon they were able to speak for themselves and name the act. This narration of pain and the act of naming provide the cathartic elements of talk shows. The act of naming offers a public language for private despair, it offers a route out of private isolation and into public life. This television genre provides a forum for the participants to discover a female self, a key moment for the formation of a feminist community.[43] Scholars such as bell hooks have argued that to have a voice that is heard marks the "movement from object to subject" and protects women from dehumanization and despair. They point out that racism, sexism, and class exploitation suppress and silence women's voices, and that the act of talking back, to speak as an equal to an authority figure, is an empowering gesture.[44] Through speaking about their experiences of rape, these guests move from object to subject position, at least for the duration of the show. As several scholars have pointed out, the privileging of the experiential voice is problematic. The storied voice of individual experience is marked by a dialectic: it affirms a female experience that often has been rendered invisible by speaking about it. These discussions do not pose a challenge to the structures that make rape possible, but only explain how and why sexual violence occurs. Nevertheless, the voice of personal experience makes visible the affective dimensions of patriarchal structures and dramatizes the embodied aspect of selected public issues.[45]

Many feminist scholars have found Michel Foucault's theories useful frameworks to understand the elaborate, ritualized discussions of sex and sexuality facilitated by contemporary television. In *The History of Sexuality*, Foucault contends that during the Victorian Era, conversations about sex were relegated to the church confessional, and sex was essentially transformed into a discourse. The confessional, Foucault believes, became "an apparatus for producing an ever greater quantity of discourse about sex" and determined the distinctions between licit and illicit behavior.[46]

The narrative structure of *Oprah* constructs an analogous situation; it enables the transformation of sex and sexual violence into discourse. The public discussions of private trauma replicate the Protestant activity of testimony or witnessing before a group.[47] Here individual identity is not constructed in secrecy or in the privacy of the confessional; the discussions enable the formation of a social citizen. Winfrey functions in a manner akin to the priest in the confessional that Foucault describes. She is the "authority who requires the confession, prescribes and appreciates it, and intervenes in order to judge, punish, forgive, console, and reconcile"; through the confession, the guest is liberated and transformed.[48] "I want to hear your side of the story," she says as she coaxes her guests to discuss private trauma in public. She provides conversational cues and adds or insists on specific details of emotions. "Were you screaming? Did you think he was going to kill you?" "In the week before you told your best friend, what were you going through? What kind of stuff were you feeling, thinking, doing?" One of the women responded to these questions by explaining, "I stopped going to parties. I stopped going out on dates." This rape survivor also admitted to a loss of confidence and to an inability to trust her judgment about people. Winfrey's role as the interlocutor allowed rape victims to articulate their pain and confusion.

Unlike the confessional, where one testifies to one's faith, *Oprah* does not promise forgiveness; the act of enunciation does not redeem the person. Instead, the act of testifying provides various participants with a public voice to make sense of their individual experiences. Shoshana Felman contends that the act of making public a previously silenced subject results in a community of witnessing and permits the formation of a collective identity.[49] In the *Oprah* shows, the collective identity coalesces around a recognition of gender-based oppression. For instance, a guest on the episode "She Asked For It" explained her reluctance to prosecute her assailant. "I didn't want to see him. I just didn't want to relive it. And nobody showed any sympathy toward me, and I just figured it was not worth my time and worth my going through everything all over again." In the discussion that followed, women in the audience not only concurred with the guest's sentiments, some even testified to their own violations. Winfrey encouraged these women's voices and incited more descriptions. "There are a million women out there who are saying, 'Oh my God. Well, this is what happened to me, but I didn't know that's what you could call it.'"

The act of bearing witness to a trauma does not provide a totalizing account of events. It provides information that is not always congruent with hegemonic definitions and often requires the transvaluation of previous categories and frames of reference. In the instance I have just cited, the different women's voices allow audiences to reconsider the reasons for low rape prosecutions: it is not just for lack of evidence, but the shame and trauma violated individuals' experience. Similarly, in conversations that were repeated on different shows with minor variations, audience members (mostly male) invoked rape myths such as, "Women are innately coy, while men are innately the aggressors." These were countered by Winfrey and women in the audience with feminist redefinitions of, "Men don't rape women because they want sex." Here the women urge that we examine the issue of sexual violence from a female perspective, not from the habitual male point of view. They insist on a new frame of reference. It is this aspect of the testimonial that makes it possible to consider *Oprah* discussions as facilitating the first step toward the formation of a counter-public sphere.[50]

Limits of the Confessional Discourse

These possibilities are tempered by *Oprah's* need to maintain a large viewership and to not alienate any section of the audience. To counter the accusation that she is "anti-male," Winfrey often goes out of her way to include male voices and to solicit men's opinions, Corrine Squire contends.[51] Further, to maintain the volatile potential of her show, the host often invokes a patriarchal definition of rape, one that should be antithetical to her description of being pro-women. The juxtaposition of incommensurable understandings of rape ensures, however, that the shows do not become a source for political activism against the system that produces sexual violence. Instead, most of the time is spent contesting ideas, as though both men and women are presenting equally valid explanations of rape.

This tendency is captured evocatively in the episode "Date Rape," which aired on December 7, 1989. The first guest was a convicted rapist who had been invited, Winfrey clarified, to "tell women how his mind worked when he was out with a woman on a date, which women he decided to rape." It is paradoxical that Winfrey should ask women to turn to a convicted rapist for advice on rape avoidance strategies. Seeking advice from the victimizer makes women indebted to the person who could potentially be a threat to them. Lauren Berlant calls this the "paradox in the social construction of female marginality," a logic that deems women should not only live with but also seek advice from those who have traditionally and institutionally denied them autonomy.[52] In "Date Rape," the rapist's account was followed by three women who described their experiences of acquaintance rape. The rapist's storied voice provided a commonsensical understanding of sexual violence as stemming from a communication breakdown between the sexes. He explained that men are socialized differently from women, and that as a rapist he exploited these differences. By giving precedence to this rapist's voice over those of the three rape survivors, *Oprah* made him, rather than sexual violence, the focus of the show. Above all, this strategy ensures that rape is seen as an individual crime and not a systemic problem. The rapist's explanations offer the shared community of women steps that they can take to communicate "no" better and thereby avoid the situations described by the rape survivors.

The limits of such a solution are revealed in the same show. Once the three women provided moving accounts of their assaults and everyone agreed that "no" really should mean "no," one male in the audience repeatedly assured one of the survivors that on a date the man is not interested in anything else but the woman's body. "Look at you there, you're gorgeous," he repeatedly asserted, as though that were explanation enough for overriding a woman's consent. Later, another male claimed unabashedly, "Every man in this audience has been with a woman, and that woman has said no repeatedly, and after the evening, sexual intercourse has happened, and you've left. Nothing else has ever been heard about it." While the guests and many in the audience tried to argue with these men, these conversations reveal poignantly that despite the storied voices of the women, the field of visibility is saturated with patriarchal ideas about women. Judith Butler's analysis of the Rodney King trial is instructive here. These men do not ignore the women's accounts but reproduce these stories within a field of visibility structured by patriarchy. The women's narratives are perceived as yet another installment of female victimage. These men's responses reveal the patriarchal production of the visible, of what can be seen. Patriarchy shapes what appears as reasonable and normal; attractive women are sexual objects, and any act of resistance can be overridden. "Attributing violence to the object of violence is part of the very mechanism that recapitulates violence."[53] As the convicted rapist pointed out, men hear what they want to hear because, "We feel entitled to have sex."

These audience voices reveal the limits of trying to alter people's attitudes without changing the systemic features that enable them in the first place. The men in the audience hear the various speakers assert that under all circumstances no means no, and yet they cannot seem to apprehend concepts of consent and resistance. These competing explanations of rape, when social conflicts are revealed, are rarely sustained or expanded. This tendency encapsulates the limits to the progressive impulses of daytime talk shows. The insistent focus on the individual erases the political context of issues. Peck characterizes this focus on the individual as being symptomatic of a therapeutic discourse that locates the individual as the cause for and solution to all problems, whether racism or anorexia.

Another limit to this genre is the emphasis placed on conflict. For instance, if no one in the audience espoused patriarchal understandings, Winfrey voiced them herself, invariably stimulating an agitated discussion. The host countered every assertion of feminism with a discourse of disbelief, one that showcased dominant stereotypes of rape. Winfrey repeatedly adhered to the journalistic formula of objectivity, posing "both sides of the issue." Pro and con, good and bad, and right and wrong are juxtaposed, allowing *Oprah* to incorporate both perspectives; to address one is to editorialize, and this, as Mimi White points out, could potentially alienate readers, advertisers, and broadcasters.[54]

For instance, on the show entitled "'She Asked For It' . . . The Rape Decision," which aired on October 17, 1989, Winfrey clarified that a woman's dress is not a "signal that she might be interested in sex or a signal to a jury that . . . she somehow asked for it." Yet, when many among the audience concurred with her, Winfrey repeatedly held up the clothes which had led a Florida jury to declare that the rape claimant's dress was "advertising for sex." Throughout the episode, Winfrey, not the audience members, returned to the idea that the alleged rape victim wore a "halter top that showed her midriff," and the discussion became recentered on the woman's "seductive" apparel when she was attacked. This focus on apparel negated the redefinitions of rape and female sexuality that *Oprah* discussions tend to promote. It should come as no surprise that audience members on these shows were emboldened to assert that men only "want" what they see, and that sex is the underlying theme of all male-female interactions. By juxtaposing radically incommensurable discourses without presenting the social context within which they evolved, *Oprah* discussions presented gender differences as biologically constituted.

The contradictory positions that Winfrey adopted foreground the centrality of conflict, interrogation, and self-disclosure on daytime narratives. This conflict model of narration reiterates binaries such as male/female and virgin/whore and limits the terms of the debates to the acceptability of lifestyles and sexual practices.

Racial Subjects

Oprah has dealt with the issue of racism in several different shows, even conducting a year-long series on the topic in 1991.[55] In the shows I examined, though, the host did not raise race as a feature that structures significantly an individual's experience of events. Even though some of the guests and experts were people of color, Winfrey did not address the issue of racial difference. Reading the transcripts of the show, it is easy to come away with the impression that the discussions on *Oprah* slide around the issue of race and evade it. Watching the show belies this conclusion. The discussions may not work through the issues of racism or racial difference, but they are obliquely worked over. The embodied presence of the host, guests, and predominantly white audience members makes it impossible to overlook race. Gender serves as a terrain across which the discussions on sexual violence allow audiences to forge a collective identity, but this is not attained by eliding race. In the shows I examined, gender identity served as a bridge across racial differences.

In her examination of the show, Squire points out that *Oprah* is permeated with race as much as it is with gender.[56] Most frequently, the show features a visual representation of racial difference without calling attention to it. Successful African-American entrepreneurs, professionals, and entertainers are featured frequently as guests. Through these choices, *Oprah* presents a picture of African-American culture and achievement rarely seen in other programming. More significantly, Winfrey, as a black woman speaking in public, has to reflect her similarity to the dominant order and represent the material effects of her difference within that order. Masciarotte argues that the "sign of Oprah Winfrey traverses not only race and gender but also declines these determinates within the cultural politics of body and presence."[57]

In the shows on rape, African Americans were present as guests, experts, and audience members, but none of these voices drew attention to the fact that racialized subjects experience sexual violence differently. The closest that one of the shows came to dealing with this topic was through an audience comment. A black male cautioned against believing acquaintance rape accusations easily. He pointed out that it was possible that a woman would think, "I was with a black man last night," and would then cry rape. It is important to note that the audience member did not point out that the woman was white—he just described her as a woman from Wisconsin. The woman's racial status was marked as white by the absence of a qualifier. He made it a point though to racially identify the male. This voice raised the specter of the post–Reconstruction practice, when white women were believed to have participated in interracial consensual sex but, fearing social reprisals, cried rape.[58] This voice draws attention to the histories surrounding the issue of interracial rape and the ways in which African-American male lives are shaped by the black male rapist myth. Winfrey though refused to discuss the issue and papered over the historical legacies of slavery and the threat of perceived miscegenation that continue to shape black-white sexual interactions.

Repeatedly, the *Oprah* show has worked hard to erase the issue of race, and Winfrey has presented rape as a deracinated subject that affects all women similarly. Yet, as Squire points out, viewing *Oprah* on a regular basis, it is impossible to avoid the realization that Winfrey's program draws on black women's writings and histories.[59] Winfrey recognizes the differences in black women's experiences of patriarchy. These acknowledgments of racial difference are introduced without preamble and become evident when Winfrey talks about her experiences. While she does not specify that hers is a black female experience, her embodied presence makes it impossible to deracinate these accounts.

Racial difference is most clearly foregrounded through linguistic markers. In her responses to individual audience members, Winfrey sometimes will adopt idioms and slang terms associated with African Americans, such as "you go girl." These linguistic choices ineluctably point out her presence as marked by race and class. Considering the show's tendency to abstract problems from their context and to present the individual as the source and solution of all issues, it is not surprising that episodes do not tackle specifically how race intersects with gender.

FEMINISM MODIFIED

While references to race are oblique, the influence of feminism on the discussion is unmistakable. Although Winfrey, her guests, and her audience never utter the word "feminism," it operates as an invisible referent, shaping their definitions of rape and possible solutions. Squire contends that Winfrey promotes a televisual feminism, one that articulates particular versions of blackness, femininity, and feminism.[60]

Oprah's emphasis on the storied voices of the guests produces a multiplicity of understandings that center on individual experiences of sexual assault. In any given episode, several guests help us clarify the nuances and differences in experiences of victimization. Both the guests and the audience articulate a range of definitions of sexual violence and provide insights on contemporary social understandings of rape. This polysemy is most noticeable in the labels attached to the various participants. For instance, on the show entitled "Date Rape," the panelists were described as "Raped by Acquaintances," "Raped by a Friend," and "Raped by a Date." Thus *Oprah* took the singular definition of rape survivor and provided multiple ways of defining this individual. In addition, through their participation in the discussion, the various audience members elaborated on these multiple definitions of rape survivor, some of them reproducing existing understandings and others broadening them. The discussions foreground a woman-centered definition that places the emphasis on violation and pain rather than institutional definitions. Through this plurality of storied voices, *Oprah* circulated discourses that were already in currency and opened them for debate. The different voices articulated a range of definitions of rape and provided insights on contemporary social understandings of sexual violence. By privileging these storied voices, the *Oprah* show has provided authority to experiential voices. Further, through the act of talking about their experiences of violence, the show has allowed women to overcome their alienation. Feminism suggests that naming the problem is an essential first step in the formation of a female self-identity, and this the show seems to achieve, at least for the duration of the hour.

The debates of rape on *Oprah* reveal that aspects of the 1970s' women's movement have entered the everyday lexicon and now seem commonsensical. Often victims and audience members invoked phrases made familiar by consciousness-raising programs: no means no; rape is not about sex, it is about violence and power; and stop victimizing the victim. When audience members voiced opinions contradicting feminist understandings, Winfrey would physically distance herself and resort to sarcasm. In one instance, when a male audience member continued to assert a male-centered definition of sexual politics, that a man speaks to an attractive woman only because he is interested in her body and not her brain, Winfrey called him Mr. Profound Thinker. In another instance, as audience members expressed their discomfort with a raped woman's attire, Winfrey coaxed them to clarify the implications of their statements. She repeatedly asked them to explain what they meant, until they assured her that, "I wouldn't wear those clothes, but it's your right," and that dress should never be an excuse for rape. Through these questions or merely by repetition, Winfrey permitted liberal feminist rhetoric to appear as common sense.

The importance given to the testifying voice and the politicization of the domestic are the two most obvious ways in which feminism shapes these discussions. Winfrey repeatedly asserts that her programs are designed to inform and empower women. Despite the numerous problematic areas I have already outlined, *Oprah* episodes on rape tended to be informative. The shows often offered viewers some factual information on sexual violence. Winfrey invariably juxtaposed individual women's narratives with statistics revealing the prevalence of this crime. "Acquaintance and date rape is more common than being left-handed," she clarified during one show. Commercial breaks on the show were punctuated by statistics on rape rates in the United States. This factual information highlighted the threat of rape and accentuated the shared plank across which women could forge a collective identity.

In the various episodes Winfrey asserted that her program was primarily an educational endeavor, and that by providing a plurality of voices she hoped to activate people into taking steps against rape. She declared repeatedly, "I'm doing this show because I want you to understand" what constitutes rape. The shows included lessons for women on how to prevent rape and cope with sexual assaults, and Winfrey repeatedly encouraged women to take self-defense courses. She thus enabled the formation of narratives that moved beyond exploring women's status as "always-already" victims and allowed women to see themselves as potential agents in their liberation from a shared threat.

In addition, the host and her guests tried to make connections between incidents of sexual violence and systemic problems such as gender-role socialization. Rape counselors and feminist scholars participating in the program enumerated the different and subtle ways in which gender-role socialization is effected, thus allowing women to believe that sexual violence is "just part of what happens." While cautioning women against such stereotypical beliefs, these experts also attempted to broaden the educational efforts to include men. For instance, Myriam Miedzian, who was identified on the show as the author of *Boys Will Be Boys*, elucidated the cultural scripts of masculinity and femininity that enable a rape culture. Echoing these sentiments on another show, Robin Warshaw, author of a *Ms.* survey on date rape, pointed out, "We imprint our children with these kinds of messages, that women somehow cause rapes to happen, that women are responsible for men's sexuality, that women make men do these things." Diverting the discussion from individual experiences, these didactic efforts offer suggestions for further action, a step toward political mobilization that is integral to feminism.

Despite these gestures toward systemic causes, the shows overwhelmingly identify communication as the cause of and solution to the problem of sexual assaults. Winfrey and her guests assert that poor communication skills, if not the complete breakdown of communications, between women and men are the central cause of rape. For instance, the convicted rapist who appeared on the "Date Rape" episode argued that the primary problem was a communication breakdown. "We're not clear with each other," he said. Similarly, all of the rape victims on the show admitted that they had sent out "mixed signals" and believed that this was the primary cause for their assaults. Winfrey too asserted that rape is an "evil" that could be confronted by telling "the truth about your experiences and to keep talking and keep talking." Through such exhortations, a commercial enterprise is transformed into a moral enterprise that could restore good in society.

Winfrey affirms the Foucauldian theory of the confession as a means to overcome repression. In a manner akin to the Victorian Era described by Foucault, in which talk about sexuality did not disappear but reappeared in particular locations, and through the use of specific rhetorical strategies, the *Oprah* show becomes a site where women (and men) talk obsessively about a taboo subject. It does not offer solutions but, like the confessional, the act of speaking is seen as important. Winfrey emphasizes as well that many of the rape survivors who appeared on her shows were once unable to identify or name their assaults as rape, thus *Oprah* appears to suggest that these women are testimony to the power of communication. Where once they were unable to define their assaults as rape, now, through the act of voicing their experiences, these women are intrinsically modified. They are able to give a name to their trauma. By overcoming their guilt and shame, they are able to discuss it in a "public" arena.

The problem and solution that this argument forwards correspond to the general tendency of talk shows to locate all solutions within the individual's grasp—that together communication and individual resolve can solve most social problems. These shows suggest that even in the absence of a final solution, the very act of communication offers a partial solution. The episodes reduce the complex operations of social and political questions to self-aware-ness and self-expression; they imply that the act of communication alone could result in the formation of a new identity. This emphasis on communi-cation to the exclusion of all other action mitigates against the emancipatory potential of these programs.

AN IMAGINED COMMUNITY

Episodes of *Oprah* teetered uncomfortably between identifying sexual vio-lence as an individual problem and valorizing the oppression of women as a group. Winfrey is particularly skillful in identifying her program and the voices within it as being representative of a community larger than the stu-dio audience. *Oprah* effects this imagined community explicitly and implic-itly. The camera work in the studio facilitates this sense that the people pre-sent are united by a shared definition of rape. Throughout the show, the camera shifts between Winfrey, the audience, and the panelists in a triangu-lated movement that captures the audience's responses of shock and sympa-thy to guests' testimonies. This symphony of shared reactions allows *Oprah* to engender a sense of a supportive, cohesive group, coalescing in this instance around the affective sense of gendered oppression.

More explicitly, both the experts and the host repeatedly point out that they are addressing a group of women that extends beyond the bounds of the studio. "Women who are watching us" and listening to these accounts may "realize for the first time" that they too had experienced rape. In these remarks, rape and the threat of rape become the catalyst for the formation of a community, a shared collective identity formation. Winfrey strength-ened this sense of a collective identity through her particular statements such as, "When I did some work for the rape center in Los Angeles," indi-cating that she had encountered similar issues. By moving the discussion geographically beyond the contours of the studio, these statements facilitate a sense that rape and the threat of sexual violence are problems that women across the country share. Elspeth Probyn points out that these representa-tions of rape articulate women and their position within the home in a com-plicated manner. By repeatedly presenting the threats that women encounter, the shows create the image of the home as a safe haven from a fearful world. But at the same time, the nature of the discussion presents the fear being aimed directly in the home.[61]

Like a lot of liberal feminism, *Oprah* discussions have identified inequitable laws as the cause of women's shared oppression. In the "Date

Rape" episode, one of the panelists asserted, "We're in a male-dominated society. State legislatures that pass laws are 95 percent male." Winfrey supplemented this position, pointing out that the crime would not exist "if men were
raped." These steps identify the problem of sexual violence and present it as a
threat that necessitates the formation of a collective identity. The various
aspects of *Oprah* facilitate the formation of a proto-feminist sphere, one where
these talking subjects could be transformed into agents in their social lives.

As Sonia Livingstone and Peter Lunt have pointed out, daytime talk
shows usually offer no conclusions; instead, various different emotions and
feelings are expressed during the allotted time. If any solutions are provided,
they are framed within individual terms, erasing the sociohistorical and systemic conditions that enable a rape culture.[62] This depoliticized aspect ultimately negates the possibility of viewing rape victims' confessions on *Oprah*
as liberating. The confessions permit only a very limited and narrow definition of female self-identity and tend to contain women's voices within the
genre of the complaint.

REVISITING "CELEBRITY" RAPES

Donahue has long been identified as an ally of the concerns raised by the
women's movement, and his talk show has dealt with topics that were considered taboo, primarily because they dealt with sexuality. In an interview, he points
out that his show explored the topic of date rape in 1977, whereas network news
addressed it only in the early 1990s.[63] Scholars have remarked that Donahue
often is the "lone feminist" on his show. He often chastises his audience for not
being feminist and reminds women of the benefits they have accrued through
the actions of the 1970s movement.[64] Nevertheless, the discussions on *Donahue*
do not provide ordinary women the speaking voice they gain on *Oprah*. There
are several reasons for this, and enumerating them helps illustrate that generic
conventions of the talk show alone do not guarantee an emancipatory potential,
the capacity to facilitate the formation of a counter-public sphere. Paolo Carpignano and others have used the example of the *Morton Downey Jr. Show* to argue
that the talk show is the exemplary public sphere because of its ability to incorporate working-class voices. I agree with Lisa McLaughlin's analysis that such a
reading is possible only if we ignore the gendered nature of the debate that
Carpignano and others privilege. Examining the discussion of prostitution on
talk shows, McLaughlin offers an excellent analysis of the problematic ways in
which talk shows incorporate the voices of marginalized groups. These voices are
included only as long as they adhere to the dominant ideology.[65]

The most obvious difference between *Oprah* and *Donahue* is the topics that are examined. During the period of analysis, discussions of rape were conducted in the context of "celebrity" cases—two shows focused on the Central Park jogger's case and one featured the William Kennedy Smith case. In all three instances, the discussion was centered on the specific nature of the rape charges rather than on individual experiences or the articulation of emotions. Even when *Donahue* addressed noncelebrity rape, the focus remained on specific trials and the ways in which the lawyers handled the cases. In this respect and in others that I enumerate below, *Donahue* replicated many of the trends observed in network news coverage of the cases.

The event-centered focus of the show was strengthened by the nature of the discussion that the host encouraged. Cultural critics often have characterized Donahue as the "sage" of talk shows, a "beacon of intelligence in the often tawdry world of afternoon soap operas and game shows."[66] His show has discussed the savings-and-loan crisis, the Watergate investigation, and the Love Canal environmental crisis, and it has regularly invited senators as guests. Pulitzer Prize-winning author David Halberstam describes *Donahue* as a televised "Ph.D. course."[67] These critics praise the show for facilitating a discussion associated conventionally with the public sphere.

In each of the instances dealing with rape, *Donahue* discussions explored the gaps between cultural and institutional definitions of rape, pointed out how the criminal and legal institutions treat the accuser and the accused, and addressed the specific lapses that victimize the innocent. These debates were facilitated by the panelists and experts who were, for the most part, journalists covering the celebrity cases, lawyers for the accused, and other experts such as social anthropologists who could help explain the sociological phenomena that make rape possible. While *Donahue* worked hard to maintain a parity between the men and women who served as guests, nonexperts were included in the panel only in one of the shows dealing with the Central Park case. The "ordinary" voices were two mothers of the teenagers accused in that case.

As is evident from this enumeration of guests, the striking difference between *Oprah* and *Donahue* is the absence of the storied voices of rape survivors.[68] The focus on experts as guests facilitates a discussion that resembles the forms of argumentation traditionally associated with the public arena. Moreover, the ways in which events are defined reflect institutional and legitimated knowledge. For instance, in the "Central Park 'Wilding' Incident," even the title, with its use of the term *wilding*, a word coined by the media, reveals how the discussion was shaped by institutional understandings of the event. The guests and the shows tried to answer the host's questions: "Who are these young men? Why are they behaving in this way?" The ensuing discussion focused on social pathology and reiterated themes underscored by the news. None of the shows included rape counselors or feminist scholars who could have provided understandings of rape that were at variance with the hegemonic definitions aired in other genres. The intertextuality between *Donahue* and network news was not limited to the topic of "celebrity" rapes but extended to the manner in which the host framed the issue of rape.

GOING BEYOND THE NEWS

The rhetorical model of objectivity characteristic of journalism was acutely visible on *Donahue*: guests were balanced evenly between oppositional understandings of rape. If there were lawyers representing the accused, their voices were counterpoised by journalists who opposed this account of events. Together, the choice of guests and the need to represent "both" sides of the issue ensured that *Donahue* provided little new information or exposed hidden insights about rape. The discussions circulated discourses that were already in currency. This tendency to adhere to traditional forms of argumentation was so pervasive that even one of the "ordinary" guests, the mother of one of the accused in the Central Park case, in "Crime and Punishment," used empirical and scientific evidence to argue her son's innocence. She pointed out the absence of any forensic evidence linking the teenagers to the crime. "Not one drop of blood connected him, not one hair, not one trace of saliva, nothing." Her son was a scapegoat, she contended. This tone would be unthinkable on *Oprah*, which focuses on the emotions engendered by the events discussed.

The hosts' styles are radically different in the two shows. Winfrey hugs her guests and audience members, cries when she is moved, and discloses details of her private life. She often elicits emotional responses by this display of her feelings. Donahue maintains the traditional opposition between public and private. He refuses to discuss his "personal" life and looks embarrassed whenever discussions bring it up. Jeffery Decker believes that on *Donahue* audiences identify and empathize with guests, while on *Oprah* they identify with the host. Jeanne Heaton and Nona Wilson concur that Donahue seems "driven to uncover and explore" while Winfrey "to share and understand."[69]

The particular host's style shapes as well the nature of audience participation. Reading transcripts of *Donahue*, audience participation seems more extensive than on *Oprah*. Here the host incorporates audience responses and telephone calls from the beginning. When viewed, these shows reveal that

Donahue tightly controls and regulates the tenor of audience participation through his posture and facial expressions. As he rushes around the floor soliciting audience remarks, he often chastises audience members for their opinions or turns his back on the speaker, effectively foreclosing discussion of the remark. The tenor of the discussion on *Donahue* is consequently more linear than on *Oprah*.

On all three shows concerning rape, most of the discussions were directed at the legal processes and the ways in which lawyers maneuvered information to secure a favorable verdict. When the discussions moved away from legal processes to sexual violence, the focus was on the alleged rapists. Like the *Oprah* episodes, the shows offered factual information on the prevalence of the crime and the rates of conviction. They did not offer victims' accounts of their experiences or feelings, nor did they attempt to clarify the definition of the phenomenon. In each show, at least one audience member would provide a feminist understanding of sexual violence, such as, it is "not a crime of sex, it's a crime of violence." These voices were drowned out by other participants, and the shows did not serve as a springboard for generalized discussions of gendered inequities. Contrary to the general perception that talk shows are an arena where private issues are discussed with abandon, the *Donahue* episodes analyzed here dealt only with the public ramifications of rape charges. Sexual violence remained a private issue, located on the periphery of public debate.

The closest that *Donahue* came to a discussion of rape per se was in the show on the William Kennedy Smith case. Every commercial break was punctuated with taped testimony from the trial, edited to juxtapose the accuser's and the accused's version of events. These clips provided two dramatically opposed versions of the same event, and recast the rape trial as a "he said, she said" case. They did not provide a better understanding of the situation; instead, they reiterated the stereotype that acquaintance rape/date rape was the result of a communication breakdown across gendered lines.

The only extended discussion of rape, and one that countered such a simplistic account, occurred among two of the female guests, a juror from the trial, Lea Haller, and Amy Pagnozzi, a *New York Post* columnist. Justifying Smith's acquittal, Haller asserted that she was a supporter of women's rights but remained unconvinced about the rape charge because the victim's clothes were not damaged. Her statement provided the opening for Pagnozzi to cite feminist criticisms of the legal definitions of resistance.

The exchanges between these two guests offered the longest discussion of sexual violence, illustrating well how some aspects of feminist reconfigurations have seemingly become commonsense ones. Haller, who identified herself as a "folk" feminist and not a male basher, proclaimed, "There's nothing to be ashamed [of] about being raped." She qualified this assertion by assigning some responsibility to the woman. "First of all, if you get the rules straight up front, possibly there's the possibility that some of it might be avoided." Pagnozzi, whom Haller called an "elite" feminist, countered that whether the accuser "drinks in bars, whether she goes out with bartenders has nothing to do with whether she was raped or not." Donahue however, did not sustain this debate. He repeatedly steered the conversation toward the legal process and provided audiences with a behind-the-scenes understanding of the trial. Like network news coverage, Donahue and his audience discussed this case as though they were on a truth-finding mission that could be gleaned only by observing both sides of the case.

While *Donahue's* discussion of rape was cursory, the shows enabled a more substantive exploration of the issue of racism. This may have been occasioned by the topics discussed rather than by any inherent quality of talk shows. When *Donahue* examined the Central Park case in two separate shows, the conversations revealed the ways in which institutionalized practices of racism affect individual African Americans. It is important to note that when addressing the issue of race, rape tended to slide out of view. The host had to be reminded by some audience members that despite the racism that structured institutional responses, the underlying event in the case was rape. In this show, as was the case with network news coverage, the host and guests effected a strategic separation between gender and race; if *Donahue* facilitated the formation of a collective identity, it was forged around race rather than gender. "If we're any good at all as a country we ought to be able to come down on the side of the people who are besieged as most certainly these young men were," the host stated, setting the foundation for the formation of a collective identity, one that asserted color blindness.

THE INJUSTICE OF RACISM

In the "Central Park 'Wilding' Incident" episode, race was a key subtext of the discussion but Donahue did not vocally draw attention to it. The show is illustrative of the ways in which whiteness saturates the field of vision and appears as a transparent category. Introducing the show, Donahue interspersed his remarks with the problematic video footage of the arrested teenagers that marked network news coverage of the case. Supplementing this network condensation symbol with slides of the individual teenagers, the show identified visually the race of the teenagers and drew attention to the interracial nature of the crime. Donahue employed other tropes to indicate racial difference. At one point, he explains, "The young men were accused of rapping in jail." Rap music becomes shorthand for the teenagers' nonwhite identity, their inner-city origins, and, above all, it marks their distance from the audience. Paul Gilroy points out that in contemporary society, people allude to racial politics with code words, inner-city, immigration laws, and so on, which are significant because they enable us to speak about race without mentioning the word.[70] Similarly, in this *Donahue* show, racial meanings are inferred by the use of words such as "wilding" and rap music. Like network news narratives, Donahue's introduction of the teenagers implies that sexual violence is a product of inner-city socialization patterns.

By repeatedly drawing attention to the violent nature of the attack, Donahue and his guests marginalized the lawyers' charges that public responses to the case reflected the anxieties and fears of whites. Ironically, in a show advertised as highlighting racist institutional practices, guests and audience members furiously sought the most rigorous punishment for the teenagers, even in the absence of any concrete evidence. The teenagers "should be executed now," one audience member demanded, while another characterized them as "savages, not humans." Their voices echoed statements made by millionaire Donald Trump and Mayor Ed Koch, which Donahue included in his introduction. Together these voices parsed the story of vigilante justice into the present tense. While some audience members opposed such language, Donahue papered over their concerns by returning to the topic of violence. On the rare instance when the discussion centered on rape, race was evacuated from the field of discussion. "I love black people, I'm not a racist," one audience member proclaimed as she called attention to rape rather than to those who had "created the crime." This and other voices reflected white privilege, "the luxury of being able to ignore race when it's convenient to do so."[71]

Nevertheless, the show created the space for a debate about the ways in which anxieties about black male bestiality shape cultural understandings about rape and rapists. The lawyers pointed out the different ways in which institutional practices, including media coverage, were weighted against their clients. Telephone callers and several African-American audience members pointed out that the media tended to ignore black rape victims, and that the Central Park case gained salience because it exemplified many deep-rooted, long-standing fears about African Americans. Donahue included a clip from a local news show that pointed out this disparity in media coverage. "And the feeling around here [Harlem] is that while the attack in Central Park was not racially motivated, it was the race of the victim that determined how much attention it received."[72] Through such inclusions,

Donahue provided information that was absent in the news. Specifically, the show offered insights into police treatment of the accused teenagers.

In this instance, racialized difference was a dominant subtext of the discussion, but Donahue repeatedly tried to redirect it in a manner that emphasized the violence. The debate, however, evoked a sentimental reading of violence rather than one that pointed out the symptomatic elements of race- and gender-based violence. There was little in the hour-long show that pointed to the intersections of gender and race in U.S. society. In the second show, "Crime and Punishment," the focus was exclusively on race and the ways in which racist institutions oppress African Americans. This show provided an opening for a discussion about the ways racism operates on a systemic level and is not simply an individual trait. These discussions enabled the formation of a collective identity around race, but this possibility was undercut each time as Donahue steered the discussion toward individual responses to racism. "This case . . . has gone from hate against women to hate against blacks . . . enough hate has been going around and that's not going to solve it," a white woman in the audience pronounced. Similarly, a telephone caller blamed the teenagers' parents for the gang rape. The focus was redirected to individual behavior rather than to the social structures that promote gendered violence or racist responses.

As the discussions of institutionalized racism were countered by individual-based solutions, Donahue introduced a New Yorker who was "involved in a car-towing incident." The white woman's story elucidated another instance of the local police's racist actions. She pointed out that as her car was being towed, she solicited the help of several passers-by. Among the numerous people who stopped to help her, the police singled out an African-American pedestrian for disrupting the peace and arrested him. Rather than develop this angle, the host directed the conversation to the expenses the woman incurred. This strategy is emblematic of the way talk shows contain discussion of irresolute problems. The show reveals the limits of forging a collective identity around race in a medium geared to attract large audiences.

MIDDLE-CLASS NORMATIVITY

The discussion on the "Crime and Punishment" episode also opened the space for an exploration of the ways in which class intersects with race and gender to mobilize identities. As "ordinary" guests, the two mothers (of convicted teenagers) introduced an element of folk wisdom. An outstanding feature of this episode was the plurality of linguistic registers that coexisted: the suave language of the lawyers and journalists resided alongside the ungrammatical, colloquial English of the mothers and audience members. Donahue vacillated between these two modes of expression. When addressing the mothers, he resorted to informal language, telling them, "I hear you."

One of the mothers, Linda McCray, spoke in a vernacular English that was in stark contrast to the other guests. Her speaking voice was testimony to the class differences that remain unarticulated in these programs; her language demarcated her from the mostly white middle-class audience. Defending her son, Ms. McCray explained that the police had "put" words into his mouth. "He wasn't satisfied to the cops. . . . They called hurts. They made you feel like you was a nothing."[73] Highlighting the linguistic differences, Donahue provided a translation. "The ominous or the frightening environment of the police lock-up . . . that over time your son was encouraged to tell what they wanted to hear." In the translation, Donahue toned down Ms. McCray's message—words such as coerced and intimidated were replaced by encouraged. While Donahue and his show failed to articulate the racial and economic differences that shape everyday lives, by translating the mother's language, the host testified to these differences.

COUNTER-PUBLIC SPHERES?

For all of their shortcomings, the *Oprah* and *Donahue* shows enable a discursive space that is substantively different from other genres. Their discussions open up the personal-political link and show the specific ways in which the private is politicized. The active participation of panelists, experts, and audience members allows for the testing of ideas about the phenomenon of rape and makes available alternate modes of understanding sexual violence and victimization. In Foucauldian terms, daytime talk shows enable a loquacious narration of sex and sexuality and blur the boundaries between expert and layperson; above all, they seem participatory, privileging the storied voice of the individual over traditional forms of building knowledge and gathering information. Daytime talk shows enable a debate about the definitions of sexual assault, its effects, and its causes.

Within Habermas's definition of the public sphere, the fragmented, emotional, and repetitive discussions of rape on talk shows would not be considered as constituting rational-critical debate. Feminist theories provide a different understanding for these public articulations of rape. Many feminist scholars, in particular, black feminist theorizers, have pointed out that oral histories and emotional narratives constitute an engendered form of knowledge building; they are alternative sites of self-definition for marginalized communities. Further, they argue that dialogues are central to the construction of an empowered community.

Talk shows contain a number of impulses toward the formation of a counter-public sphere. *Oprah* is a site where women (and men) talk obsessively about a taboo subject and through specific rhetorical strategies. The show does not offer solutions but, like the confessional, the act of speaking is seen as important. Through this speech act, these women appear to be intrinsically modified; they are able to identify a shared oppression. The discussions on *Oprah* critique cultural practices from the standpoint of women as an oppressed group in society. They generate a female-specific identity grounded in a consciousness of the fear of rape and seek to convince society of the validity of women's claims and assertions. The show facilitates the formation of a counter-public sphere that affirms and critiques the construction of female identity as "always-already" victims. The discussions empower an alienated class of women to speak. Sometimes *Donahue* facilitates a similar shared identity around racial oppression. These shows assert that knowledge of rape cannot be produced without taking account of women's disparate experiences. But, they do not undertake the next step that feminists have insisted upon— that knowledge of rape should not be confined to these subjective experiences, it is simultaneously always also embodied and conceptualized in discourses, through institutions and other social practices. Both shows though fail to specify the institutionalized practices and paths of praxis that connect the "private" and "social" bodies.[74] Nevertheless, they permit a tenuous link between community and politics, social change and television.

Oprah and *Donahue* enable discussions that are ambivalent about feminism; they espouse some aspects of it and ignore others. This permits the shows to discuss rape in a problematic manner: they frame rape in individualist terms; the discussions reveal the presence of structural barriers, yet the shows exhort individuals to transcend obstacles.[75] Self-actualization takes precedence over any sense of structural change.

The talk show focus on individual solutions has co-opted the real changes that feminists have sought. As a genre, daytime talk shows reject radical structural changes and work only within existing structures. According to Jane Shattuc, talk shows enact a "disingenuous game of appealing to the rebellious spirit of disenfranchised citizens through appeals to empowerment" but close down this avenue by "ending their programs within the conservative confines of middle-class reformism."[76] In the shows analyzed here, although feminist definitions of rape were aired, the hosts tended to go out of their way to "balance" the conversation. This resulted in a majority or consensus discussion that ensured that the terms of the debate never strayed toward the "extremes." Impulses toward the formation of a counter-public sphere are sharply regulated by the commercial logic within which these shows operate.

Both *Donahue* and *Oprah* emphasize subjective change; social structures and institutionalized practices are subordinated to individual choices and perception. As a result, conversations tend to spiral into endless talk about individual experiences and individual cures. They are denuded of political force. Indeed, these shows generate a collective identity grounded in a consciousness of a shared problem, whether violence against women or racism, and produce solidarity among participants. However, neither *Oprah* nor *Donahue* makes possible a response to this realization of a shared problem; they do not rouse people into action.

Serving merely as arenas for opinion formation, the episodes do not enable decision making but simply privilege commonsense understandings of rape. However, while these can be read as empowering moments, if we take into account Gramsci's definition of common sense as the "sub-stratum of ideology," it is difficult to find liberatory impulses within hegemonic, that is, patriarchal, discourses of gender and race. This was evident in the definitions of rape that the various audience members articulated—viewers were provided only with mainstream definitions premised on a binarized male/female definition of gender identity. It was left to the experts and to some women in the audience to vocalize an alternative definition of female sexuality and rape, one that went against the grain of patriarchal definitions. The commonsense wisdom postulated by the majority was not empowering (to women), nor could it be conceived as constituting a liberatory sphere of debate and discussion.

Daytime talk shows have broadened the nature of debate enabled by other television programs, providing a plurality of positions from which one can approach the issues of rape, gender, and sexuality. They have enabled a discursive space in which nonhegemonic definitions can be articulated and have also pointed out a way in which the concept of the public sphere could accommodate bodily and affective aspects of human existence within the realm of debate and discussion. *Oprah* has revealed the possibility of introducing the feminine style of one-on-one intimate conversations within the larger project of social change. It is not so much that it has allowed women to participate in the public arena as much as it had insinuated a rhetoric associated with the private into the public arena of community formation. In the counter-public sphere enabled by daytime talk shows, particularly *Oprah*, women have the authority to define their experiences of pain and violation.

Through the articulations of women's sense of self as a collective identity, this genre arouses deep passion about injustice, thus providing affective empowerment but it does not promote actual political resistance. Both *Oprah* and *Donahue* have privileged a private voice. As the above discussion enumerates, these "populist" shows have approached the topic of rape from various perspectives, enabling a broader discussion of the problem, if not the solution. The conversations on these shows have highlighted the impossibility of abstracting the democratic public sphere from issues pertaining to identity, illustrating the complex ways in which issues of culture and social identity shape deliberative practices.

6

Fragmented Counternarratives

Women are depicted in a quite different way from men—not because the feminine is different from the masculine—but because the "ideal" spectator is always assumed to be male.

—John Berger[1]

In the previous chapters I outlined the ways in which different genres of television programming open up or foreclose discussions of rape, gender, and race. The Berger quotation cited above may seem dated, but it continues to be relevant when examining representational practices produced in a system framed by capitalist logic. The previous chapters elucidate that television programs may no longer present/produce women *only* as objects to be seen. Nevertheless, male ways of seeing dominate and inform debates of rape. In most television genres, with the exception of *Oprah* and some prime-time fictional narratives, the male viewpoint of sexual violence predominates, leading to a focus on the rapist and/or the credibility of the accuser. Women's experiences of sexual violence are rare, but not completely absent. Television genres are far more problematic when confronted with the intersection of gender and race; often they isolate one of the categories, focusing exclusively on either gender or race. In this chapter I examine the counter-public spheres enabled by alternative forms of programming whose oppositional representational practices sometimes necessitate different ways of seeing. Under the rubric of alternative forms, I have included a broad range of televisual products. Some belong to well-defined genres, such as the made-for-TV-movie and newsmagazines, and others fall outside of the realm of commercial programming, such as video art. Through a juxtaposition of these disparate forms, I illustrate the potential for debate and discussion that is available in the television apparatus.

This book has thus far pointed out the variability within individual genres, illustrating the uneven development of rape representations on television. This chapter, with its inclusion of a broad range of television discourses, accentuates the diversity of rape imagery that exists. Turning to alternative forms underscores the need to develop a more nuanced and variegated understanding of television representational practices. The chapter illuminates the manner in which artifacts influenced by feminist and critical race theories broaden debates about sexual violence.

Since the 1970s, feminist filmmakers, film theorists, and art historians have developed and expanded Berger's concept of the male gaze in a sophisticated and complex manner. Focusing initially on Hollywood films and canonical art, feminists developed the modalities through which the male gaze is effected. Scholars such as Laura Mulvey have theorized how Hollywood films constitute female subjectivity.[2] These efforts point out the now-familiar themes of representational practices that assume the "ideal" viewer is male and hence produce women primarily as (sexual) objects of male desire and as lacking agency. Within the traditional representational grammar, women rarely emerge outside the shadow of male ways of seeing. The theories not only identified the problem, they also provided feminist filmmakers with clues for envisaging new ways of imaging women. This challenge was most specifically undertaken in the arena of rape representations, since sexual violence had been one of the primary issues that mobilized the 1970s' women's movement.

Feminist filmmakers' efforts since the 1970s attest to the possibility of new ways of seeing, ways of imaging rape that do not assume a normative male viewer. Experimental works such as Mitchell Block's controversial film *No Lies* and JoAnn Elam's *Rape* altered significantly the practices of imaging rape. For instance, Elam's *Rape* deploys different camera techniques to shatter the voyeuristic tendencies that are the hallmark of traditional film images of sexual violence. It also uses a participatory narrative structure to make the viewer confront the numerous myths surrounding rape. These experimental films enable viewers to rethink and reorganize the terrain from which representational practices emerge. They do not offer an essentialized women's way of seeing as an alternative. They destabilize, instead, the axis of rape narratives and present a defamiliarized rape representation that requires the viewer to rethink women outside of their object-victim status. They raise questions rather than offer prescriptive responses to rape images. And above all, they are significant because they allow women to represent themselves rather than be represented. Later in this chapter I discuss in greater detail how these altered perspectives are constituted.

This form of "writing" against the grain has been a persistent narrative tradition in slave cultures and among other subaltern groups. Counternarratives attempt to demythologize stereotypes that essentialize racial difference and humanize the marginalized. Television has not been immune from these attempts to rewrite traditional practices. Lorraine Gamman and Margaret Marshment assert that at least since the 1980s, aspects of female autonomy and control have found expression in television genres, and they often involve more than a simple reversal of gender roles.[3]

Highlighting the problems involved in such resistive inscriptions, poet-scholar Audre Lorde asserts that the master's tools can never dismantle the master's house. She is making specific reference here to liberal feminist efforts which, like patriarchy, unfortunately replicate an ideology where gender and race are produced as separate and different forms of oppression. At best, these efforts offer gender and race as additive forms of domination, not as constituted by interdependent systems of domination. Lorde's evocative phrase poses questions underpinning this book: Is there any space outside of patriarchy from which television can address rape as it affects women (white and nonwhite women)? Is there any space uncontaminated by hegemonic ideologies (patriarchy and capitalism) from which television can enable a counterpublic sphere? Heeding the warnings posed by these questions, I turn to television's interstitial spaces from which counter-hegemonic narratives could potentially be articulated. My concern here is with examining imaging techniques and narrative strategies of rape that move beyond a representation of the unified subject of modernism to a fragmented subject, shaped by multiple and often contestatory identities.[4]

In this chapter I examine programming that intervenes in television's public culture by exposing the cracks and fissures in hegemonic rape representational practices. Through an examination of a documentary, made-for-TV movies, network educational efforts, and video art, I argue that alternative sites of television production effect displacements that enable a new series of questions and understandings about rape and its television representation. They are unable to subvert culturally sanctioned rape metanarratives. Nevertheless, they (some more effectively than others) are able to critique television's ways of imaging rape, gender, and race. They foreground also the ways race mediates gender identity formation in television narratives. Yet, none of the sites I examine here is able to capture effectively the ways in which race and gender intersect to mobilize the subject of rape differently for men and women, whites and nonwhites. Most of these alternative sites self-consciously enact a strategic essentialism—choosing to focus on either gender or race—in their critique of television rape. For the most part, in its critique of mainstream representational practices, alternative programming necessarily replicates the focus on the rapist-attacker and the valences of racialized masculinity. The woman-victim is bracketed off from these attempts to unmask patriarchal practices. Hazel Carby has criticized the majority of feminist theory for ignoring "the hierarchical structuring of relations between black and white women" and often presenting the concerns of middle-class, articulate white women as the norm.[5] In their portrayal of women, the alternative forms I examine in this chapter implicitly tend to ignore race as a factor that structures women's lives differently.

In what follows, I examine the made-for-TV movie which, though now routinized into a formulaic genre of programming, offers the greatest possibility for dissenting from network ideology.[6] Through an analysis of Barbara Kopple's *Fallen Champ: The Untold Story of Mike Tyson*, I explore the ways in which this made-for-TV movie provides a space for the articulation of subjugated knowledges produced by African-American women and other marginalized groups. Most networks offer, through their newsmagazine shows, in-depth coverage of topical issues. In this chapter, I examine the discursive space made possible by rape programs geared to educate viewers. Finally, in sharp contrast to these representational practices that are still governed by television's institutional apparatus, I venture into the art studio, where artists have used news portrayals to offer pungent analyses of mainstream images of rape, gender, and race. In each instance, I examine the possibilities for the formation of counter-public spheres, those that foreground the possibility of an imagined community of (racialized) women.

Examining the theoretical framework and the material conditions that could enable the formation of a feminist counter-public sphere, Rita Felski provides a useful definition for this discursive space that affirms women's collective gendered identity. It is grounded in gender politics, and the shared experience of an oppressive situation (in this case, rape) unites people beyond their specific differences. A feminist counter-public sphere "serves a dual function: internally it generates a gender-specific identity grounded in a consciousness of community and solidarity among women; externally it seeks to convince society as a whole of the validity of feminist claims, challenging existing structures of authority through political activity and theoretical critiques."[7] Most significantly for this analysis, which explores the possibility of a counter-public sphere that valorizes the intersections of gender and race,

Felski adds, "It is perhaps more appropriate to speak of coalitions of overlapping subcommunities, which share a common interest in combating gender oppression but which are differentiated not only by class and race positions but often by institutional locations and professional allegiances, and which draw upon a varied range of discursive frameworks."[8]

MELODRAMATIC OVERDETERMINATIONS

In theory, the made-for-TV movie comes closest to affirming Felski's definition of a counter-public sphere. Originating in the 1960s, the genre was supposed to be an antidote to routine television scheduling, a must-see event. The few scholars who have examined made-for-TV movies have isolated the following features as being characteristic of the genre.[9]

The made-for-TV movie is cheap to produce (between $3 and $4 million per movie) and garners high ratings, especially among women. Together these institutional factors explain partially their presence as staples on the weekly schedule. In addition, the made-for-TV movie is designed to deal with contemporary socially vexing issues; the narratives often are derived from "real" events. They provide "cultural capital" for the networks, which can draw audiences while appearing serious and informative.[10] Listing these structural features allows us to see clearly that they shape the kinds of narratives undertaken by the genre.

These movies are produced by organizations not affiliated with the networks. They draw large audiences by presenting social issues in an audacious manner. Since they are intended for a single screening, made-for-TV movie producers can be more adventurous and take greater risks in developing story lines than in other prime-time genres. The devalued status of the genre also allows producers to undertake topics and issues foreclosed to other "respectable" genres.

As a rule, the made-for-TV movie develops topics that emanate from the public arena, but the narratives invariably present the issues as family problems. The genre reworks and produces conflicts in the family. It has become a site where anxieties pertaining to the stability of the family are worked out. Most often these instabilities are shown as emerging from contemporary sexual politics. Blending fact and fiction, the story lines in this hybrid genre tend to follow a formulaic trajectory: they begin with a problem that threatens or at least has an impact on the functioning of the nuclear family; at midpoint, the crisis escalates, but by the end of the movie, the family is rehabilitated. With their focus on the family, the made-for-TV narrative domesticates social issues, personalizes them, and allows the viewer to respond to them emotionally.[11] As Todd Gitlin points out, even movies such as *Bitter Harvest* (1981), which addresses the issue of chemical poisoning, are personalized to present the problem only as it relates to the family. The made-for-TV movie narrates small stories that can reveal the larger society.[12] It may explore grim, downbeat issues, but it offers neat and tidy endings.

Some of the characteristic features of this genre echo themes that I have elucidated in my discussion of daytime talk shows. In an effort to sustain a female audience, these movies explore issues raised by the women's movement, especially those pertaining to the perils that women encounter within the family. They have explored the issues of rape, domestic violence, incest, and a range of other feminine topics.[13] In each of these instances, the story lines focus on the victim's point of view and constitute a spectatorial subject different than those in Hollywood films, Elayne Rapping contends. Made-for-TV movies attempt a female gaze: the narratives chronicle a woman's experiences as she lives and understands them. They also portray women as strong, independent, and supportive of each other, Rapping argues.[14]

The genre may be effective in enabling discussions of issues pertaining to women and the domestic arena, but it has had less success in examining racial issues; its coverage of race can best be characterized as benign neglect. Despite the unprecedented success of *Roots*, producers and networks refuse to explore topics pertaining to race for fear of alienating white audiences. Gitlin contends that racial conflict is either marginalized or bleached. Issues emerging from racist behavior are displaced onto white characters, thereby transforming the nature of the issue at hand.[15]

Narratives that center on (white) women's experiences of oppression and women as victims of various kinds of violence have been a favorite topic for television movies.[16] Nevertheless, in the late 1980s and early 1990s, just as legitimated genres of television, such as the news, explored the issue of rape in a widespread fashion, themes of sexual violence burgeoned in the made-for-TV genre. The prevalence of this theme led critic Claudia Dreifus to dub 1992 the "Season of Rape." In these narratives, the female protagonist is invariably an independent woman who is assaulted. She turns to the authorities for assistance, but they fail at their task. The woman, through her own efforts but most often with the aid of a male mentor, eventually avenges her rape. In these narratives, women are rehabilitated to society through some act of revenge.[17]

When He's Not a Stranger (1989) would qualify as a typical television rape drama. It undertakes the troubled terrain of acquaintance rape on a college campus. Here a first-year pre-med student is raped by the college football captain. He takes her up to his coed dorm for a cup of coffee, and once she is in his room he refuses to take no for an answer. The woman finds that no one believes her account: her roommate, her family, college authorities, or the legal system. She feels ashamed for letting the rape occur and can no longer trust anybody. Finally, with the assistance of a male friend, she is able to find an assistant district attorney to take up her case and successfully prosecutes her assailant. According to John Leonard, *When He's Not a Stranger* plays it "safe." The woman is portrayed as "buttoned up instead of provocative." She goes to the football captain's room thinking that her best friend would be there and not "on a lark."[18] The film successfully draws attention to the issue of acquaintance rape, but it is nevertheless problematic. Susan Faludi believes that such a narrative performs a controlling function—it keeps women in line by frightening them. Gitlin, in a more cynical assessment contends that women in jeopardy films serve an economic function. "In one shot they [networks] can pull in women who are interested in the subject, other women who want to expose the problem, still other women who might want to feel some mastery of it vicariously, and some men who enjoy—consciously or unconsciously—programs about women getting raped."[19]

While most story lines explore women's victimization inside and outside of the home, a few have examined the ways in which women can be mobilized politically to act against oppression. For instance, *Silent Witness* (1985) explores the ways in which a woman could help a rape survivor successfully prosecute her assailants, while *A Matter of Sex* (1984) depicts female bank employees who collectively seek higher wages and better treatment. Whether they focus on victimization or agentic action, in these women-centered movies the female protagonist is conceptualized in relation to and as representative of a gendered collective identity. This is the first step toward the formation of a feminist public sphere, Felski contends.

Taking Back My Life: The Nancy Ziegenmeyer Story was the exception to the women in jeopardy trend (March 15, 1992, CBS). Although the story line is premised on a rape, it does not portray the woman only as a victim. The movie presents the aftermath of rape rather than simply focusing on sexual assault. Nancy Ziegenmeyer, a white resident of Iowa, was kidnapped and raped. Before her assailant was brought to trial, Ziegenmeyer decided to let the *Des Moines Register* interview her and use her name to describe the impact of rape on her life.[20] *Taking Back My Life* offers a postrape narrative and details the ways in which women cope with rape. According to Claudia Dreifus, the story line is "messy like life itself" and presents the protagonist in context, which is rarely accomplished in television dramas.[21] Further, sexual assault does not result in permanent victimization, nor does it preclude a woman's agency; in this movie, Ziegenmeyer is shown to have an active life before and after her rape. She becomes a subject through rape rather than merely remaining subjected to its violation. In the film she asserts, "I'm not a statistic. I'm a person with a name."

Ziegenmeyer's assailant was a black male, but the movie does not focus sensationally on the interracial character of the assault. In fact, the narrative points out that interracial rape cases are statistically the exception, not the norm. The film, however, does not explore how stereotypes of black criminality and bestial sexuality may have informed Ziegenmeyer's decision to reveal her identity. In Helen Benedict's memorable phrase, she is not a "good" victim. Ziegenmeyer had extramarital affairs and continued to live with the husband she had divorced. According to Leonard, the movie emphasizes that she is not "St. Theresa."[22] However, the resemblance to real rape and the interracial nature of the assault may have helped position her relationally as a reliable claimant of rape. Given the conventions of made-for-TV movies, *Taking Back My Life* presents a narrative of an individual's triumph over the system, marginalizing broader social issues.

Feminist practices of representation, Annette Kuhn believes, embody "the quest for a 'new voice,' a transformation of vision." They resist and transform existing imaging practices. Woman as spectacle and object of the male gaze is metamorphosed into "women as historical subjects."[23] *Taking Back My Life* sheds the formulaic narrative of the women in jeopardy genre and acknowledges the fact of rape in stark, brute terms as the very premise upon which this narrative is built. Ziegenmeyer's character encapsulates the revisionist view of rape offered by the film when she asserts, "Bobby Lee Smith made me a victim. My family and friends made me a survivor. The criminal justice system made me a witness. The media made me a news source. Now, I am an advocate." Through such assertions that emphasize multiple identities, *Taking Back My Life* valorizes a woman's experience of sexual assault and its aftermath. It also provides the space for the assertion of female autonomy and a limited (political) empowerment. These two steps, the affirmation of a gender-specific identity and the narrative's efforts to convince society of the validity of women-centered knowledge, allow the movie to facilitate Felski's definition of a counter-public sphere. Unlike news narratives, where the male perspective predominates, the movie offers avenues for a radically different debate and discussion of sexual assault. Like daytime talk shows, the movie facilitates the formation of an affective public sphere that can include emotions, the body, and subjective experiences of pain.

BIOGRAPHY OF A CULTURAL ICON

During this period, only one made-for-TV movie addressed the "celebrity" rapes that were discussed in network news or fictionalized in prime-time entertainment. Barbara Kopple's *Fallen Champ: The Untold Story of Mike Tyson* (1993) was commissioned by NBC following the boxer's rape conviction, but like *Taking Back My Life*, it does not deal with rape per se.[24] Combining elements of the documentary and the star biography genres, *Fallen Champ* displaces rape to discuss other discourses surrounding and inseparable from the boxer's rape conviction.[25] Tracing the life of a cultural-athletic icon, the movie is a restorative to the images of bestial masculinity produced by network coverage.[26] Although elegiac in tone and texture, the movie is not an apologia for Tyson's criminal behavior. It does not offer a cause-effect narrative to explain the boxer's violent behavior; it maps out instead the field of forces that shapes his actions.

Kopple, who received two Academy Awards for *Harlan County, U.S.A.* (1976) and *American Dream* (1991), does not speak to the boxer directly or narrate his account of the events. Instead, she constructs her film through a series of post-conviction interviews with sportswriters, feminist scholars, friends and business associates of the boxer, juxtaposed with pre-conviction footage from home films, news clips, and a German documentary.[27] Through these multiple voices, the film offers a collective storytelling about the rise and fall of a folk hero. While *Fallen Champ* was the first network documentary to air in a prime-time slot, NBC officials preferred to call it a "reality" film for fear of alienating viewers.[28]

I have illustrated in Chapter 3 of this book the specific ways in which network news coverage of the trial (and print media accounts) explicitly and implicitly linked the boxer's criminal behavior "to his color, to his gang past, to what black men to the ghetto born are destined to do by nature."[29] The news media constructed a discourse that rationalizes sexual violence, not as a product of patriarchal society but as an effect of inner-city black culture. Network news coverage of this case is epitomized in a triptych of images that shows the boxer fulfilling his racial destiny: Tyson being fingerprinted, Tyson being patted down, and Tyson being handcuffed.[30] Kopple's film provides a poignant and an evocative response to such characterizations of "always-already" black male criminality. Discarding this simplistic account, *Fallen Champ* oscillates between the present and the past to outline some of the complex forces that informed Tyson's behavior.

Enclosed within two clips from an interview with the incarcerated boxer, the narrative arc of the film does not lead up to the moment of the rape conviction but instead charts how different discourses cumulatively shaped Tyson and his actions. The opening clip from the prison cell shows Tyson avowing his innocence to a news worker and is followed by a clip from a newsmagazine interview, where Desirée Washington proclaims that the boxer hurt her and that he must seek professional help. The juxtaposition of these two clips produces a conversational effect, as though the two were addressing each other; it reproduces a hackneyed "he said, she said" account of rape. Having disclosed the denouement of her narrative in the pre-credits segment, Kopple sets aside the specific nature of the rape to shuttle between Tyson's boxing career and his youth, delineating the factors that enabled his rags-to-riches dream and facilitated his fall from grace.

Fallen Champ explains partially why Tyson's story transcended the sports segments of the news and became a fertile site for television programming.[31] As the film reveals, the boxer's body became a site where several cultural myths came to reside. To most Americans, particularly African Americans, the boxer's success attested to the veracity of the rags-to-riches dream. As Jeffrey Decker has noted in *Made in America,* the Horatio Alger myth continues to resonate deeply in U.S. society and remains the bulwark of the ideology of individualism.[32] Simultaneously, for white America in particular, the boxer, because of his violent behavior, became the site where a range of cultural anxieties about black male sexuality and criminality coalesced. According to Felicia Feaster, Kopple allows viewers to see how "what white Americans ordinarily feared in black men became awesome in Tyson" as a boxer, and yet myths of black male deviance return to centerstage in light of his activities outside of the ring.[33]

Fallen Champ does not contain a voice-over that outlines any of this information. Instead, this rich cultural commentary is produced by the clever juxtaposition of visual and verbal clips. For instance, the film begins with a clip of a young Tyson jogging in the fog-shrouded Adirondack mountains. Against this bucolic vision of middle America, which the African-American youth seems to inhabit comfortably, a trainer's voice narrates the specific crimes Tyson committed as a child growing up in Brooklyn. The visual and verbal texts encapsulate the contradictions that have come to reside in the Tyson iconography that the culture has produced. In an interview, Kopple confirms that her film depicts "a man with many layers, a story of rags to riches and back to rags."[34]

Using the accounts of a range of sportswriters, business associates and people associated with the boxer at various stages of his career, *Fallen Champ* charts Tyson's growing athletic proficiency. His ability to mold his body to perform incredible feats within the sports arena is contrasted against his inability to control his emotions. For instance, a clip shows Tyson sobbing and crying helplessly against his trainer's shoulder the night before an important fight. The following day, the trainer informs viewers, the boxer defeated his opponent easily and convincingly. Through a series of similar clips, the film captures the contradictions that constitute the boxer's persona.

The film does not follow a chronological order but moves across different moments in the boxer's life to construct a narrative that is both a celebration and a warning. It reveals that the rags-to-riches dream was accomplished by cultivating violence. While the film does not draw attention to racialized subject formations, it is strikingly clear that the initial part of Tyson's life, marking the trajectory from rags to riches, is dominated by white male mentors. As the various white sportswriters and trainers describe it, boxing trainer Cus D'Amato spotted Tyson's talent while he was in a juvenile detention center. Impressed by his raw pugilistic abilities, D'Amato offered to train him, providing Tyson with a way out of criminality. D'Amato later became the white substitute for the absent African-American father, and Tyson his pygmalion.[35] D'Amato's death resulted in an unfinished product, malleable to the designs of various greedy and covetous African Americans who entered Tyson's life.

Interviews celebrating Tyson's athletic potential also present him as the stereotypical black male, "always-already" bestial and criminal.[36] Recounting in detail the numerous crimes committed by the young Tyson, the sportswriters and business associates produce a narrative where the boxer becomes the logical and legitimate object of surveillance and policing, of containment and punishment. Even though Kopple does not explicitly comment on the ways in which sportswriters and the culture of boxing construct Tyson as a racial subject, her deft editing underscores this constituted identity.

Taken together, these voices restore faith in the rags-to-riches Horatio Alger myth, even as Tyson's biography undermines it. These voices assert that the ideology of individualism is not to blame; it is the boxer who is at fault. Tyson had already completed the trajectory into success when his inner-city socialization erupted to impede his continued access to the American ideal. It was race and environment that led Tyson to failure.

A CULTURE OF MISOGYNY

Initially, *Fallen Champ* focuses almost exclusively on the destruction of the rags-to-riches dream, but gradually it starts to point out as well the gendered nature of its subject. The narrative develops slowly the subtle and seemingly

inconsequential ways in which the boxing world that Tyson inhabits cultivates misogyny. His identity as a boxer, the clips show, is defined by outbursts
of violent energy (within the ring) and a cultivated distrust of women.
D'Amato's injunctions to control the libido and explode with destructive
force in the ring are juxtaposed with stories from different sources that
recount the ways in which violence and violation intersect on women's bodies. The different clips reveal that Tyson is surrounded by people who view
women only as sexual objects. The prosecutor in the Tyson case, Gregory
Garrison, recounts in his book an incident that cultivates this objectification
of women. D'Amato is supposed to have once presented the young boxer
with a baseball bat. This prompted Tyson to ask, "What's this for?" The
trainer is said to have responded, "For the women. When you're the champion, you're going to need something to beat them off you."[37]

The trainers and business associates surrounding Tyson perceived all
women to be a threat to the boxer, destructive forces determined to undermine his athletic prowess. These stories reveal the climate in which the boxer's
attitudes toward women were engendered. They explain, but do not excuse,
his criminal behavior. While Tyson's offenses as a juvenile delinquent have
been well documented, these clips reveal how sportswriters participated in a
collusion of silence that concealed the boxer's violation of women. In a particularly poignant clip, one of Tyson's childhood sweethearts, Nadia Hutjyn,
recounts an early instance of his refusal to accept female resistance. Hutjyn
herself seems unaware of how damaging her affectionate account is. She tells
the filmmaker that as a young boy Tyson was very shy and refused to ask girls
to dance with him for fear of rejection. He would wait until the music
started, grab a girl's arm, and rush her onto the floor before she could demur.
He was convinced that once on the dance floor girls would acquiesce rather
than draw undue attention. Kopple juxtaposes this clip with one of D'Amato advising Tyson that women are a distraction and that he should exercise
discipline to resist them.

Fallen Champ shows how masculinity is authorized in the world of boxing and evokes the atmosphere of a male sport's club, where women are seen
as one more round. Different aspects of boxing culture reflect this objectification of women.[38] Most of the people around Tyson, including sportswriters, characterized his marriage to actor Robin Givens a disaster. Notwithstanding her status as a Hollywood star, the commentators repeatedly
presented Givens as a gold digger and a vamp, intent on destroying the boxer.
They held her responsible for Tyson's loss of the heavyweight title. In contrast
to these images, Kopple includes a clip from *20/20*, where Givens testifies on
national television that Tyson physically abused her. In what can only be

described as a disconcerting and chilling segment, the camera shows Tyson sitting quietly beside Givens with a smile on his face as his wife excoriates him in public. He does not contest battering his wife.

The objectification of women and the gendered nature of his violent outbursts are underscored repeatedly by the boxer's chauffeur and bodyguard. They testify that women seek Tyson's company only for sex, ergo there could be no rape. Rudy Gonzalez, the boxer's chauffeur, explains, "The world has this impression of us as 'Here's a guy who goes around grabbing people' and stuff like that. And that is not true. First of all, for me to grab you, you have to be within my reach." Similarly, Tyson's bodyguard asserts, "Girls want their butts grabbed." These statements are meant to defend Tyson but end up indicting him.

The most unsettling clips of this film emerge from a Free Mike Tyson rally organized in Indianapolis, where the boxer was recoded as a persecuted martyr. As the keynote speaker, Nation of Islam leader Louis Farrakhan denounces all women, Washington in particular, to a rousing ovation. "You bring in a hawk into the chicken yard and wonder why the chicken got eaten up. You bring Mike to a beauty contest, and all these foxes just parading in front of Mike." He goes on to elaborate, "I mean, how many times, sisters, have you said no, and you mean yes all the time. She said, 'No, Mike, no.'" These scenes reveal the ways in which the African-American community valorized only Tyson's experiences and erased Washington's victimization.[39] They present Tyson as a poster child to indict a racist law and order system. But this imagery of black victimhood is derived at the expense of black women. As I have already mentioned, Kopple does not provide any commentary throughout the film, but here her silence is damning. These images of a hall filled with black men cheering Farrakhan as he berates black women produce a patronizing message that "they just don't get it."

In sharp contrast to these accounts, June Jordan in a compelling essay, "Requiem for the Champ," points out the structural conditions that produced Tyson's criminality. Even as she empathizes with Tyson's feeling of victimization by a racist system, she points out how discourses of gender reconfigure this racism differently for black men and black women. She argues that masculinity is socialized to express itself aggressively. Specifically she points out that as a black man, Tyson "was given a choice of violence or violence: the violence of defeat or the violence of victory."[40]

The seemingly simplistic image of a misguided, patriarchal African-American community raised by the Free Mike Tyson rally is countered by clips of an informal discussion, conducted by a group of black women, on the rape charges. Some of the women offer eloquent analyses of the ways in which the cultural landscape continues to valorize the cliché that "all the women are white and all the blacks are men." They highlight the silencing of black women's experiences of sexual assault. Outlining the polyvocality of African-American women's responses to the rape trial, these clips reveal why some of them conceptualize Washington as a race traitor. These women do not accede to the valorization of race over gender; they express "an identification of interest with a particular configuration of race and gender over a different one."[41] They identify with the figure that most closely symbolizes their sense of shared oppression. From these clips it is clear that although most African-American women recognize that gender and race intersect to mobilize different experiences for black men and black women, many approach gender politics hesitantly. It is important to recognize that to facilitate a public sphere of debate and discussion, television narratives should not prescribe the "correct" response to rape but should make available a multiplicity of avenues to explore the issue. Kopple provides African-American women's support for the boxer within a broader context of prevalent race relations and allows for an analysis of sexual violence that could potentially be framed by insights from feminist and critical race theories.

AN ABSENT PRESENCE

Through this range of voices, including those of some feminist scholars, *Fallen Champ* makes available on prime time an intervention that is grounded in the subjugated and marginalized knowledges produced by African-American women. Although the film offers insight into how African-American women understand intraracial rape, it remains silent on the specific nature of the charges filed against Tyson. The accounts of the Indianapolis rape are filtered through the numerous voices that characterize the film. Apart from avowing his innocence, the film does not offer Tyson's account of the event. The closest we come to this is through Farrakhan's denunciation of the rape charge. The victim's perspective is presented only in proxy through *Sports Illustrated* reporter Sonja Steptoe, who recounts in detail Washington's version of the events. Here the black body of Steptoe substitutes for Washington.

Fallen Champ's powerful analysis of the masculine world of professional sports and African-American patriarchy is articulated by evacuating the rape survivor from the field of vision. The film title attests that the narrative is about Tyson, and that the Indianapolis rape charge is only one of several instances relevant to his star biography. Nevertheless, the few references that the movie makes to Washington, through an emotional clip from her father and her white schoolmates, present her only as a victimized subject. Washington's life seemingly begins and ends with her victimization. Similarly, although the film points out the black male response to the rape charge, it fails to reveal the ways in which African-American women mobilized protests against Free Mike Tyson rallies. For instance, Aaronette White chronicles how black women in St. Louis, Missouri, initiated a two-step campaign, which included black men, to protest the misogynistic characterizations of black women that underpinned African-American support for Mike Tyson. Through an advertisement campaign, the collective challenged the notion that black women must identify as black or women, black first and women second, or women first and black second. They insisted on a recognition of the complex ways in which race intersects with gender—that African-American men and women experience racist systems differently.[42] By marginalizing these women's voices, the sexual nature of Tyson's criminality is displaced and presented as a generic crime. Simultaneously, it reinforces a male-centered definition of the African-American experience of rape. It does not break the silence that feminist scholars have pointed out surrounds the African-American female experience of sexual assault.

The documentary works against a racist explanation for Tyson's criminal behavior; instead it reveals how athletic socialization, combined with the misogyny expressed by those around him, facilitated the boxer's behavior. It points out as well that individual influences alone cannot account for Tyson's behavior. According to Kopple, America got what America demanded. Her film allows us to see "what we do as Americans, as people, to other human beings, and how they become meal tickets."[43] *Fallen Champ* offers some possibilities for an alternative television representational practice, one that avoids what Stuart Hall calls the fetishization, objectification, and negative figuration that are so much a feature of the representation of the black subject.[44] While it explores only one configuration of the race-gender intersection, the African-American male, the film creates an awareness that the African-American female experience would be more complex.

AN EVERYDAY ACT

Apart from the made-for-TV movies, yet another genre of programming, newsmagazines, addressed repeatedly the issue of rape, as the topic gained widespread media attention in the 1990s. Newsmagazines such as *20/20*, *Prime Time Live*, and *48 Hours* and other specially commissioned programs such as ABC's *Men, Sex and Rape* (1991) developed issues pertaining to various aspects of rape. All were cast as educational anti-rape efforts, devices meant to explain the phenomenon of sexual assault to their viewers and seek to help men in their audience understand how women experience violation. Although these programs seemed to gain salience from the prevalence of "celebrity" rapes, these educational efforts were divorced from news events and presented the phenomenon of sexual assault in a depoliticized manner. Their aim was to create an understanding, not to challenge the phenomenon.[45]

Unlike the other genres addressed so far in this book, these efforts by the newsmagazines to introduce rape into the public arena of discussion were structured by a different set of production practices: their presentation was shaped by a mandate to educate and instruct viewers, forwarding in effect an anti-rape politics. They were governed, however, by the economic imperatives and marketing practices that characterize the U.S. television apparatus, which limits what they say and how they say it. Although in what follows I enumerate the problematic aspects of such programming, I still welcome them for presenting the issue of sexual violence as an everyday phenomenon that most women cope with rather than as an extraordinary event that occasionally makes for sensational headlines.

The majority of newsmagazine coverage of rape was either part of a larger special issue on violence against women, such as in *20/20*, or stand-alone programs dealing with specific aspects of the phenomenon, such as ABC's *Men, Sex and Rape*. Like many feminist anti-rape films from the 1970s, these programs focused on awareness, prevention, or self-defense. They were directed primarily at female viewers, drawing their attention toward the potential for rape and to strategies that they could develop to avoid "dangerous situations." For instance, in a *20/20* special edition on violence against women, Barbara Walters addressed the issue of rape preventive measures in an interview with a Houston resident, who had experienced rape and subsequently established a victim support group. The woman delineated the self-defense and rape-avoidance strategies that her program advocated. Her voice was supplemented by those of rape counselors, who offered other individual efforts that could help prevent sexual assault and thereby empower women. This was important information that could potentially move women out of the object-victim status. Pauline Bart and Patricia O'Brien have provided empirical evidence to show that when women resist their attackers, the rape often is not completed.[46]

Walters' interview recreated the rape, both visually and verbally, a problematic aspect that I discuss below. Above all, these programs valorized self-defense strategies and individual-based solutions over social change.[47] The narratives may have enumerated legal and social injustices but did not elaborate on how these affected women's experiences of rape, for instance, why so many women fail to press charges or even to report the crime.

Newsmagazines are designed to offer critical accounts of events, and it is significant that none of them offers a critique of television's representational practices and how popular culture may contribute toward the devaluation of women. Most of the programs do not examine the rape culture within which they operate. An exception to this is *Men, Sex and Rape*, which presented women in revealing clothes to argue that the erotic nature of these images cannot condone sexual assault.[48] In their refusal to address media practices that enable a rape culture, these programs appear to address the issue from a space far removed from television images.[49]

Further, these newsmagazines present rape only as nighttime stranger assaults, where the woman is attacked in her home or kidnapped on a dark street. Apart from reifying several myths pertaining to "real" rape, these programs invariably present only white women as rape victims. A beneficial aspect of such a focus on white-on-white rape is that the programs effectively destabilize the cultural position accorded to white men as protectors of women. These narratives, however, echo the silencing of nonwhite women's rape that pervades the culture at large.[50]

THE RAPIST'S STORY

Another striking aspect of these educational specials is the attention they provide to rapists. For instance, both ABC's *Why Rapists Rape* (1992), about a rapist rehabilitation center in Vermont,[51] and *Men, Sex and Rape*, an hour-long program hosted by ABC news anchor Peter Jennings, focus on the victimizers. These programs are set in prisons and rehabilitation centers, focus on rapists' perspectives of events, and seem to offer therapy as an important solution to the epidemic of sexual assault.

These programs are disturbing for a variety of reasons. They explain that their focus on rapists is meant to instruct women on preventive measures. What advice can you give, the programs repeatedly ask, and the rapists offer the limited advice of asking women to be more cautious and to ensure that their windows and doors are locked. The programs invariably include extended interviews with rapists to help viewers understand the assailant's mind. Newsmagazine narratives, as a whole, enumerate relevant statistical information and include information on the low conviction rates of rapists.

It is paradoxical then that these two programs turn to these convicted rapists, who represent a small minority, to understand the phenomenon of sexual assault and its perpetrators.

Further, most of these programs, including the *20/20* episode I referred to earlier, reproduce rape; the rapists describe in vivid detail their assaults, and on screen the camera work replicates the attack with dark, grainy footage and voyeuristic shots of women from handheld cameras. Ominous music underscores these visuals; the background music orchestrates a particular rhythm of experience and helps reproduce the sense of fear, anticipating the violence that is enacted off camera. These reenactments are counterproductive, because they are presented from the rapist's point of view and position the viewer within the same angle of vision. While these descriptions may convince viewers of the horrors of sexual assault, they do not enumerate how the victims experience the assault. Instead, they highlight women's vulnerability and intensify the fear that spectators may feel. The rapist himself remains a dark, shadowy, and menacing figure.

In an even more troubling replication of rape, often the newsmagazines elaborate on behavioral modification therapy programs undertaken by the various centers. For instance, they show the rapists watching pornography or videos of violent rapes as part of aversion therapy. Various sensory devices indicate the rapists' responses to these images. If they find them erotic rather than horrifying, they receive a strong dose of ammonia or a shock. On screen, the viewer gets to see these images heightening and duplicating the representation of rape. Inadvertently, these practices reproduce women's fear as stimulating.

The majority of men interviewed in these programs are serial rapists, and the programs imply that rehabilitating even one will contribute significantly toward rape prevention. Most of them cry on camera and appear to have been "rebirthed" by the therapeutic process, but their responses inspire little hope that they will not rape again. Once again, these programs offer individual solutions and effectively abstract these individual rapists from larger social and cultural processes that enable rape. As the rapists address the doctors or the camera, it becomes clear that these men have appropriated the language of feminism and therapy, but they confess that even they are not confident that their attitudes toward women have changed.

The discussions enabled by these programs are very limited and replicate most of the problematic aspects of network news programming. The absence of race is very striking and could be interpreted positively as a rejection of the black rapist myth. The absence of nonwhite women as rape victims is troubling, since it reiterates white women's status as the only ones who can occupy the position of rape victim. The didactic function of newsmagazines allows them to broaden the scope of debate and discussion beyond those made available by network news. The educational programs offer salient information on rape prevention strategies, but through their exclusive focus on gender, they replicate trends that I have elucidated in the news.

ENGENDERING RAPE

At different moments during the period examined in this book, each of the networks aired at least one report in their news segments on rape. These reports addressed the issue of sexual violence in a broad manner and did not link it to the "celebrity" rapes that had preoccupied the news.

For instance, soon after the networks halted their coverage of the Central Park case, *ABC Nightly News* aired a show on acquaintance rape and its increasing prevalence on college campuses. Similarly, midway through the Smith case, *CBS Evening News* aired a report spurred by a Senate study that found that rape was a "particularly American problem."[52]

Apart from providing statistical information, these reports clarified popular understandings of rape, particularly date rape. "What is a woman saying when she agrees to go to a man's home?" an NBC report asked. And several college male students elaborated:

> Just because a woman says no and because you have sex, those are the two facts: a woman said no and you had sex, then you are a rapist automatically because of that?

These rhetorical questions posed by the news worker and aggrieved college students point out the gaps between hegemonic understandings of the phenomenon and feminist efforts to rewrite these definitions. The voices I have just cited emanate from the ideological center of society, where overriding a woman's refusal is "just being smooth."[53] Eileen Rooney points out the consequences of such a sensibility. "If all feminine behavior can be read as seduction, women cannot avoid complicity."[54] In a field of vision saturated by patriarchal thought, women's resistance goes unread. As the statements I have just cited illustrate, it is women's sexual behavior that is recast as the real menace to society. Nevertheless, by including the voices of rape counselors, these news stories pointed out as well that rape is not an inevitable aspect of contemporary sexual relations.

These reports reiterated many of the problematic elements in the news-magazines, even as they rewrote rape as an everyday act. The reports offered rape resistance strategies, yet they suggested that both men and women must work to repair the lines of communication between the genders. These non-celebrity texts demystified the myth of "real" rape by incorporating feminist research findings and including the voices of rape counselors. Broadening definitions of the crime and destigmatizing it, these reports indicated that assaults occur in safe spaces and include "a much broader range of people than was thought." Simultaneously, the camera work re-produced the threat of rape as an inescapable aspect of women's everyday lives. These texts eventually reiterate understandings that rape can only be feared, since there are few viable recourses to resistance.

The inclusion of newsmagazines and noncelebrity narratives may seem incongruous in the context of alternative forms of television programming. Nevertheless, if we are to consider the flow of television programming, it is essential that the debate and discussion enabled by these narratives be taken into account. They work within the imperatives of the news, but they make significant contributions to discussions of rape.

AESTHETIC EXPRESSIONS

Normally art tells us what we don't know. The news tells us what we should know, or what is known by some and not by others. Art tells us more than what we know. It tells us what we could know.

—Anna Deveare Smith[55]

In this chapter, I have examined two sites of television programming and the discussions of rape that they enable. Although both genres articulate ideas about sexual violence that are not available in other programming, only the made-for-TV movie offers even an implicit critique of mainstream representational practices. As I have enumerated above, the organizational structure of television and its economic underpinnings delimit the kinds of critiques that they can offer. I move out of the television apparatus to the realm of art to examine how rape is articulated in this alternative, seemingly noncommercial space.[56]

Various artists, from the canonical works of Western art through feminist filmmakers, have thematized rape in their artifacts and produced a grammar for the aesthetic representation of sexual violence. In this chapter, though, I limit my examination of artwork to that which specifically refers to television representations of rape, those pieces that incorporate television clips to question dominant ways of seeing rape and offer alternative representational practices. At least two exhibits at the Whitney Museum of American Art in New York City specifically address the issues raised in this book. *The Subject of Rape* offered feminist critiques of dominant understandings of sexual violence and its representation in popular culture. *Black Male* addressed the representation of racialized masculinity in popular culture and integrated many of the issues raised by critical race theorists. The artwork and the critiques embedded in them are informed by feminist film criticism and feminist cultural studies. In what follows, I first outline briefly the dominant trends in artistic representations of rape and the ways in which feminist film criticism has offered new ways of imaging rape. Given the broad scope of both of these fields, my review is necessarily schematic and selective rather than comprehensive.

Art historians have recognized and analyzed variously the numerous references to rape in a range of Western art. As the discursive point where sex and violence intersect, rape generates a series of anxieties but also becomes a very fertile site from which to delineate good from bad and to define social proscriptions and prescriptions.[57] Outlining the centrality of rape to the narrative grammar of Greek mythology, Froma Zeitlin traces its representation in art objects from antiquity. She argues that the themes of male domination and violent appropriation of the female perform an ideological function. In the stories told on Greek pottery from 5 B.C. onward, rape became a way of crossing the boundary between gods and men; it also became a device to express identity and the boundaries of the self. In Greek mythology, rape was a heuristic device to address existential, theological, and political questions.[58] This metaphorical use of rape to articulate larger issues is not an atavistic practice but continues to structure the ways in which ideas pertaining to licit and illicit sexuality continue to be addressed in the public arena.

David, Titian, Poussin—a long list of illustrious painters housed in prestigious museums across the (Western) world—all depicted rape in their paintings. In these works, rape functions in one of two ways: either allegorically or as the site for the depiction of erotic images. For instance, the rape of the Sabine women often stands in for the foundation of Rome in most canonical art.[59] A violent act is transformed into a way of defining relations between nations; in this decontextualized portrayal, the brutish and sexual use of force against women is erased. For example, in the works of Fragonard, this event of violation is re-presented as an erotic encounter; here the absence of consent is transformed and sanitized into consent.

Art historians and feminists have vehemently criticized these two forms of representing rape, either through a representational form, where the violence is displaced, or a seduction, where the violence is erased. For instance, Diane Wolfthal argues that most artists and art historians who study such art adopt the rapist's viewpoint and can thus recast sexual violence as abduction. In *Images of Rape*, she provides a critical feminist analysis of medieval and early modern representations of rape. Looking beyond the canon where rape has been sanitized and aestheticized, Wolfthal recovers practices that offer if not a woman's perspective of sexual violence at least one that is critical of it.[60]

Feminist film theorists have expressed a similar set of concerns over the cinematic representation of rape. In this medium, too, sexual violence functions as an allegory for other issues, or it is presented as erotic. Susan Jeffords notes that in movies, the bodies of women become the currency through which men communicate with each other, most often to assert their masculinity. Similarly, bell hooks outlines how rape often is transformed into consensual sex—women's resistance is rewritten as consent and desire.

CINEMATIC EYE

Unlike in art, in Hollywood cinema, rape often becomes the site where issues of racial difference and national identity are worked through. The violation of women's bodies allows movies to address anxieties surrounding the transgression of racial boundaries. Further, men are neatly divided into rapists (or potential rapists) and women's protectors and embody national identity, the sense of belonging and unbelonging. The violence inherent in rape is displaced onto this set of oppositions.[61] Most often, white women's bodies become the site on which these transgressions are inscribed. White men are depicted as their protectors, while men of color are presented as lascivious, hypersexualized, and always a threat to white women. Women of color either remain unrepresented or are presented as "unrapable." When they are raped, the sexual assault is rewritten as consensual "exotic" sex. In each of these formulations, the camera work treats both rape and women's bodies exploitatively, Julia Lesage contends. The films show women as powerless and pathetic. The camera itself tracks the woman's body voyeuristically and intrusively. Even more problematically, the viewer is positioned in the space of the rapist and sees events from his point of view.[62]

Feminist filmmaking that developed in conjunction with the 1970s' women's movement attempted to work on both of these problematic areas: the representational grammar of rape and the constitution of the viewing subject. Like the women's movement, the early feminist films relied on the act of storytelling and speaking out. First-person testimonials and biographical accounts were the defining features of early anti-rape films. They were designed to demystify sexual violence and presented women who addressed the viewer about their experiences, their isolation from friends and families, and their processes of recovery. Significantly, the women who experienced rape are not shown crying. They are depicted instead as being in control. The films allowed women to define their oppression and how they experienced rape. Most of the filmmakers thought the act of speaking about their rape would restore women's identity and self-esteem. This process can be seen in Martha Coolidge's *Not a Pretty Picture* (1975) or JoAnn Elam's *Rape* (1974), movies that attempted to disrupt the classical viewing subject by using hand-held cameras and presenting multiple points of view; these strategies ensured that the spectator could not identify with a singular perspective of rape. Other films, such as Yoko Ono's *Rape* (1969) or Mitchell Block's more problematic *No Lies* (1973), deployed the camera to reproduce the violence and the sense of intrusion and violation that raped women experience.

The feminist films of the 1980s, such as *Rape, An Act of Hate* (1986) and *Waking Up to Rape* (1985), address some of the gaps in these early anti-rape productions. They point out how issues of class, race, and heterosexism are glossed over in an effort to effect a collective gender identity. They address the need for a new cultural literacy, one that acknowledges the ways in which representational practices are shaped and limited by the language and camera work used. They insist that previously marginalized voices should be recognized. And they insist on the dispersal of the collective gender identity into one that is fragmented by the intersections of race, class, nationality, and so on.

POLITICS OF REPRESENTATION

The video art I examine works through the concerns of these two strands of feminist criticism; it borrows elements from feminist art theories and feminist filmmaking. The cultural artifacts that the artists produce are images of images (multimedia work that includes a taped news clip, for instance) that call attention to the politics of representation. Each of the works reveals that language is implicated in the ways in which we understand rape and talk about it. Each explores the connections between language, sexuality, and representational practices.[63] And each is concerned with not just what we see about rape but how we see it.

Andrea Slane's *The Alleged* (1992) fractures homogeneous conceptualizations of white masculinity. Her film foregrounds the ways in which class produces different valences of whiteness. Unlike the early feminist films in which women narrated their experiences of violation, here the narrator is the sister of a man incarcerated for statutory rape. She testifies about the experiences that her family underwent when her brother committed suicide in jail; the film evocatively points out the ways in which rape affects people beyond the alleged rapist and his victim. The televised rape trial of William Kennedy Smith plays in counterpoint to this narrative. The juxtaposition of these two rape charges exposes the ways in which class differences inform social and institutional understandings of sexual violence. In one case, a white man from a privileged family is able to hire a defense team that successfully casts doubt on the rape charge, and in the other, a white, working-class male is unable to effect a similar result for the sexual assault charges filed by his girlfriend's mother.[64]

The film calls into question the ways in which issues of consent, resistance, coercion, and proscribed sex are defined. By including clips of several local rape trials, the film calls for a more nuanced and careful understanding of sexual violence. Like African-American feminists who have asked for a more complicated understanding of patriarchy, Slane's film demands a more complex nomenclature for sexual violence. *The Alleged* develops as well a genealogy of rape representational practices; Slane locates the defendant's suicide within images of lynching and hanging that dominate Hollywood westerns. These filmic images of sanctioned and celebrated violence force a reevaluation of the discourses of crime and punishment, within which the subject of rape often is discussed. The film, including its title, suggests that the binary category of the victim and the accused needs to be supplemented with a more complicated discourse of rape.

REWORKING THE SMITH TRIAL

Two works by Lutz Bacher in the *Subject of Rape* exhibition similarly used televised images from the Smith trial to raise a different set of questions. These projects are concerned specifically with the ways in which language socializes women and enables a rape culture; they interrogate as well who can speak in society and whose voice is considered legitimate. *Corpus Delecti* displays the depositions provided by three women in the Smith trial that were never entered in the courtroom record. The multimedia installation highlights excerpts from their depositions and draws attention to the silences and erasures that surround the testimony of rape survivors. It simultaneously underscores the limited vocabulary of rape and probes the circumstances under which women are heard. Unlike early feminist art, *Corpus Delecti* does not instruct viewers on how to interpret the material, it only reveals women's accounts of rape and points out that women's voices in general are imbricated in patriarchal ideology. Susan Estrich contends that the case would have followed a different trajectory if the "other" women's testimonies had been included. It would have directed more attention to Smith's credibility rather than make determinative the accuser's inconsistencies in her testimony. Estrich notes that a similar testimony was rendered invisible in the Tyson case too.[65]

Bacher's multimedia installation introduces into the debate of the Smith trial aspects that were previously unavailable to the public. Significantly, it introduces into the discussion a broader range of women's voices. Further, by making the politics of enunciation its central theme, the installation draws into the public arena new vectors along which popular culture's representations of sexual violence can be understood.

In *My Penis*, Bacher uses a video clip from the Smith rape trial and plays it on a loop. The resulting video installation has Smith repeatedly admitting in court, with a wince, "I did have my penis." The curator of the exhibition, Monica Chau, contends that this serial repetition undermines Smith's testimony, and the video "becomes a social commentary on the media's role in reinscribing dominant social codes of male privilege and power."[66] In both of Bacher's pieces, the alleged victim, the person who appeared on television screens with a blue blob covering her face, is absent.

None of these pieces that work with television representations addresses people of color and their experiences of rape. This erasure echoes the absence of racialized subjects in television representations in the first instance. Nevertheless, these video artifacts acknowledge different voices and contest the silences, myths, and fallacies that have been the hallmarks of rape representations. *The Alleged* can be included in the Whitney curator's assertion that the videos "represent multiple vantage points on the part of the women and the men who are both the speaking subject(s) or object(s); the works also explore new ways to define rape in the hope of increasing the dialogue among different communities and audiences."[67]

Other art in the *Subject of Rape* highlights the ways in which racist stereotypes locate women of color within discourses of rape.[68] Women also figure in some artwork that specifically addresses media representations of "celebrity" rapes. For instance, Laura Field's *Mansion of Despair* uses images and texts from popular media about hysteria as the background against which she offers her critique of rape representations. She juxtaposes medical statements about the hysteric with excerpts from Charlotte Perkins Gilman's *The Yellow Wallpaper*. Further, the piece includes photographs of Anita Hill, Patricia Bowman, and Desirée Washington, and quotes from newspaper articles that present these women's testimonies as fantasies. This montage shows how the concept of the hysteric continues to inform, repress, and silence women's voices.

Mansion of Despair joins a small group of artwork that introduces race as an axis through which to understand cultural discourses of sexual violence. In *Images of Rape*, Wolfthal isolates a seventeenth-century Dutch painting variously called the *Rape Scene*, *Rape of the Negro*, and *Rape of the Negress* to illustrate the ways in which rape representations function to articulate racialized discourses of national identity. In Christian van Couwenbergh's painting, three well-clad white men are depicted in a small room holding down a terrified black naked woman. With the men clearly presented as violators, this little-known painting comments on and enters into the discourse of the sexualized black woman, a phenomenon contemporaneous with slavery and imperialism, which Sander Gilman has analyzed (see Chapter 2 of this book). Wolfthal believes that the painting could be seen as an antidote to the myth of the promiscuous black woman, because it shows her resisting the men's advances, or it could be perceived as legitimizing Dutch imperialism in Africa. Nevertheless, the painting performs an important function. "Black women who are raped have traditionally been silenced and the event erased from history, but Couwenbergh offers a reminder of such violations."[69]

Addressing the issue of interracial rape from a slightly different perspective, Glenn Ligon's *Profile Series* confronts the twin myths of black male sexual deviance and criminality. Included in the Whitney show *Black Male*, Ligon's piece consists of eight separate works that address the ways in which the New York City media constructed the identities of the accused teenagers in the Central Park rape case. Each of the eight accused teenagers gets his own piece. To construct this commentary on media representational practices, Ligon has selected excerpts from local media coverage about each teenager. Through the juxtaposition of these statements, Ligon reconstructs the profiles for each of the teenagers that were developed by the media. Consequently, initial commentary puzzling over the "goodness" of the boys, the absence of any criminal records, is juxtaposed with later characterizations of wolf packs and wilding. According to the curator of the exhibit, Thelma Golden, Ligon's play with "the language of visual and textual description . . . heightens the contradictions inherent in the descriptions of the stereotyped black male."[70] The resultant artifacts reveal the processes through which the black male body becomes a "site upon which the nation's crisis comes to be dramatized, demonized, and dealt with."[71] His work reveals that the contradictory images of the eight defendants draw on myths of rape as well as stereotypes of black male brutishness and lust. The reconstituted profiles force us to interrogate media representational practices.

In each of these works relating to the media, the art does not show rape. Sexual violence is shown to be engulfed by various institutions, particularly the media. These works are powerful, because they insist that rape cannot be represented through a single representation. They recognize implicitly that they are capturing only one or at most a few of the moments that constitute rape. They resist what Frederic Jameson calls the ideology of form as they contest television representational practices.[72] They assert the need to recognize that rape is spoken for, about, and by the agencies of law, medicine, media, and criminal justice systems in dramatically different ways. These discourses constitute rape, the rapist, and the rape victims in dramatically different ways.

Each piece of art locates rape in a multiplicity of discourses. The artifacts specify that an understanding of sexual violence that is structured singularly along the male/female binary cannot account for the ways in which people experience the phenomenon. Implicit in such representations is the recognition that patriarchy alone is not a sufficient explanatory frame for rape. Whether Slane's movie, Laura Field's art, or Glenn Ligon's profiles, each work that I examine selects one vector of difference, such as class or race, to intersect with gender. The artists are self-consciously participating in a strategic essentialism. Foregrounding race or class works here, because the artists' selections are made specifically to provide provisional and polemical definitions. These works open up the space for a new kind of exchange, one that requires a discussion of rape culture and television's role in reifying it. They also attest to the idea that there is no space to discuss the intersection of race and gender within the language and representational system of television. On mainstream commercial networks the subaltern seemingly cannot speak.

Each of the genres and video art that I have examined in this chapter creates the space for new kinds of debates and discussions on sexual violence that have not been made available by other television genres. For instance, the made-for-TV movie, for all of its drawbacks, foregrounds a woman's perspective of rape. It also tends to provide a narrative that moves beyond the moment of violation. Countering the sentimentality that marks postrape story lines, Slane's movie offers us a different avenue to understand the aftermath of sexual violence and how it is dispersed.

In contrast to the other genres examined in this book, the general reports on rape aired on the networks provide an opportunity to read against the grain of patriarchal understandings that rape is inevitable and can only be feared. They provide women with an avenue to fight back and gain some agency. Further, they hint at long-term solutions rather than a legal bandage—they suggest education, self-defense, and political organization as possible ways to redress women's structural vulnerability.

As Melissa Deem points out, the contemporary public arena makes available a very limited and cramped space for the articulation of a feminist politics. Consequently, "grasping at fragments" becomes a necessary strategy to facilitate a counter-public sphere. The alternative forms that I have examined in this chapter could be seen as occupying this "space of the minor." They contribute to the erosion and questioning of previously established boundaries of the public. One must concur with Deem that, "While falling short of a transformative politics, artistic forms of feminism do open up the possibility for such a politics." The alternative forms as a whole contribute to a radically reformulated debate and discussion of sexual violence.[73] Each form explodes the topic of rape and compels a reexamination from a new angle of vision. Significantly, not only do these forms invigorate new debates and discussions of sexual violence, they also facilitate an examination of imaging practices prevalent in conventional television genres.

Each of the alternative forms of representation I examined in this chapter constitutes the first step toward the formation of a counter-public sphere. The made-for-TV movie, with its focus on the domestic arena and women, enables discussions about the gender-specific nature of sexual violence. It allows women to voice their experiences of rape and its aftermath. It goes beyond presenting women as object-victims and transforms them, for at least the space of the film, into subjects who can take steps toward autonomy. *Fallen Champ*, with its focus on Tyson, unravels the formation of violent masculinity. Demythologizing the black male rapist myth, the film reveals the multiple forces that shape the boxer's behavior. Even as it focuses on black masculinity, the film clears the space for an exploration of the multiplicity of African-American experiences, including women, feminist or otherwise. Kopple's film allows for the formation of a counter-public sphere that coheres around a racialized identity. The artwork that I examined in the final section reveals a different axis along which sexual violence could be conjugated. While some pieces address issues pertaining to female or black male experiences, others, like Slane's movie, reveal the ways in which popular culture's representational practices shape the material lives of everyday people, how we come to understand events. Both Slane and Bacher force an examination of legal practices, the ways in which the law addresses rape, rape victims, and rape defendants. These works together allow for a debate and discussion of sexual violence that is unavailable in other genres of programming. They fragment the seemingly unified subject of rape and reveal the multiple and contestatory discourses that constitute it. And they enact shifts in the regimes of representation that could potentially facilitate new understandings of sexual violence.

Conclusion

The analysis that I have conducted in this book reveals that the various television genres follow different trajectories in producing narratives of rape. Some of them, such as daytime talk shows and certain prime-time programs, provide viewers with a multiplicity of approaches to address the issue of sexual violence. Others, such as the news, tend to offer monolithic understandings that are framed primarily by patriarchal definitions of rape. The diversity of rape imageries within each genre is striking and reveals the complex ways in which discourses of gender, race, and sexuality are circulated, produced, and rewritten in television space. The range of rape images stems in part from the tendency of each genre to think of the issue in discrete terms. On network television, there is no unified discussion of sexual violation. Separate contexts—law, women's perspectives, postfeminism—govern how rape is presented. Television representations of rape have a broad range of tone and meaning. Some portray rape symbolically as a sign for something else, and others do this explicitly; some clearly condemn rape, and others blur the distinction between rape and seduction; and some explicitly address race, while others speak from a position of (white) transparency.

Amidst this diversity, the discussions promoted by television rape narratives rarely offer new insights into the continued prevalence of rape. Instead, rape becomes a site where a contestation between discourses of gender and race is enacted. In the public spheres enabled by various genres of programming, discourses of gender and race are strategically separated to offer clean, coherent narratives, with a single explanatory cause for sexual violence. The programs either address rape as it affects (white) women or as an effect of black masculinity. Some shows focus their attention on the dark side of (black) masculinity. Rarely do television programs present sexual violence as a site where gender and racial discourses intersect in problematic ways to mobilize people differently. This valorization of either gender or race allows television programming to hail the white male subject as the normative citizen of democratic debate and discussion.

Examining narratives across genres, I have pointed out repeatedly that the one subject position that is consistently addressed by television programs is the white male. Television narratives do not present the white male in a monolithic manner or within a stable position; they present a diversity of understandings of (white) masculinity. But rape is presented consistently from the "normal" position of the white male subject. From this vantage point, gender or race becomes the only explanatory framework for the crime. Rape occurs because of bad masculinity (often black masculinity) or because a woman sends "wrong messages," or it is an instance of a woman "crying rape." In other instances, this white male angle of vision explains rape by tapping into myths of racialized (male and female) sexuality.

Whether they engage with interracial or intraracial rape, no single genre is able to include unproblematically the marginalized voices of women and racialized subjects. Few programs are able to produce a woman-centered understanding of rape; most present women only as victims. The most productive understandings of sexual violence that could lead to the formation of a counter-public sphere can be found in the devalued genres of the daytime talk show or in the made-for-TV movie. These two sites are able to highlight the pain and trauma experienced by raped women; they foreground as well the different ways in which people in the United States understand the issue. The discussions in daytime talk shows facilitate the formation of a community based on a shared sense of identity, primarily gender oppression. Here women often are shown taking control of their lives. While *Oprah* and *Donahue* rarely address the intersectionality of race and gender, they at least obliquely work through the understanding that race alters the ways in which individuals experience and understand rape. They reveal that historical, social, and political factors shape the ways in which white and black women experience sexual violence. Similarly, they underscore that institutions such as the criminal justice and legal systems treat black and white men differently when they are accused of rape. This genre draws attention to the fact that only in arenas resembling the intimate conversations of the domestic sphere is the complex topic of race even undertaken. Daytime talk shows facilitate an affective public sphere, where identity and difference are the modes through which individuals engage in debate.

Genres that replicate the rational-critical mode of argument, such as the news, engage with rape, gender, and race only in stereotypical ways. The rhetorical strategies of objectivity that they employ and the institutional sources from which they derive their information permit a focus only on the rapists/accused men. It should be noted that news narratives no longer focus singularly on the rape survivor and her sexual history, as they once did. Nevertheless, the shift in focus to the rapist results in an unrelenting focus on the male fear of false accusations, or suggestions to women to lock their doors. In the rhetoric associated with public modes of discussion, incidents of rape permit a reification of hegemonic understandings.

In all genres, the issue of race remains nebulous and caught in stereotypical formulations. In the news, race figures only in the marked bodies of African Americans, primarily men. News programs introduce the topic of race only to discuss the violent and criminal nature of inner-city culture. News workers do not introduce the topic of whiteness or white privilege; instead, it remains an unmarked category and retains its status as the norm. Prime-time entertainment repeatedly uses racial difference as a generative moment for its dramatic narratives. Often, though, when the story lines focus on race, rape tends to slide out of view. Racial oppression and gender oppression are rarely shown occurring simultaneously. As Stuart Hall has pointed out, on television the spaces for difference are carefully regulated and policed by the dominant ideology.[1] I argue that it is prime-time narratives' reliance on some insights from liberal feminism that leads to such racial blindness. These fictional accounts often attest to various feminist insights. For instance, they highlight that legal systems often discredit women's experiences of violation. Yet, they are rarely able to clarify how black women's experiences within the criminal justice and legal systems are significantly different from those of white women's.

On daytime talk shows, *Oprah* rarely addresses directly the issue of race, but Winfrey's embodied presence and her tendency to be one of her own guests make it impossible to elide the topic. *Donahue,* on the other hand, dealt specifically with the topic of racial structures of oppression, but only as it was perpetuated by social institutions. The show opens up the space for a debate about the ways in which the legal and criminal justice systems treat nonwhites. It broadens the parameters of news discourses, but it does not discuss how individuals experience racial oppression. In the last chapter I included specific works of art to show the ways in which it is possible to effect a strategic essentialism, focusing either on race or gender, and yet outline the complexity of rape.

A central argument I make in this book is that television programs, if they are to enable the existence of public spheres, must be able to facilitate a wide-ranging debate and discussion of sexual violence. This would require including voices that are in opposition to hegemonic understandings, such as those offered by feminists. It is evident that the various genres of television programming have incorporated feminist arguments selectively. Most reveal that men and women are affected differently by the experience of sexual violence.

Repeatedly, the programs present these two gendered experiences, the rapist and the rape survivor, as commensurable and often set up one against the other. These narratives assume that men and women can enter into public deliberative processes as if they are equals. They do not take into account the specific ways in which differences shape who can and how they can speak in the public arena. They also do not elucidate the ways in which race and class mediate gender identities. These programs provide a biologically essentialist understanding of gender, suggesting that this is the central axis along which we should understand sexual violence. Specifically, feminist voices are either absent, as in the news, or they function as confrontational devices, as in *Oprah* and some prime-time programs. As a result, television narratives do not facilitate a wide-ranging discussion of sexual violence. Above all, by selecting only some aspects of feminist arguments, those that are characterized as stemming from liberal feminism, television programs posit gender as the single axis around which to make sense of rape. These programs replicate the racial blind spots of these theories, presenting gender-based victimization as the single unifying factor for women.

This focus on the gendered dimensions of sexual violence is produced by erasing the effects of racial structures. Television narratives of rape gloss over the historical legacies of slavery that continue to mark black male and female sexuality in a distorted manner. Nevertheless, these understandings of sexualized black bodies continue to be the invisible referents for discussions of sexuality, even white sexuality. By ignoring the ways in which discourses of gender and race intersect to constitute racialized men's and women's experiences, the programs ultimately reify hegemonic understandings of rape and do not contribute to a broadening of the discussion.

It is important to recognize that, although no single genre can be identified as facilitating inclusive democratic formations, any discussion of television and the public sphere should include different genres. As is clear from the analysis that I have conducted, each genre explores some of the discourses that have accumulated around the topic of rape. The news provides us with insights into the ways in which social institutions deal with sexual violence, primarily in the criminal justice and legal systems. News narratives rarely depict rape as a violent sexual act whose determining moment is the exercise of power over subordinated subjects. They do not foreground the social factors or gendered nature of social relations that create a climate where rape is possible. Sexual violence is instead portrayed as the individual eruption of male sexual desire.

Prime-time entertainment programs broaden these understandings to include the ways in which individuals apprehend rape. They promote multiple understandings by offering plural points of view from the survivor, the rapist, bystanders, the police, and so on. The asymmetry between these multiple definitions creates the discursive space, which Edwin Ardener calls "the zone of difference," from which viewers can discuss sexual violence outside of patriarchal understandings.[2] Further, these narratives rely on representations of ambivalence and contradictions. It is this relative openness, the ideological uncertainty, that creates a space for debate. However, in these programs, women are primarily presented as vulnerable and lacking agency; they are sexually and socially subordinate to men. These narratives present a masculinized version of feminism where the male characters espouse counter-hegemonic understandings, while the female characters either present themselves as postfeminist or they reiterate patriarchal definitions and are distinctly antifeminist. This gender role reversal highlights the fragility of feminist discourses and suggests that they require the stamp of approval of male authority to be recognized as valid. This blind spot in theories of the public sphere merits reiteration. Habermas's theory assumes that we can all participate as equals in the public sphere and engage in rational-critical debate. However, as prime-time fictional accounts do point out there are significant differences in who can espouse counter-hegemonic ideologies with authority. White males can speak about feminism and adopt a feminist rhetoric in television space with greater ease than women. Identity and differences shape who can participate in public deliberative practices and how they do so.

Daytime talk shows and made-for-TV movies reveal the individual experience of sexual violence. As I have mentioned already, they focus on the trauma experienced by rape survivors, the ways in which both rapists and rape survivors apprehend the crime, and the "average" American's understanding of the issue. They offer a narrative grammar that foregrounds women's experiences of rape.

What constitutes the public sphere, and what can be deliberated within such a sphere, is shaped by racial and gender formations and by who has the power to authoritatively define where the line between the public and the private would be drawn. It depends as well on who has the power to police and defend that boundary. These issues are broached only in alternative genres, such as the commissioned made-for-TV movie, *The Fallen Champ*, or video art. They offer a critique of television's representational practices and how these imaging practices may contribute to the prevalence of patriarchal understandings of rape.

The tightly focused time frame within which I conduct my analysis allows us to understand the specificity of rape representations at a particular historical moment. It allows us to examine the complex relationships among television genres. We can observe that prime-time entertainment, daytime talk shows, made-for-TV movies, and network news all borrow ideas and representational strategies from each other. Notwithstanding the production practices that are characteristic of a particular genre, we find that television programs exhibit a complex relationship with each other; sometimes critiquing but at other times mimicking each other. This analysis reveals not only the fragility of the distinctions made between fictional and nonfictional programs, but it asserts the need to study the flow of television programming. It is only when genres are taken together that we can understand the variegated, nuanced debates and discussions that television representations could promote. It is the totality of television rape representations across genres, not those in one single program or genre, that allows us to see the potential the medium has to facilitate democratic debate and discussion.

The debates facilitated by television's commercial culture rarely consider how gender and race intersect to create multivalent, shifting definitions of private and public arenas. Television's intervention into the topic seemingly dismantles the public/private binary, even as it reifies it. As I mentioned earlier, television genres that imitate the sphere of intimate conversation, "feminine" modes of speaking associated with the private arena, are able to underscore the complexity of rape. Those genres associated with rational-critical debate such as the news provide very simplistic accounts that elide the female experience of violation.

This analysis has used a feminist–Foucauldian approach to reveal the shortcomings in Habermas's conceptualization of the public sphere. Habermas and Foucault offer radically different views of critiquing society and social discourses. Habermas tends to seek solutions by positing a neo-Enlightenment paradigm, while Foucault's formulation of power, knowledge, and social discourses ignores the issue of human agency. A feminist approach, though, facilitates a way to envisage emancipatory discourses, one that can begin to incorporate subjects who are multiply intersected by discourses of race and gender.

In his reassessment of the public sphere, Habermas concedes that he had not problematized the gendered assumptions of the bourgeois public sphere.[3] The racial exclusions of the public sphere are rarely discussed. He continues to rely, however, on the notion of rational-critical debate as the defining feature of the public sphere. As this analysis has shown, in feminist reinterpretations of democracy where the public/private divide is radically reconceptualized, Habermas's reliance on the public sphere is clearly inadequate.

It is precisely because topics such as rape, gender, and race do not lend themselves to rational-critical debate that traditional forms of democratic theories are unable to account for these subjects in the public realm. So-called entertainment genres are able to introduce a broader range of discussion, especially the different ways in which society apprehends the culturally constructed categories of race, gender, and sexuality.

It would be foolhardy to suggest that these entertainment genres be perceived as the primary sites of the public sphere. Information genres, such as news and newsmagazines, despite their flaws, remain useful sites from which we can become cognizant of the dominant institutional understandings of rape. Habermas's main critique of the media as public sphere directs our attention toward the role of the marketplace and its effects on media content. This remains a valid criticism for all genres. For instance, the scripts of the various prime-time entertainment programs reveal the control that advertisers and network authorities can exercise over the content of the shows. By comparing the revisions in these scripts to the advertisements that accompanied the programs, one can infer that some of the changes were shaped by the interests of the networks and commercial sponsors. Similarly, talk show hosts have consistently skirted the issue of structural change as a possible solution to the multitude of problems that they enumerated.

This book highlights the limits of traversing the public/private divide and addressing the plurality of race when the debates are undertaken in a medium structured by the logic of the marketplace. I have offered a critique of both theories of feminism and democracy that continue to facilitate an either/or understanding of citizenship, one that cannot account for the multiple and intersecting identities of racialized and gendered subjects. As Angela Davis has pointed out, rather than discuss race only in terms of racism, it is important to see how race constitutes difference.[4]

The discussions and debates that various genres of programming enable are partial and limited. Further, not one facilitates democratic participation beyond discussion. To this extent, television programming can only be characterized as forming "weak public spheres." Nancy Fraser characterizes arenas that facilitate only debate and counter-hegemonic narratives, which could lead to opposition formation, as weak public spheres. In contrast, strong public spheres are those arenas where debate and discussion result in decision making.[5]

Despite the numerous problematics involved in conceptualizing television as a public sphere, even after diffusing the reliance on rational-critical argument and masculine modes of theorizing I do not seek to abandon this concept. This analysis suggests that we reconceptualize television as facilitating a weak public sphere. The discussions in this reconceptualized public sphere are not expected to guide the state; they are supposed to provide individuals with a better understanding of the operations of social power, of how individuals' experiences are discursively constituted, and of how the individual's social location shapes personal experience. Within such a redefined public sphere, television would be expected to air a range of storied voices, articulating many perspectives, so individuals could be made aware of their situated selves and thereby form a shared community.

Notes

NOTES TO INTRODUCTION

1. Kristal Brent Zook has offered a marvelous analysis of the ways in which the emergence of the Fox network created a space for the articulation of black identity. A confluence of technological changes permitted the formation of the fourth network. In an effort to distinguish itself from the established networks and to sustain a viewership base, Fox geared its programming primarily toward a black audience and in the mid-1990s offered the largest crop of black-produced programming in television. See Zook's *Color by Fox: Fox Network and the Revolution in Black Television* (New York: Oxford University Press, 1999). Herman Gray, on the other hand, cautions against celebrating the representations of black masculinity in *In Living Color*. See Gray's *Watching Race: Television and the Struggle for "Blackness"* (Minneapolis: University of Minnesota Press, 1995).

2. For an analysis of Indian television representations of rape and gender in general, see Ammu Joseph and Kalpana Sharma, "Rape: A Campaign Is Born," in *Whose News? The Media and Women's Issues* (New Delhi: Sage, 1994), 43–50. Also see Flavia Agnes, "The Anti-Rape Campaign," in *The Struggle against Violence*, edited by Chhaya Datar (Calcutta: Stree, 1993), 99–150.

3. Angela Davis, *Women, Race, and Class* (New York: Vintage, 1983), points out that the dominant images of rape in America are a legacy of slavery and racism. Also see, Michele Wallace, "Negative Images: Towards a Black Feminist Cultural Criticism," in *Cultural Studies*, edited by Lawrence Grossberg, Cary Nelson, and Paula Treichler (New York: Routledge, 1992), 654–71; Traci West, *Wounds of the Spirit: Black Women, Violence, and Resistance Ethics* (New York: New York University Press, 1999).

4. Lawrence Grossberg, "Cultural Studies and/in New Worlds," *Critical Studies in Mass Communications*, vol. 10, no. 1 (1993): 1–22.

5. Michel Foucault has elaborated on this concept in several of his books. See *The Archaeology of Knowledge*, translated by Sheridan Smith (New York: Pantheon, 1972); *The History of Sexuality*, vol. 1, translated by Robert Hurley (New York: Vintage, 1978) and *Power/Knowledge: Selected Interviews and Other Writings, 1972–1977*, translated by Colin Gordon (New York: Pantheon, 1980).

6. Joan Scott provides a useful synopsis of this term and the ways in which feminists could deploy it, while John Fiske modifies it for analyzing media products in the United States. See Joan Scott, "Deconstructing Equality-versus-Difference: Or, the Uses of Poststructuralist Theory of Feminism," *Feminist Studies*, vol. 14, no. 1 (1988): 33–50; John Fiske, *Media Matters: Everyday Culture and Political Change*, rev. ed. (Minneapolis: University of Minnesota Press, 1996).

7. Raymond Williams, *Television: Technology and Cultural Form* (New York: Schocken, 1975); Nick Browne, "The Political Economy of the Television (Super) Text," *Quarterly Journal of Film Studies*, vol. 9, no. 3 (1984): 74–82.

8. In a different manner *Boys Don't Cry*, a movie adaptation of the Teena Brandon story, introduced a new angle of vision into the crime: sexual identity. The movie documents the experiences of a transgender person who was brutally raped and killed in 1994. The fictional account underscores rape as a weapon of power. Similarly, the U.S. Supreme Court's decision in May 2000 to invalidate a section of the Violence Against Women Act stimulated debate over the effects of rape. The Violence Against Women Act permitted women to sue their attackers for monetary damages and underscores the feminist belief that the effects of rape on women's lives are multifarious and pervasive. Meanwhile, the publication of Randy Thornhill's and Craig Palmer's *A Natural History of Rape: Biological Bases of Sexual Coercion* (Cambridge, Mass.: MIT Press, 2000) has brought feminists such as Susan Brownmiller back into center stage. Returning to the enduring question of why men rape, the authors suggest that males are responding to biological impulses. Echoing some of the issues raised by sociobiologists, this book presents rape as a necessary component of the evolution of the species.

9. Jürgen Habermas, *The Structural Transformation of the Public Sphere: An Inquiry into a Category of Bourgeois Society*, translated by Thomas Burger, with Frederick Lawrence (Cambridge, Mass.: MIT Press, 1989).

NOTES TO TELEVISION AND THEORIES OF THE PUBLIC SPHERE

1. See Benedict Anderson, *Imagined Communities: Reflections on the Origin and Spread of Nationalism*, rev. ed. (New York: Verso, 1991).

2. Several scholars have examined the role that television plays in promoting and reproducing a particular understanding of nation, however, no one, to my knowledge, has examined how the medium has been constitutive in articulating a new sensibility. See Purnima Mankekar, *Screening Culture, Viewing Politics: An Ethnography of Television, Womanhood, and Nation in Postcolonial India* (Durham, N.C.: Duke University Press, 1999); David Morley and Charlotte Brunsdon, *The Nationwide Television Studies* (New York: Routledge, 1999); Martin Jésus, *Communication, Culture and Hegemony: From the Media to Mediations* (Newbury Park, Calif.: Sage, 1993).

3. Lynn Spigel, "Installing the Television Set: Popular Discourses on Television and Domestic Space, 1948–1955," in *Private Screenings: Television and the Female Consumer*,

edited by Lynn Spigel and Denise Mann (Minneapolis: University of Minnesota Press, 1992), 3–38; Raymond Williams, *On Television: Selected Writings*, edited by Alan O'Connor (New York: Routledge, 1989), xv.

4. See the writings in the two anthologies: Lynn Spigel and Denise Mann, eds., *Private Screenings*; Charlotte Brunsdon, Julie D'Acci, and Lynn Spigel, eds., *Feminist Television Criticism: A Reader* (New York: Oxford University Press, 1997).

5. Elayne Rapping has argued that programs such as *Melrose Place* have altered this gendered divide. She points out that particularly in its first season, the program "rejected the notion of gendered difference and inequity, as well as the stereotypical gender images that have informed classic TV genres." See "Gender, *Melrose Place*, and the Aaron Spelling Legacy," *Mediated Women: Representations in Popular Culture*, edited by Marian Meyers (Cresskill, N.J.: Hampton Press, 1999), 271–85, 272.

6. Gray, *Watching Race*, 2.

7. Avtar Brah, Mary Hickman, and Maírtin Mac an Ghail, eds., *Thinking Identities: Ethnicity, Racism and Culture* (New York: St. Martin's Press, 1999), 1–24.

8. Andrea Press and Elizabeth Cole, *Speaking of Abortion: Television and Authority in the Lives of Women* (Chicago: University of Illinois Press, 1999), 125.

9. These ideas of serving the public good have been codified in the broadcast licensing regulations formulated by the Federal Communications Commission (FCC). Providing a history of the origins of the television industry, William Boddy traces how the competing forces of market interests and the public interest have shaped regulatory practices. See William Boddy, "The Beginnings of American Television," in *Television: An International History*, edited by Anthony Smith (New York: Oxford University Press, 1995), 35–61. R. Randall Rainey and William Rehg provide a nuanced account of the ways in which deregulation has affected FCC practices. See "The Marketplace of Ideas, the Public Interest, and Federal Regulation of the Electronic Media: Implications of Habermas' Theory of Democracy," *Southern California Law Review*, vol. 69, no. 6 (1996): 1923–87.

10. See Sylvia Walby, "Is Citizenship Gendered?" in *Gender Transformations* (New York: Routledge, 1997), 166–79.

11. Stuart Hall, "Media Power and Class Power," in *Bending Reality: The State of the Media*, edited by James Curran (London: Pluto Press, 1986), 6–14, 9.

12. For an extended discussion, see Mary Ellen Brown, ed., *Television and Women's Culture: The Politics of the Popular* (Newbury Park, Calif.: Sage, 1990), 15–24; Todd Gitlin, *The Whole World Is Watching: Mass Media in the Making and Unmaking of the New Left* (Berkeley: University of California Press, 1981), 249–82; Hebert J. Gans, *Deciding What's News: A Study of CBS Evening News, NBC Nightly News, Newsweek, and Time* (New York: Vintage, 1979), 79.

13. Stanley Aronowitz believes that arguments that evoke the ghost of Greece to posit an authentic democratic practice, as in the Athenian agora, rest on a mythic town in the sky, a phantasmagoria. The concepts of democracy and public participation in governance have "long served as a rallying cry against private greed, a demand for attention to the general welfare as against propertied interests, an appeal for openness to scrutiny as opposed

to corporate and bureaucratic secrecy, an arena in which disenfranchised minorities struggle to express their cultural identity." See "Is Democracy Possible? The Decline of the Public in the American Debate," in *The Phantom Public Sphere*, edited by Bruce Robbins (Minneapolis: University of Minnesota Press, 1993), 75–92.

14. Raymond Williams, *Keywords: A Vocabulary of Culture and Society*, 2d ed. (New York: Oxford University Press, 1976), 93–98.

15. John Keane, *Public Life and Late Capitalism: Toward a Socialist Theory of Democracy* (New York: Cambridge University Press, 1984), 9.

16. Walter Lippmann, *The Phantom Public* (New York: Macmillan, 1927); John Dewey, *The Public and Its Problems* (New York: Holt Rinehart, 1927); C. Wright Mills, *Power, Politics and People*, edited by Irving Horowitz (New York: Oxford University Press, 1967). James Carey provides an excellent overview of Dewey's philosophy in *Communication As Culture: Essays on Media and Society* (Boston: Unwin Hyman, 1989).

17. Carey, *Communication As Culture*; Raymond Williams, *Culture and Society, 1780–1950* (New York: Columbia University Press, 1958); Lawrence Grossberg, "Interpreting the 'Crisis' of Culture in Communication Theory," *Journal of Communication*, vol. 29, no. 1 (1979): 55–68; John D. Peters, "Democracy and American Mass Communication Theory," *Communication* 11 (1989): 199–220.

18. Peter Dahlgren, *Television and the Public Sphere: Citizenship, Democracy, and the Media* (Thousand Oaks, Calif.: Sage, 1995).

19. See Jürgen Habermas, *The Inclusion of the Other: Studies in Political Theory*, edited by Ciaran Cronin and Pablo De Greiff (Cambridge, Mass.: MIT Press, 1998) and *Between Facts and Norms: Contributions to a Discourse Theory of Law and Democracy*, translated by William Rehg (Cambridge, Mass.: MIT Press, 1996), among others.

20. Habermas, *The Structural Transformation of the Public Sphere*.

21. Prior to the seventeenth century, the public sphere was the arena where the ruler's power was represented. With the emergence of capitalism, this model gave way to one where state authority was publicly monitored through informed, critical discourse by the people. These changes in forms of publicity were facilitated by economic transformations that reconfigured the contours of civil society and the state.

22. James Curran, "Rethinking the Media As a Public Sphere," in *Communication and Citizenship: Journalism and the Public Sphere in the New Media Age*, edited by Peter Dahlgren and Colin Sparks (New York: Routledge, 1991), 27–57.

23. The literary salons in France, the coffeehouses in England, and the literary societies in Germany were characterized by three features: (1) they disregarded status and focused on rationality; (2) discussions in these sites centered on issues of "common concern," including criticism of governmental authority; and (3) they were established on the principle of inclusivity. See Patricia Roberts, "Habermas, Philosophes, Puritans: Rationality and Exclusion in the Dialectical Public Sphere," *Rhetorical Society Quarterly*, vol. 26, no. 1 (1996): 47–68.

24. Houston Baker, "Critical Memory and the Black Public Sphere," in *The Black Public Sphere: A Public Culture Book*, edited by the Black Public Sphere Collective (Chicago: University of Chicago Press, 1995), 11–21.

25. See Andrew Calabrese and Barbara Burke, "American Identities: Nationalism, the Media, and the Public Sphere," *Journal of Communication Inquiry*, vol. 16, no. 2 (1992): 52–73; Juha Koivisto and Esa Valiverronen, "The Resurgence of the Critical Theories of the Public Sphere," *Journal of Communication Inquiry*, vol. 20, no. 2 (1996): 18–36; Hans Verstraeten, "The Media and the Transformation of the Public Sphere," *European Journal of Communication*, vol. 11, no. 3 (1996): 347–70.

26. Nancy Fraser, "Rethinking the Public Sphere: A Contribution to the Critique of Actually Existing Democracy," *Social Text*, vol. 9, no. 3 (1990): 56–80; Rita Felski, *Beyond Feminist Aesthetics: Feminist Literature and Social Change* (Cambridge, Mass.: Harvard University Press, 1989).

27. Michael Schudson, "Was There Ever a Public Sphere? If So, When? Reflections on the American Case" in *Habermas and the Public Sphere*, edited by Craig Calhoun (Cambridge, Mass.: MIT Press, 1992), 143–63.

28. Eva Gamarnikow et al., eds., *The Public and the Private* (London: Heinemann, 1983).

29. Carol C. Gould, ed., *Beyond Domination: New Perspectives on Women and Philosophy* (Totowa, N.J.: Rowman & Allanheld, 1984); Michèle Barrett, *Women's Oppression Today: The Marxist/Feminist Encounter*, rev. ed. (New York: Verso, 1988); Sarah Franklin, Celia Lury, and Jackie Stacey, eds., *Off-Centre: Feminism and Cultural Studies* (New York: Harper Collins, 1991).

30. Gould, ed., *Beyond Domination*; Nancy Fraser, *Unruly Practices: Power, Discourse, and Gender in Contemporary Social Theory* (Minneapolis: University of Minnesota Press, 1989); Barrett, *Women's Oppression Today*.

31. Nancy Fraser, "Sex, Lies, and the Public Sphere: Some Reflections on the Confirmation of Clarence Thomas," *Critical Inquiry*, vol. 18, no. 3 (1992): 595–612, 606.

32. Aída Hurtado, *The Color of Privilege: Three Blasphemies on Race and Feminism* (Ann Arbor: University of Michigan Press, 1996).

33. Carole Pateman, *The Disorder of Women: Democracy, Feminism, and Political Theory* (Stanford, Calif.: Stanford University Press, 1989), 121.

34. Carol Smart and Barry Smart, "Accounting for Rape: Reality and Myth in Press Reports," in *Women, Sexuality, and Social Control* (Boston: Routledge and Kegan Paul, 1978), 89–103.

35. Seyla Benhabib, "Models of Public Space: Hannah Arendt, the Liberal Tradition, and Jürgen Habermas," in *Habermas and the Public Sphere*, 73–98, 93.

36. Susan Bourque and Jean Grossholtz, "Politics an Unnatural Practice," in *Women and the Public Sphere: A Critique of Sociology and Politics*, edited by Janet Siltanen and Michelle Stanworth (New York: St. Martin's Press, 1984), 103–21, 105.

37. Iris Marion Young, "Impartiality and the Civic Public: Some Implications of Feminist Critiques of Moral and Political Theory," in *Feminism As Critique: On the Politics of Gender*, edited by Seyla Benhabib and Drucilla Cornell (Minneapolis: University of Minnesota Press, 1987), 56–76.

38. Laura Kipnis, "(Male) Desire and (Female) Disgust: Reading *Hustler*," in *Cultural Studies*, edited by Lawrence Grossberg, Cary Nelson, and Paula Treichler (New York: Routledge, 1992), 373–91.

39. Mary Ryan, "Gender and Public Access: Women's Politics in Nineteenth-Century America," in *Habermas and the Public Sphere*, 259–88.

40. Susan Herbst, "Gender, Marginality, and the Changing Dimensions of the Public Sphere," *Communication Research*, vol. 19, no. 3 (1992): 381–92.

41. Joan Landes, ed., *Feminism, the Public and the Private* (New York: Oxford University Press, 1999), 16.

42. Warren Montag, "The Universalization of Whiteness: Racism and Enlightenment," in *Whiteness*, edited by Mike Hill (New York: New York University Press, 1997), 281–93; Houston Baker, "Critical Memory and the Black Public Sphere," in *The Black Public Sphere*, 16.

43. See Paolo Carpignano, Robin Andersen, Stanley Aronowitz, and William diFazio, "Chatter in the Age of Electronic Reproduction," *Social Text*, vol. 9, no. 3 (1993): 33–55; John Keane, *Public Life and Late Capitalism*; Curran, "Rethinking the Media As a Public Sphere," in *Communication and Citizenship*, 27–57.

44. Curran, "Rethinking the Media As a Public Sphere," in *Communication and Citizenship*, 27–57.

45. Lisa McLaughlin, "Gender, Privacy and Publicity in 'Media Event' Space," in *News, Gender and Power*, edited by Cynthia Carter, Gill Branston, and Stuart Allen (New York: Routledge, 1998), 71–90.

46. For an extended debate, see Ien Ang, *Watching Dallas: Soap Opera and the Melodramatic Imagination*, translated by Della Couling (New York: Methuen, 1985); Tony Bennett, "Putting Policy into Cultural Studies," in *Cultural Studies*, 23–33; Janice Radway, *Reading the Romance: Women, Patriarchy, and Popular Culture* (Durham, N.C.: Duke University Press, 1984); Ellen Seiter, "Semiotics, Structuralism, and Television," in *Channels of Discourse, Reassembled: Television and Contemporary Criticism*, 2d ed., edited by Robert C. Allen (New York: Routledge, 1992), 17–41; Jane Feuer, "Melodrama, Serial Form, and Television Today," in *The Media Reader*, edited by Manuel Alvarado and John Thompson (London: BFI Pub., 1990), 253–64.

47. Press and Cole, *Speaking of Abortion*.

48. See Jane Mansbridge, "Feminism and Democratic Community," in *Democratic Community*, edited by John W. Chapman and Ian Shapiro (New York: New York University Press, 1993), 339–95; Helán E. Page, "Authoring and Authorizing 'Black Male' Imagery," unpublished paper; Janet Siltanen and Michelle Stanworth, "The Politics of Private Woman and Public Man," in *Women and the Public Sphere*, 185–208.

49. Mills, *Power, Politics and the People*, 371.

50. Geoff Eley, "Nations, Publics, and Political Cultures: Placing Habermas in the Nineteenth Century," in *Habermas and the Public Sphere*, 289–339.

51. Felski, *Beyond Feminist Aesthetics*, 67–68.

52. "Thomas Holt, "Mapping the Black Public Sphere," in *The Black Public Sphere*, 325–28.

53. Lisa McLaughlin, "Feminism, the Public Sphere, Media and Democracy," *Media, Culture & Society*, vol. 15, no. 4 (1993): 599–620.

NOTES TO THE FEMINIST SUBJECT OF RAPE

1. Elisabeth Bumiller, "Deny Rape or Be Hated: Kosovo Victims' Choice," *New York Times*, June 22, 1999.

2. Associated Press Report, "Woman in Jeans Cannot Be Raped," February 11, 1999.

3. When I introduced this news item for discussion in one of my classes, I was surprised to hear a number of my female students concur with the judge's ruling. It must be noted that most media coverage of this case was disdainful of the seemingly atavistic ruling.

4. As I discuss later in this chapter, Catharine MacKinnon and Andrea Dworkin are most commonly associated with presenting all heterosexual intercourse as nonconsensual. They arrive at this position through a careful consideration of the options for refusal and nonconsent available to women in a patriarchal society; rape is paradigmatic of all sexual relations, they argue. Critics of the feminist movement negate these nuances, however, when they point out that it comprises women who would like to label all heterosexual sex as rape. For instance, see Norman Podhoretz, "Rape in Feminist Eyes," *Commentary*, vol. 92, no. 4 (October 1991): 29–35.

5. See Margaret Gordon and Stephanie Riger, *The Female Fear: The Social Cost of Rape* (Urbana: University of Illinois Press, 1991); Suzanne Sunday and Ethel Tobach, eds., *Violence against Women: A Critique of the Sociobiology of Rape* (New York: Gordian Press, 1985).

6. National Victim Center and Crime Victims Research and Treatment Center, *Rape in America: A Report to the Nation* (Arlington, Va.: National Victim Center, 1992).

7. There are numerous regional differences in these statistics. As early as 1974, Diana Russell pointed out that over 46 percent of women in the San Francisco area will be raped in their lifetime. Similarly, Mary Koss and others revealed that over 38 percent of college female students experience sexual assault. See Diana Russell, *The Politics of Rape: The Victim's Perspective* (New York: Stein and Day, 1974); Mary Koss et al., "The Scope of Rape," *Journal of Consulting and Clinical Psychology* 55 (1987): 162–70; Allan Johnson, "On the Prevalence of Rape in the United States," *Signs*, vol. 6, no. 1 (1980): 136–46.

8. The Uniform Crime Report is compiled from data gathered in over 16,000 law enforcement agencies.

9. The National Crime Victim Survey is administered by the Bureau of the Census for the Bureau of Justice. According to the Bureau of Justice National Crime Survey, this

figure rose to 307,000 in 1996. Although the Uniform Crime Report and the National Crime Victim Survey provide more contemporary statistics, I have listed only those obtained in 1991 to maintain uniformity with the figures uncovered by the *Rape in America* survey. For more current estimates, see http://www.ojp.usdoj.gov/bjs/cvict_c.htm.

10. Norman Bryson, "Two Narratives of Rape in the Visual Arts: Lucretia and the Sabine Women," in *Rape*, edited by Sylvana Tomaselli and Roy Porter (London: Basil Blackwell, 1986), 152–73. For an overview of the dominant strands of rape theories, see Julie Allison and Mark Wrightsman, *Rape: The Misunderstood Crime* (Newbury Park, Calif.: Sage, 1993); Linda Bourque, *Defining Rape* (Durham, N.C.: Duke University Press, 1989); Lee Ellis, *Theories of Rape: Inquiries into the Causes of Sexual Aggression* (New York: Hemisphere, 1989).

11. Mieke Bal, *Lethal Love: Feminist Literary Readings of Biblical Love Stories* (Bloomington: Indiana University Press, 1987).

12. There is a vast and contested body of work that tries to pin down the contours of feminist epistemology. For instance, see Margrit Eichler, "Feminist Methodology," *Current Sociology*, vol. 45, no. 2 (1997): 9–36; Sandra Harding, "Is There a Feminist Method?" in *Feminism and Methodology* (Bloomington: Indiana University Press, 1987), 1–14; Maria Mies, "Women's Research or Feminist Research? The Debate Surrounding Feminist Science and Research" in *Beyond Methodology*, edited by Judith Cook and Margaret Fonow (Bloomington: Indiana University Press, 1991), 60–84.

13. I use the term *women of color* to refer to African-American, Chicana, Latina, Native American, and Asian-American women. The most sustained criticism of the anti-rape movement and feminism in general has been produced by black feminists, and I mark this specificity by referring to them individually rather than using the women of color label.

14. The London Rape Crisis Centre, *Sexual Violence: The Reality for Women* (London: Women's Press, 1984), x.

15. Catharine MacKinnon, *Toward a Feminist Theory of the State* (Cambridge, Mass.: Harvard University Press, 1989).

16. Susan Griffin, "Rape: The All-American Crime," *Ramparts*. vol. 10, no. 3 (1971): 26–35.

17. Andra Medea and Kathleen Thompson, *Against Rape* (New York: Farrar, Straus and Giroux, 1974); Russell, *The Politics of Rape*.

18. Medea and Thompson, *Against Rape*, 11.

19. See Barbara Sichtermann, "Rape and Sexuality: Essay on a Borderline," in *Femininity, The Politics of the Personal*, translated by John Whitlam (Minneapolis: University of Minnesota Press, 1986), 32–40.

20. Peggy Reeves Sanday, "Rape and the Silencing of the Feminine," in *Rape*, 84–101; Gordon and Riger, *The Female Fear*.

21. Medea and Thompson, *Against Rape*, 145.

22. Lorenne Clark and Debra Lewis developed a sophisticated Marxist reading of rape within capitalist societies. They assert that women and female sexuality have been treated as property. Rape, therefore, is perceived as the violation not of women but of male property. See *Rape: The Price of Coercive Sexuality* (Toronto: Women's Press, 1977).

23. Susan Brownmiller, *Against Our Will: Men, Women and Rape* (New York: Bantam, 1976), 315.

24. Tomaselli, "Introduction," in *Rape*, 1–15. See Hazel Carby, "'On the Threshold of the Woman's Era': Lynching, Empire, and Sexuality in Black Feminist Theory," *Critical Inquiry* 12 (1985): 262–77; Jacquelyn Hall, "'The Mind that Burns in Each Body': Women, Rape, and Racial Violence," in *Powers of Desire: The Politics of Sexuality*, edited by Ann Snitow, Chrtistine Stansell, and Sharon Thompson (New York: Monthly Review Press, 1983), 329–49; bell hooks, *Talking Back: Thinking Feminist, Thinking Black* (Boston: South End Press, 1989).

25. See Camille Paglia, *Sex, Art, and American Culture* (New York: Vintage, 1991).

26. Sanday, "Rape and the Silencing of the Feminine," in *Rape*, 84–101. Similarly, the Senate Judiciary Committee, Majority Staff Report, "The Response to Rape: Detours on the Road to Equal Justice" (Washington: U.S.G.P.O., May 1993), found that the United States has the highest rape rate among industrialized nations; Britain's rate is thirteen times lower, Germany's four times, and Japan's twenty times.

27. Susan Estrich, *Real Rape* (Cambridge, Mass.: Harvard University Press, 1987); see also Gordon and Riger, *The Female Fear*.

28. Peggy Reeves Sanday traces acquaintance rape in the United States since the seventeenth century, marking the changing sociocultural attitudes toward sexual violence and female sexuality. See *A Woman Scorned: Acquaintance Rape on Trial* (New York: Doubleday, 1996).

29. Nancy Gibbs believes that headline writers coined the term *date rape*, suggesting "an ugly ending to a raucous night on the town." See Nancy Gibbs, "When Is It Rape?" *Time* (June 3, 1991): 48–54. Also see Sue Lees, "Media Reporting of Rape: The 1993 British 'Date Rape' Controversy," in *Crime and the Media: The Post-Modern Spectacle*, edited by David Kidd-Hewitt and Richard Osborne (East Haven, Conn.: Pluto Press, 1995), 107–30.

30. Mary Koss, "Stranger and Acquaintance Rape," *Psychology of Women Quarterly* 12 (1988): 1–24.

31. See Diana Russell, *Rape in Marriage*, rev. ed. (Bloomington: Indiana University Press, 1990); Robin Warshaw, *I Never Called It Rape: The Ms. Report on Recognizing, Fighting, and Surviving Date and Acquaintance Rape* (New York: Harper & Row, 1988); Mary Koss et al., "The Scope of Rape," *Journal of Consulting and Clinical Psychology* 55 (1987): 162–70; Vikki Bell, *Interrogating Incest: Feminism, Foucault, and the Law* (New York: Routledge, 1993).

32. Pauline Bart and Patricia O'Brien, *Stopping Rape: Successful Survival Strategies* (New York: Pergamon, 1985); William Sanders, *Rape and Woman's Identity* (Beverly Hills, Calif.: Sage, 1980).

33. As scholarly interest in this topic grew, a number of sociological and psycholog-ical studies were undertaken to identify characteristics of rape victims and rapists. See Philip Belcastro, "A Comparison of Latent Sexual Behavior Patterns between Raped and Never-Raped Females," *Victimology* 7 (1982): 224–30; Rosalind Hall and Patrick Flan-nery, "Prevalence and Correlates of Sexual Assault Experiences in Adolescents," *Victimol-ogy* 9 (1984): 398–406; Gary LaFree, "The Effect of Sexual Stratification by Race on Offi-cial Reactions to Rape," *American Sociological Review* 45 (1980): 842–54.

34. The anti-rape literature refers to cultural stereotypes and popular perceptions as myths. This is significantly different from the ways in which the term *myth* is used in anthropology, where it signifies stories that address those problematic aspects of human experience that resist rational exploration. Myths explore and express the complexity of cultural norms, values, and preoccupations.

35. Menachem Amir, *Patterns in Forcible Rape* (Chicago: University of Chicago Press, 1971), 44.

36. According to a 1991 *Time* magazine survey of junior high school students, 20 percent believed that if a man spent a lot of money on a date, he had the right to sexual intercourse with the woman; 61 percent believed that if the couple had had a sexual rela-tionship previously, the man had a right to intercourse at any subsequent date. See *Time* (June 3, 1991): 51.

37. Since the 1970s, activists from the anti-rape movement worked actively with the police to ensure that law enforcement agencies were more sensitive in recording com-plaints of sexual violence.

38. See Susan Griffin, *Rape, The Politics of Consciousness*, 3d ed. (San Francisco: Harper & Row, 1985); Estrich, *Real Rape*.

39. In rape cases, the state is the prosecutor, not the individual victim. According to Gregory Matoesian, if a complaint is to result in a trial, the police must formally accept the complaint and investigate it. The police could declare a rape as unfounded for any one of the following reasons: if the report is filed late, lack of physical evidence, if the woman refuses to submit to a medical examination, if the victim refuses to prosecute, if the police fail to apprehend the accused, if there is evidence of a prior relationship between the woman and the offender, or if the police make unfavorable judgments about the woman's character. See Gregory Matoesian, *Reproducing Rape: Domination through Talk in the Courtroom* (Chicago: University of Chicago Press, 1993).

40. Lisa Cuklanz offers a very useful time line charting the highlights of rape law reform efforts. See *Rape on Prime Time: Television, Masculinity, and Sexual Violence* (Philadelphia: University of Pennsylvania Press, 2000).

41. Susan Estrich cautions that these legal reforms do not translate very well in the courtroom. The woman is still put on trial, she insists. See Susan Estrich, "Palm Beach Stories," *Law and Philosophy* 11 (1992): 5–34.

42. In 1993, marital rape became a crime in all fifty states, including the District of Columbia. In seventeen states and the District of Columbia, there are no exemptions from rape prosecution granted to husbands. However, in thirty-three states, there are exemp-

tions given to husbands from rape prosecution. For more details on these laws, see *http://www.vaw. umn.edu/\/awnet/mrape.htm*. Diana Russell, *Rape in Marriage*, documents the silence that surrounds the topic of spousal rape as well as some troubling discrepancies in legal definitions. For instance, in some jurisdictions if the accused is less than eighteen years old, he cannot be charged with rape, yet the age of consent for girls is lower.

43. Linda Fairstein, *Sexual Violence: Our War against Rape* (New York: William Morrow and Co., 1993); Alice Vachss, *Sex Crimes: Ten Years on the Front Lines Prosecuting Rapists and Confronting Their Collaborators* (New York: Random House, 1993).

44. Sue Lees, "Media Reporting of Rape," in *Crime and the Media*, 109.

45. Roy Porter, "Rape—Does It Have a Historical Meaning?" in *Rape*, 216–36, 226.

46. Carol Smart, *Feminism and the Power of Law* (New York: Routledge, 1989), 99.

47. Matoesian, *Reproducing Rape*; Zsuzsanna Adler, *Rape on Trial* (New York: Routledge and Kegan Paul, 1987).

48. Andrew Taslitz, *Rape and the Culture of the Courtroom* (New York: New York University Press, 1999), 9.

49. For a nuanced outline of the various legal reforms, see Estrich, "Palm Beach Stories," *Law and Philosophy* 11 (1992), 5–34. She points out specifically how defense teams have managed to get around rape shield laws to discredit a woman's account.

50. Catharine MacKinnon, "Rape: On Coercion and Consent," in *Writing on the Body: Female Embodiment and Feminist Theory*, edited by Katie Conboy, Nadia Medina, and Sarah Stanbury (New York: Columbia University Press, 1997), 42–58, 50.

51. Similarly, Carole Pateman has pointed out that, "Consent as ideology cannot be distinguished from habitual acquiescence, assent, silent dissension, or even enforced submission. Unless refusal of consent or withdrawal of consent are real possibilities, we can no longer speak of consent in any genuine sense." See her *The Disorder of Women* (Stanford, Calif.: Stanford University Press, 1989).

52. See Sandra Harding, *The Science Question in Feminism* (Ithaca, N.Y.: Cornell University Press, 1986); Joan Cocks, *The Oppositional Imagination: Feminism, Critique, and Political Theory* (New York: Routledge, 1989).

53. Keith Burgess-Jackson, "A Theory of Rape," in *A Most Detestable Crime: New Philosophical Essays on Rape* (New York: Oxford University Press, 1999), 92–117, 94.

54. Katie Roiphe, *The Morning After: Sex, Fear, and Feminism* (Boston: Little Brown, 1994); Christina Hoff Sommers, *Who Stole Feminism? How Women Have Betrayed Women* (New York: Simon and Schuster, 1994).

55. Naomi Wolf, *Fire With Fire: The New Female Power and How It Will Change the Twenty-First Century* (New York: Random House, 1993), 147.

56. Sharon Lamb, ed., *New Versions of Victims: Feminists Struggle with the Concept* (New York: New York University Press, 1999).

57. Chris Atmore, "Brand News: Rape and the Mass Media," *Media Information Australia* 72 (May 1994): 20–31.

58. Lesbian and queer theorists have, along with women of color, intervened and interrupted a feminist discourse that was anchored to the single axis of gender as difference. These marginalized voices have offered a feminist critique of feminism.

59. Abdul R. JanMohamed defines racialized sexuality as "the site where discourses of race and sexuality intersect." It exists where "the virtual powerlessness of certain subjects intersects with the massive prohibitive power of various state and civil apparatuses, power that . . . is always underwritten by the actual or potential use of massive coercive violence." See "Discourses On/Of the Racial Border: Foucault, Wright, and the Articulation of Racialized Sexuality," in *Discourses of Sexuality: From Aristotle to AIDS*, edited by Domna Stanton (Ann Arbor: University of Michigan Press, 1992), 94–116.

60. Elizabeth Pleck, *Rape and the Politics of Race, 1865–1910* (Wellesley, Mass.: Wellesley College, Center for Research on Women, 1990).

61. Hall, "The Mind That Burns in Each Body," in *Powers of Desire*, 332; Michele Wallace, *Black Macho and the Myth of the Superwoman* (New York: Dial Press, 1978).

62. See Harriet Jacobs, "The Perils of a Slave Woman's Life," in *Invented Lives: Narratives of Black Women, 1864–1960*, edited by Mary Helen Washington (Garden City, N.Y.: Doubleday, 1987); Alice Walker, *The Color Purple* (New York: Washington Square Press, 1982); Toni Morrison, *The Bluest Eye* (New York: Washington Square Press, 1970).

63. Sander Gilman, "Black Bodies, White Bodies: Toward an Iconography of Female Sexuality in the Late Nineteenth Century," *Critical Inquiry*, vol. 12, no. 1 (1985): 204–42.

64. For a more nuanced account of the representations of the black male rapist myth in popular culture, see Donald Bogle, *Toms, Coons, Mulattoes, Mammies, and Bucks: An Interpretive History of Blacks in American Films*, rev. ed. (New York: Continuum, 1989).

65. Pleck, *Rape and the Politics of Race*, 2.

66. During his run for the 1988 presidential election campaign, Vice President George Bush tapped into this racialized stereotype. An advertisement endorsing his candidacy invoked the image of the black rapist to disparage his opponent's position on crime. The Republican Party ran a series of national advertisements that came to be known as the Willie Horton commercials. William Horton, a murderer serving a life sentence, was permitted a furlough under a Massachusetts prison program. While on release, he raped a white woman and stabbed her and her fiancé. The campaign commercials blamed the Democratic candidate for Horton's furlough but did not show the prisoner's face or reveal his race. However, state television advertising and flyers mailed to voters used Horton's photograph, making clear that he was black. During the 1988 election, Horton symbolized the purported menace from violent black crime and the advertisements are credited with securing Bush's electoral success.

67. Angela Davis, "Rape, Racism, and the Capitalist Setting," *Black Scholar*, vol. 9, no. 7 (1978): 24–30.

68. Micaela di Leonardo, "Racial Fairy Tales," *Nation*, vol. 253, no. 20 (December 9, 1991): 752–54, 753.

69. The National Association for the Advancement of Colored People (NAACP) conducted a study revealing that between 1889 and 1918, less than one in five victims had been accused of rape. See *Thirty Years of Lynching in the United States, 1889–1918* (New York: Arno Press, 1970).

70. Helen Benedict, *Virgin or Vamp: How the Press Covers Sex Crimes* (New York: Oxford University Press, 1992), 27.

71. Black feminists, such as Angela Davis, Susan Edwards, and Kimberlé Crenshaw, have criticized sharply Brownmiller's account of the cases. They argue that she privileges gender-based oppression over race-based discrimination. Bat-Ami Bar On outlines these arguments and reveals the stakes in asserting the primacy of gender or race as the central category for the analysis of rape. See "The 'Scottsboro Case': On Responsibility, Rape, Race, Gender, and Class," in *A Most Detestable Crime*, 200–10.

72. Brownmiller contends that the anti-lynching efforts mobilized outside of the black community gained support primarily by presenting the Southern white woman as hysterical, frigid, and masochistic. See Brownmiller, *Against Our Will.*

73. Paula Giddings, *When and Where I Enter: The Impact of Black Women on Race and Sex in America* (New York: W. Morrow, 1984); Sara Evans, *Personal Politics: The Roots of Women's Liberation in the Civil Rights Movement and the New Left* (New York: Knopf, 1979).

74. Patricia Hill Collins, *Black Feminist Thought: Knowledge, Consciousness, and the Politics of Empowerment* (New York: Routledge, 1991).

75. New York Radical Feminists Newsletter (October 1974): 243–45.

76. Michele Wallace develops this idea and reveals the devastating impact of this belief. See her *Black Macho and the Myth of the Superwoman.*

77. W. J. Musa Moore-Foster, "Up from Brutality: Freeing Black Communities from Sexual Violence," in *Transforming a Rape Culture*, edited by Emilie Buchwald, Pamela Fletcher, and Martha Roth (Minneapolis: Milkweed, 1993), 419–26.

78. Medea and Thompson, *Against Rape*, 145.

79. See Jane Flax, *Thinking Fragments: Psychoanalysis, Feminism, and Postmodernism in the Contemporary West* (Berkeley: University of California Press, 1990), 175.

80. Angela Davis, *Violence against Women and the Ongoing Challenge to Racism* (Latham, N.Y.: Kitchen Table, 1985), 9.

81. Kimberlé Crenshaw, "Color-Blind Dreams and Racial Nightmares: Reconfiguring Racism in the Post–Civil Rights Era," in *Birth of a Nation'hood: Gaze, Script, and Spectacle in the O.J. Simpson Case*, edited by Toni Morrison and Claudia Lacour (New York: Pantheon, 1997), 97–168; June Jordan, "Requiem for a Champ," *Progressive*, vol. 56, no. 4 (1992): 15–16; Hurtado, *The Color of Privilege.*

82. Kimberlé Crenshaw, "Beyond Racism and Misogyny: Black Feminism and 2 Live Crew," in *Feminist Social Thought*, edited by Diana Meyers (New York: Routledge, 1997), 246–63, 247.

83. Nadya Burton, "Resistance to Prevention: Reconsidering Feminist Antiviolence Rhetoric," in *Violence against Women: Philosophical Perspectives*, edited by Stanley French, Wanda Teays, and Laura Purdy (Ithaca, N.Y.: Cornell University Press, 1998), 182–200, 185.

84. Susan Friedman uses this phrase to describe feminist discussions of gender and race. She argues that they tend to get caught in various iterations of the white/other binary, recapitulating instead of moving through and beyond ignorance, anger, guilt, and silence. See *Mappings: Feminism and the Cultural Geographies of Encounter* (Princeton, N.J.: Princeton University Press, 1998).

85. Foucault, *The History of Sexuality*, vol. 1, 81.

86. Caroline Ramazanoglu, *Up against Foucault: Explorations of Some Tensions Between Foucault and Feminism* (New York: Routledge, 1993), 11–12.

87. Foucault, *The History of Sexuality*, vol. 1, 100–101.

88. For instance, Machiavelli, in *The Discourses*, has a chapter entitled, "How Women Have Brought the Downfall of States," where he discusses the significance of rape in the matter of government and the political danger it constitutes. Quoted in Tomaselli and Porter, eds., *Rape*, 3.

89. Anna Clark, *Women's Silence, Men's Violence: Sexual Assault in England, 1770–1845* (New York: Pandora, 1987), 3.

90. Vikki Bell believes that "a concern with women's oppression barely flickers in the vast majority" of Foucault's writing, yet he is of interest to feminist scholars because of the topics of his work. See her *Interrogating Incest*, 4. Also see, Monique Plaza, "Our Damages and Their Compensation," *Feminist Issues*, vol. 1, no. 3 (1981): 23–35; Vikki Bell, "Beyond the Thorny Question," *International Journal of the Sociology of Law* 19 (1991): 83–100; Linda Martin Alcoff, "Dangerous Pleasures: Foucault and the Politics of Pedophilia," in *Feminist Interpretations of Michel Foucault*, edited by Susan Hekman (University Park: Pennsylvania State University Press, 1996).

91. Catharine MacKinnon, *Feminism Unmodified: Discourses on Life and Law* (Cambridge, Mass.: Harvard University Press, 1987), 86.

92. See Susan Hekman, ed., *Feminist Interpretations of Michel Foucault*; Ramazanoglu, *Up against Foucault*; Bell, *Interrogating Incest*; Irene Diamond and Lee Quinby, *Feminism and Foucault: Reflections on Resistance* (Boston: Northeastern University Press, 1988).

93. See Robert Young, "Foucault on Race and Colonialism," *New Formations* 25 (1995): 57–65; JanMohamed, "Sex On/Of the Racial Border," in *Discourses of Sexuality*, 94–116; Gayatri Spivak, "Can the Subaltern Speak?" in *Marxism and the Interpretation of Culture*, edited by Cary Nelson and Lawrence Grossberg (Urbana: University of Illinois Press, 1988), 271–313; Ann Laura Stoler, *Race and the Education of Desire: Foucault's History of Sexuality and the Colonial Order of Things* (Durham, N.C.: Duke University Press, 1995).

94. The Enlightenment characterizes a shift in European thought from the eighteenth century. During this period, the notion of reason being superior to other modes of

thought became dominant, along with a belief in the progress of humanity and the superiority of scientific method as a means of discovering the truth. Although these thoughts have been contested on many counts, they have remained powerful in affecting commonsense assumptions about what is true, how we discover the truth, and the superiority of reason over emotion, objective over subjective, and mind over body.

95. Susan Hekman, "Introduction," in *Feminist Interpretations of Michel Foucault*, 1–11.

96. Friedman, *Mappings*.

97. Michel Foucault, *Language, Counter-Memory, Practice*, edited by Donald Bouchard and translated by Donald Bouchard and Sherry Simon (Ithaca, N.Y.: Cornell University Press, 1977), 185.

98. Amy Farrell, "Feminism and the Media," *Signs*, vol. 20, no. 3 (1995): 642–45, 643.

99. Ibid.

100. Wendy Kozol, "Fracturing Domesticity: Media, Nationalism, and the Question of Feminist Influence," *Signs*, vol. 20, no. 3 (1995): 646–67.

101. Lauren Berlant, "The Female Complaint," *Social Text* 19/20 (1988): 237–57.

NOTES TO THE RIGHT OF SIGHT IS WHITE

1. Peggy Reeves Sanday has examined this case at some length in *A Woman Scorned* (New York: Doubleday, 1996).

2. Jonathan Markovitz, "Collective Memory, Credibility Structures, and the Case of Tawana Brawley," *Discourse*, vol. 22, no. 1 (2000): 31–52.

3. Within media studies, Stuart Hall's theory of the encoding and decoding process has been central in this formulation. See "The Encoding/Decoding Model in Television Discourses," in *Culture, Media, Language: Working Papers in Cultural Studies, 1972–79*, edited by Stuart Hall et al. (London: Hutchinson, 1980), 128–38. The concept of situated knowledge has been deployed by critical thinkers across various disciplines, but it is most commonly associated with Donna Haraway's work and other feminist theorizing. See "Situated Knowledges: The Science Question in Feminism and the Privilege of Partial Perspective," *Feminist Studies*, vol. 14, no. 3 (1988): 575–600.

4. Helán Page, "'Black Male' Imagery and Media Containment of African American Men," *American Anthropologist*, vol. 99, no. 1 (1997): 99–111; Wendy Kozol, "Fracturing Domesticity," *Signs*, vol. 20, no. 3 (1995): 646–67; Helen Benedict, "Blindfolded: Rape and the Press's Fear of Feminism," in *Feminism, Media, and the Law*, edited by Martha Fineman and Martha McCluskey (New York: Oxford University Press, 1997), 267–72.

5. Numerous ethnographic studies and organizational information reveal that newsrooms are no longer a male domain. Women are represented at various levels there. My use of the phrase "masculine gaze" includes these female news workers.

6. Ruth Frankenberg, *White Women, Race Matters: The Social Construction of Whiteness* (Minneapolis: University of Minnesota Press, 1993); John Fiske, *Media Matters*, rev. ed. (Minneapolis: University of Minnesota Press, 1996); David Roediger, "White Looks: Hairy Apes, True Stories, and Limbaugh's Laughs," in *Whiteness*, 35–46.

7. Hazel Carby, "Multicultural Wars," in *Black Popular Culture*, edited by Gina Dent (Seattle: Bay Press, 1992), 187–99; George Lipsitz, *The Possessive Investment in Whiteness: How White People Profit From Identity Politics* (Philadelphia: Temple University Press, 1998).

8. Fiske, *Media Matters*, 42.

9. Mary Louise Pratt, *Imperial Eyes: Travel Writing and Transculturation* (New York: Routledge, 1992).

10. See Henry Louis Gates, "Preface," in *Black Male: Representations of Masculinity in Contemporary American Art*, edited by Thelma Golden (New York: Whitney Museum of American Art, 1994), 11–14.

11. Sandra Gunning adds that the threat of interracial rape functions as a "multilayered metaphor to structure and articulate the latent anxieties over black and white self-construction in terms of gender, class, and citizenship roles." See her *Race, Rape, and Lynching: The Red Record of American Literature, 1890–1912* (New York: Oxford University Press, 1996).

12. Stuart Hall, "New Ethnicities," in *"Race," Culture, and Difference*, edited by James Donald and Ali Rattansi (Newbury Park, Calif.: Sage, 1992), 252–59, 255.

13. Nancy Fraser, "Sex, Lies, and the Public Sphere," in *Critical Inquiry*, 597.

14. Benedict, "Blindfolded," in *Feminism, Media, and the Law*, 267–72; Jack Katz, "What Makes Crime 'News'?" *Media, Culture & Society* 9 (1987): 47–75.

15. See Daniel Linz, Edward Doonerstein, and Steven Adams, "Psychological Desensitization and Judgments about Female Victims of Violence," *Human Communication Research*, vol. 15, no. 4 (1989): 509–22; David Phillips and John Hensley, "When Violence Is Rewarded or Punished," *Journal of Communication*, vol. 34, no. 3 (1984): 101–16.

16. Helen Benedict, *Virgin or Vamp*; Marian Meyers, "Good Girls, Bad Girls, and TV News," in *News Coverage of Violence against Women: Engendering Blame* (Thousand Oaks, Calif.: Sage, 1997), 52–69.

17. Lisa Cuklanz, *Rape on Trial: How the Mass Media Construct Legal Reform and Social Change* (Philadelphia: University of Pennsylvania Press, 1996).

18. Sylvia Walby, Alex Hays, and Keith Soothill, "The Social Construction of Rape," *Theory, Culture and Society*, vol. 2, no. 1 (1983): 86–98; Keith Soothill and Sylvia Walby, *Sex Crime in the News* (New York: Routledge, 1991).

19. Leon Higginbotham, "The Hill-Thomas Hearings—What Took Place and What Happened: White Male Domination, Black Male Domination, and the Denigration of Black Women," in *Race, Gender, and Power in America: The Legacy of the Hill-Thomas Hearings*, edited by Anita Hill and Emma Jordan (New York: Oxford University Press, 1995), 26–36.

20. Chris Grover and Keith Soothill find similar stereotypical portraits in British press coverage of interracial rapes. See their "Ethnicity, the Search for Rapists and the Press," *Ethnic and Racial Studies*, vol. 19, no. 3 (1996): 567–84; Michael Awkward, "Representing Rape: On Spike, Iron Mike, and the 'Desire Dynamic'," in *Negotiating Difference: Race, Gender, and the Politics of Positionality* (Chicago: University of Chicago Press, 1995), 95–135; Jack Lule, "The Rape of Mike Tyson: Race, the Press and Symbolic Types," *Critical Studies in Mass Communication*, vol. 12, no. 2 (1995): 176–95.

21. George Cunningham, "Body Politics: Race, Gender, and the Captive Body," in *Representing Black Men*, edited by Marcellus Blount and George Cunningham (New York: Routledge, 1996), 131–54.

22. Evelynn Hammonds, "Toward a Genealogy of Black Female Sexuality: The Problematic of Silence," in *Feminist Genealogies, Colonial Legacies, Democratic Futures*, edited by Jacqui Alexander and Chandra Talpade Mohanty (New York: Routledge, 1997), 170–82.

23. Medea and Thompson, *Against Rape*, 36.

24. In New York State, juveniles are not accorded anonymity.

25. In a study of local television news, Robert Entman points out that accused black criminals are depicted as particularly threatening. In television news, they are "usually illustrated by glowering mug shots or by footage of them being led around in handcuffs," unlike the majority of accused white criminals. See Robert Entman, "Modern Racism and the Images of Blacks in Local Television News," *Critical Studies in Mass Communication* 7 (1990): 332–45.

26. See Edward Diamond, "Anatomy of a Horror," *New York*, vol. 22, no. 22 (May 15, 1989): 41–45, for a detailed description of the various crimes the teenagers were believed to have perpetrated.

27. *ABC World News Tonight*, April 24, 1989; *NBC Nightly News*, April 24, 1989.

28. Benedict, *Virgin or Vamp*, 203.

29. Helán Page, "'Black Male' Imagery and Media Containment of African-American Men," in *American Anthropologist*, 99–111.

30. *ABC World News Tonight*, April 24, 1989; *CBS Evening News*, April 24, 1989.

31. According to *Village Voice* reporter Barry Cooper, wilding was "used to broadstroke young Aframerican males as subhumans who rape, pillage, and throw themselves into urban bacchanalia." See Barry Cooper, "Cruel and the Gang," *Village Voice* (May 9, 1989): 27–38.

32. *ABC World News Tonight*, April 24, 1989.

33. Stuart Hall, "The Whites of Their Eyes," in *The Media Reader*, 7–23, 13.

34. Paul Gilroy, *Problems in Anti-Racist Strategy* (London: Runnymede Trust, 1987), 5.

35. Initially, the local media presented the accused teenagers as "normal" children, and their participation in the brutal gang rape seemed inexplicable. Later, though, the media discovered that some of them were neighborhood bullies and thus these teenagers

were portrayed as archetypal, inner-city youth with a history of malfeasance. Only alternative newspapers such as the *Village Voice* pointed out that the accused teenagers may have participated in acts of vandalism. They also participated in everyday activities, such as playing in the school band. Similarly, only the alternative press pointed out that there was little evidence linking the accused teenagers to the rape, and that the videotaped confessions, which were central to the prosecution, were obtained irregularly. Writing in the *Village Voice* about the controversy surrounding the teenagers' confessions, Rick Hornung pointed out that some police officers had "admitted in pretrial hearings that they failed to inform at least three defendants of the Fifth Amendment right to remain silent and [the] Sixth Amendment right to consult a lawyer." See Rick Hornung, "The Central Park Rape," *Village Voice* (February 20, 1990): 30–36.

36. George Cunningham believes that this trend is paradigmatic. See his "Body Politics," in *Representing Black Men*, 131–54.

37. Syndicated columnist and television host Patrick Buchanan is quoted by Edwin Diamond as offering the following solution to such violence. If the oldest member was "tried, convicted, and hanged in Central Park by June 1 . . . the park might soon be safe again for women." See Edwin Diamond, "Anatomy of a Horror," *New York*, vol. 22, no. 22 (May 15, 1989): 41–45.

38. As sociologist Jane Hood wrote in the *New York Times*, "Americans see everything but gender at work in the April 19 assault. . . . Given more than 30 years of research on rape, our myopia is hard to explain. . . . To get to the root of this particular brand of violence, we need to [go] beyond race and class to look at gender relations in the United States." See Jane Hood, "Why Our Society Is Rape-Prone," *New York Times*, May 16, 1989. Similarly, an editorial in the *Nation* pointed out that rather than focus on racial tensions and class antagonism, "any understanding of what happened in Central Park must begin with the wider problem of violence against women." See "The Rape in Central Park," *Nation*, vol. 242, no. 21 (May 29, 1989): 721.

39. Benedict, *Virgin or Vamp*, 194.

40. A year after they first started to report the story, a network news report listed the names of the three teenagers on trial. Until that moment, the accused teenagers were nameless. *CBS Evening News*, July 23, 1990.

41. *CBS Evening News*, September 11, 1990; *ABC World News Tonight*, September 11, 1990. These reports ignored African-American criticisms of the unusually harsh sentences meted out to nonwhite criminals.

42. For a detailed analysis of the issues at stake in this case, see Timothy Sullivan, *Unequal Verdicts: The Central Park Jogger Trials* (New York: Simon and Schuster, 1992).

43. Sanday, *A Woman Scorned*, 1–49.

44. Marcia Ann Gillespie draws attention to feminists' silence over this case. See "A Crime of Race *and* Sex," *Ms.* 16 (April 1988): 18–19. For a description of media coverage of the case, see Edwin Diamond, "The Selling of Tawana," *New York* (May 30, 1988): 22–25. Also see his "The Brawley Fiasco," *New York* (July 18, 1988): 21ff.

45. Charlotte Pierce-Barker and Valerie Smith each document the effects of such silences. See Charlotte Pierce Barker, *Surviving the Silence: Black Women's Stories of Rape* (New York: Norton, 1998) and Valerie Smith, "Split Affinities: Representing Interracial Rape," in *Not Just Race, Not Just Gender: Black Feminist Readings* (New York: Routledge, 1998), 1–32.

46. I am using the accusers' names in this and the Tyson case, because the media had revealed their names during the coverage, and after the trials, both women provided their version of events in televised interviews.

47. Courtroom Television Network premiered in July 1991, and this was among one of the first cases it covered. See Elayne Rapping, "Gavel-to-Gavel Coverage," *Progressive*, vol. 56, no. 3 (March 1992): 34–37.

48. Cuklanz, *Rape on Trial*, 37.

49. This includes four *Nightline* specials on the case. A substantial amount of network coverage functioned to construct what Marjorie Garber and others have called a media spectacle of "real" politics and "real" life, which is made spectacular by the media themselves as they report on their own coverage as much as on the event itself. See Marjorie Garber, Jann Matlock, and Rebecca Walkowitz, eds., *Media Spectacles* (New York: Routledge, 1993).

50. Gibbs, "When Is It Rape?" *Time*, 48–54.

51. An editorial in the *New York Post* highlights this tendency. It declared, "If the sexual encounter, *forced or not*, has been preceded by a series of consensual activities—drinking, a trip to the man's home, a walk on a deserted beach at 3 in the morning—the charge that's leveled against the alleged offender should, it seems to us, be different from the one filed against, say the youths who raped and beat the jogger" (emphasis in original).

52. *CBS Evening News*, December 1, 1991.

53. Williams, *Television*, 78–118. Also see Stephen Heath and Gillian Skirrow, "An Interview with Raymond Williams," in *Studies in Entertainment: Critical Approaches to Mass Culture*, edited by Tania Modleski (Bloomington: Indiana University Press, 1986), 3–17.

54. Tania Modleski, "Introduction," in *Studies in Entertainment*, ix–xix, xiv.

55. For a detailed account of the ways in which the flow of texts helps constitute specific discourses, see John Fiske and John Hartley, *Reading Television* (London: Methuen, 1978).

56. *NBC Nightly News*, April 5, 1991.

57. *ABC World News Tonight*, May 10, 1991.

58. *ABC World News Tonight*, April 7, 1991.

59. *CBS Evening News*, May 7, 1991.

60. *ABC World News Tonight*, April 7, 1991.

61. *CBS Evening News*, May 11, 1991.

62. Frankenberg, *White Women, Race Matters*, 1. As Helán Page points out, the "we" is invoked from an unexamined position of whiteness.

63. *CBS Evening News*, May 9, 1991.

64. *Nightline*, April 17, 1991.

65. Nancy Fraser, "Sex, Lies, and the Public Sphere," in *Critical Inquiry*, 595–612.

66. *NBC Nightly News*, April 5, 1991.

67. Sylvia Walby et al., "The Social Construction of Rape," in *Theory, Culture, and Society*, 86–98.

68. Matoesian, *Reproducing Rape*.

69. *Nightline*, November 1, 1991.

70. *ABC World News Tonight*, December 11, 1991.

71. *NBC Nightly News*, December 11, 1991.

72. *NBC Nightly News*, April 16, 1991.

73. Jann Matlock, "Scandals of Naming: The Blue Blob, Identity, and Gender in the William Kennedy Smith case," in *Media Spectacles*, 137–59.

74. *CBS Evening News*, May 11, 1991.

75. Walby et al., "The Social Construction of Rape," in *Theory, Culture, and Society*, 86–98.

76. *NBC Nightly News*, December 5, 1991. All three networks reproduced large segments of the defense attempt to redefine the rape as consensual but violent sex. These extended sound bites reiterate Catharine MacKinnon's argument that women's consent is meaningless in a society saturated by the eroticization of dominance. See her "Rape," in *Writing on the Body*, 42–58.

77. *CBS Evening News*, December 7, 1991.

78. Referring to post-trial talk show appearances, where Smith's lawyers emphasized Bowman's mental instability, Susan Estrich points out the specific ways in which the conduct of rape trials has circumvented some of the reforms initiated by the anti-rape movement. Specifically, she says, defense teams are turning to psychological evidence to prove that the accuser is troubled. This tactic comes into play especially when the woman lacks traditional motives to fabricate: embarrassment over her nonvirginity, or fear of her parents' reactions. See Susan Estrich, "Palm Beach Stories," *Law and Philosophy* 11 (1992): 5–33.

79. Katha Pollitt, "Media Goes Wilding in Palm Beach," *Nation* (June 24, 1991): 833ff.

80. For instance, see Phil Berger, *Blood Season: Tyson and the World of Boxing* (New York: Harper Collins, 1990); Peter Heller, *Bad Intentions: The Mike Tyson Story* (New York: New American Library, 1989); and Montieth Illingworth, *Mike Tyson: Money, Myth, and Betrayal* (Secaucus, N.J.: Carol Publications, 1991).

81. I am once again referring to the accuser by name, only because she revealed her identity at the end of the trial.

82. Richard Corliss, "The Bad and the Beautiful," *Time* (February 24, 1992): 25–26.

83. *Nightline*, February 7, 1992.

84. *CBS Evening News*, February 7, 1992.

85. *Nightline*, February 7, 1992.

86. Judith Mayne, "*L.A. Law* and Prime-Time Feminism," *Discourse*, vol. 10, no. 2 (1988): 30–47.

87. *NBC Nightly News*, February 11, 1992.

88. *Nightline*, February 7, 1992.

89. *NBC Nightly News*, January 26, 1992; *CBS Evening News*, January 27, 1992.

90. Morrison and Lacour, eds., *Birth of a Nation'hood.*

91. Anne duCille, "The Unbearable Darkness of Being: 'Fresh' Thoughts on Race, Sex, and the Simpsons," in *Birth of a Nation'hood*, 293–338.

92. *CBS Evening News*, February 11, 1992.

93. *CBS Evening News*, January 27, 1992.

94. *ABC World News Tonight*, February 8, 1992.

95. Norman Mailer, *The White Negro* (San Francisco: City Lights Books, 1957).

96. *ABC World News Tonight*, February 10, 1992.

97. *CBS Evening News*, March 26, 1992; *Nightline*, February 10, 1992.

98. Lule, "Rape of Mike Tyson," in *Critical Studies in Mass Communication*, 181.

99. Awkward, "Representing Rape," in *Negotiating Difference*, 95–135.

100. Judith Butler, "Endangered/Engendering: Schematic Racism and White Paranoia," in *Reading Rodney King, Reading Urban Uprising*, edited by Robert Gooding-Williams (New York: Routledge, 1993), 15–22, 16.

101. Jeff Benedict points out that Alan Dershowitz used this defense effectively in the appeals process, where six of the jurors recanted their guilty verdict. He argues that this reveals the continuing cultural fear of false accusations and the ease with which women can be cast as incredible victims. See Jeff Benedict, *Athletes and Acquaintance Rape* (Thousand Oaks, Calif.: Sage, 1998). In an article he wrote for *Penthouse*, "The Rape of Mike Tyson," Dershowitz co-opts feminist rhetoric of the rape trial as a second rape to present the boxer as the true victim.

102. It must be noted that defense arguments themselves were structured around stereotypes of black male sexuality.

103. Bogle, *Toms, Coons, Mulattoes, Mammies, and Bucks*, rev. ed.

104. *CBS Evening News*, February 11, 1992. A *Sports Illustrated* cover story on the verdict exemplifies this theme. It describes the boxer as a "single purpose organism, bred

for bad intentions and well maintained for its unique ability to enact violent public spectacle, but entirely unsuited for real life." See Richard Hoffer, "Destined to Fall," *Sports Illustrated* (February 17, 1992): 24–25.

105. *NBC Nightly News*, January 31, 1992.

106. *ABC World News Tonight*, March 26, 1992.

107. *Nightline*, February 7, 1992.

108. *ABC World News Tonight*, February 12, 1992; *CBS Evening News*, February 11, 1992; *NBC Nightly News*, February 11, 1992.

109. *CBS Evening News*, February 11, 1992.

110. *NBC Nightly News*, February 21, 1992.

111. Charles Lawrence contends that the accuser was cast in the role of Miss Anne, a pejorative characterization of an African-American woman who was in a position of power. He argues further that the guilty verdict was inevitable within the master narrative of race, gender, and sexuality that structures American life. It proved that "'good' girls will be protected from the unwanted advances of 'bad' men." See Charles Lawrence, "The Message of the Verdict: A Three-Act Morality Play Starring Clarence Thomas, Willie Smith, and Mike Tyson," in *Race, Gender, and Power in America*, 105–28, 109.

112. Catharine MacKinnon, "Rape," in *Writing on the Body*, 46.

113. *CBS Evening News*, January 27, 1992.

114. *NBC Nightly News*, January 26, 1992.

115. *NBC Nightly News*, February 21, 1992.

116. *CBS Evening News*, February 13, 1992.

117. *Nightline*, February 10, 1992.

118. Lawrence, "The Message of the Verdict," in *Race, Gender and Power in America*, 105.

119. Hammonds, "Toward a Genealogy of Black Female Sexuality," in *Feminist Genealogies, Colonial Legacies, Democratic Futures*, 170–82.

120. Ruth Frankenberg, "Local Whitenesses, Localizing Whiteness," in *Displacing Whiteness: Essays in Social and Cultural Criticism* (Durham, N.C.: Duke University Press, 1997), 1–33, 16.

121. *CBS Evening News*, February 13, 1992.

122. Foucault, *The History of Sexuality*, vol. 1, 83.

123. Stuart Hall uses the metaphor of the articulated lorry to explain this subject: in Britain an articulated lorry refers to a vehicle where the front (cab) and the back (trailer) can, but need not necessarily, be connected to one another. For an elaboration on this concept, see Lawrence Grossberg, "On Postmodernism and Articulation: An Interview with Stuart Hall," *Journal of Communication Inquiry* 10 (1986): 45–60.

124. Kobena Mercer, "Engendered Species: Danny Tisdale and Keith Piper," *Artforum* 30 (1992): 75.

125. Helen Benedict, "When to Blame the Victim—The Media Rules on Rape," *Ms.*, vol. 2, no. 1 (1991): 102–3.

126. Teresa de Lauretis, "Eccentric Subjects: Feminist Theory and Historical Consciousness," *Feminist Studies*, vol. 16, no. 1 (1990): 115–50.

NOTES TO WHITE MEN DO FEMINISM

1. *In the Heat of the Night*, "Rape," aired on August 21, 1989.

2. Todd Gitlin calls this creativity of least imagination "recombinant thinking." He believes that prime-time narratives proliferate from a limited repertoire of basic models. This thinking is a response to institutional pressures for novelty and constancy. See "Prime Time Ideology: The Hegemonic Process in Television Entertainment," in *Television: The Critical View*, 3d ed., edited by Horace Newcomb (New York: Oxford University Press, 1982), 426–55; David Buxton, *From the Avengers to Miami Vice: Form and Ideology in Television Series* (New York: St. Martin's Press, 1990); Cuklanz, *Rape on Prime Time*.

3. Todd Gitlin, "Prime Time Ideology," in *Television*, 426–55; Jane Feuer, *Seeing through the Eighties: Television and Reaganism* (Durham, N.C.: Duke University Press, 1995), reveal the different ways in which prime-time programming papers over contradictions in an effort to solicit the largest viewing audience.

4. According to Robert Deming, viewers have television archives—memories of past programs and surrounding discourses—that frame their interpretations of programming. See "*Kate and Allie*: 'New Women' and the Audience's Television Archives," in *Private Screenings*, 203–16. In the episodes I examine, some story lines go beyond viewers' television archives; they are premised on a familiarity with news events.

5. Under the term *entertainment*, I am examining a range of self-avowed fictional programs. While several different genres exist within prime-time entertainment, together they represent a way of telling a collective story about issues considered important to our common social well-being.

6. John Fiske is primarily associated with theories that emphasize the polysemy of media texts. He has argued that media texts are open to multiple oppositional interpretations that render marginal authorial intention. See his *Television Culture* (New York: Routledge, 1987). Criticizing this theory, Celeste Condit postulates instead that media texts are polyvalent. The meanings of a text are bounded; media texts offer viewers a multiplicitous but structured meaning system. See her "The Rhetorical Limits of Polysemy," *Critical Studies in Mass Communication* 6 (1989): 103–22.

7. At least twenty-seven episodes during the time period of this study mention rape, but I have included only those that center on sexual violence. I have not included shows that deal with child abuse or same-sex rape. A database search since 1968 showed that over

190 episodes dealt with the issue of sexual violence; only a quarter of them made more than a passing mention of rape. All references in this chapter to scripts allude to these documents.

8. David Buxton defines serials as "continuing narratives, usually in a soap opera mode," and the series as "the use of recurring characters in discrete episodes." The majority of the shows I examine combine elements of the series and the serials. See his *From the Avengers to Miami Vice.*

9. In the United States, the police series has integrated formal properties of the soap opera, such as the construction of in-depth personalities for the protagonists and a focus on the continuing dramas of everyday life, only since the early 1980s. This trend was heralded by *Hill Street Blues,* where the dynamics of the workplace family shared equal time with the detection of crime.

10. Carol Deming, "*Hill Street Blues* As Narrative," *Critical Studies in Mass Communication,* vol. 2, no. 1 (1985): 1–22.

11. Jane Feuer, "The MTM Style," in *MTM: Quality Television,* edited by Jane Feuer, Paul Kerr, and Tise Vahimage (London: BFI, 1984), 32–60; Todd Gitlin, "Prime Time Ideology," in *Television,* 426–55.

12. Todd Gitlin, "*Hill Street Blues*: 'Make It Look Messy'," in *Inside Prime Time* (New York: Pantheon, 1983), 273–324, 313.

13. Buxton, *From the Avengers to Miami Vice,* 135.

14. Ibid.

15. Sonia Livingstone, "Watching Talk: Gender and Engagement in the Viewing of Audience Discussion Programmes," *Media, Culture & Society,* vol. 16, no. 3 (1994): 429–47, classifies cop shows as masculine programs. They focus on judgment, abstract principles, and cause and effect, all considered masculine characteristics. John Fiske offers a similar assessment in *Television Culture.* He asserts that the cop show displays male achievement and uses the male as the savior to distract attention from the ideologically problematic role of the male as privileged oppressor.

16. John Brigham, "*L.A. Law,*" in *Prime Time Law: Fictional Television As Legal Narrative,* edited by Robert Jarvis and Paul Joseph (Durham, N.C.: Carolina Academic Press, 1998), 21–32, 32.

17. In the early 1980s, family-centered shows such as *All in the Family* dealt with the issue of sexual violence. In the period examined in this study, prime-time programs about families did not deal with rape.

18. Todd Gitlin points out that NBC's Broadcast Standards guarded against negative portrayals of African Americans and other minorities. Consequently, certain topics were avoided for fear of offending some viewers. See his "*Hill Street Blues,*" 273–324.

19. For an overview, see Julie D'Acci, *Defining Women: Television and the Case of Cagney & Lacey* (Chapel Hill: University of North Carolina Press, 1994); Bonnie Dow, *Prime-Time Feminism: Television, Media Culture, and the Women's Movement since 1970* (Philadelphia: University of Pennsylvania Press, 1996); Susan Douglas, *Where the Girls*

Are: Growing Up Female with the Mass Media (New York: Random House, 1995); Lauren Rabinovitz, "Sitcoms and Single Moms: Representations of Feminism on American TV," *Cinema Journal*, vol. 29, no. 1 (1989): 3–19.

20. According to a *Newsweek* cover story (March 13, 1989), women-centered programs have proliferated as television executives have pursued a female audience for prime time and as women's participation behind the scenes has increased.

21. Serafina Bathrick, "*The Mary Tyler Moore Show*," in *MTM*, 99–131.

22. For a critique of postfeminist representations, see Elspeth Probyn, "New Traditionalism and Post-feminism: TV Does the Home," *Screen*, vol. 31, no. 2 (1990): 147–59; Sarah Projansky, "Working on Feminism" (Ph.D. diss., University of Iowa, 1995).

23. Probyn, "New Traditionalism and Post-feminism," 147–59. Finding an exception to this trend, Elayne Rapping has pointed out that in its first season *Melrose Place* presented women and the relations between the sexes in surprisingly new ways. See "Gender, *Melrose Place*, and the Aaron Spelling Legacy," in *Mediated Women*, 271–85.

24. Claudia Dreifus, "Women in 'Jep'," *TV Guide* (March 14, 1992): 22–25.

25. Barbara Wilson et al., "The Impact of Social Issue Television Programming on Attitudes toward Rape," *Human Communication Research*, vol. 19, no. 2 (1992): 179–208.

26. David Phillips and John Hensley, "When Violence Is Rewarded or Punished: The Impact of Mass Media Stories on Homicide," *Journal of Communication*, vol. 34, no. 3 (1984): 101–16.

27. Naomi Wolf, *The Beauty Myth: How Images of Beauty are Used Against Women* (New York: William Morrow and Co., 1991), 137.

28. Susan Faludi, "Fetal and Fatal Visions: The Backlash in the Movies," in *Backlash: The Undeclared War Against Women* (New York: Crown, 1991), 112–39.

29. Molly Haskell, *From Reverence to Rape: The Treatment of Women in the Movies*, 2d ed. (Chicago: University of Chicago Press, 1987).

30. Tania Modleski, *Feminism without Women: Culture and Criticism in a "Postfeminist" Age* (London: Routledge, 1991).

31. bell hooks, "Selling Hot Pussy: Representations of Black Female Sexuality in the Cultural Marketplace," in *Black Looks: Race and Representation* (Boston: South End Press, 1992), 113–28.

32. Awkward, "Representing Rape," in *Negotiating Difference*, 95–153.

33. Susan Brinson, "TV Rape: Communication of Cultural Attitudes Toward Rape," *Women's Studies in Communication*, vol. 12, no. 2 (1989): 23–36. While praising the "gender equity" underlying the premise of female cops shows such as *Cagney and Lacey*, David Buxton believes that scenarios such as this rape allows the story line to present women in "the crudest sex symbol terms." See his *From the Avengers to Miami Vice*, 159.

34. Cuklanz, *Rape on Trial*.

35. Using FBI data and National Crime Victim Survey rape statistics, Robert Lichter, Linda Lichter, and Stanley Rothman, *Prime Time: How TV Portrays American Culture* (Washington, D.C.: Regnery Publications, 1994), argue that television portrayals are unrealistic. "In the real world forcible rape is usually an opportunistic and violent act. Victim and rapist are almost often unknown to one another, and the rape is a fairly brief assault, which leaves the victim traumatized but alive" (279–80).

36. Judith Mayne, "*L.A. Law* and Prime-Time Feminism," in *Discourse*, 30–47.

37. Sarah Projansky, "Working on Feminism" (Ph.D. diss., University of Iowa, 1995).

38. Lisa Cuklanz, "The Masculine Ideal: Rape on Prime-Time Television, 1976–1978," *Critical Studies in Mass Communication*, vol. 15, no. 4 (1999): 423–48.

39. Walter Benjamin, *The Origin of German Tragic Drama*, translated by John Osborne (London: Verso, 1985).

40. Gayatri Chakravorty Spivak divides allegory into three broad historical periods, depending on the relationship between iconography and modes of interpretation. See Spivak's "Thoughts on the Principle of Allegory," *Genre*, vol. 5, no. 4 (1972): 327–52.

41. The final edition of the script lists this episode title "Business As Usual." Overall, in this instance there are significant differences between the final script available at the Television Script Archive and the televised version. The final script indicates a closer resemblance to the Central Park case, sometimes imitating the rhetoric of newspaper coverage of the accused to describe the assailants, than the televised version.

42. While all of the assailants are male, the episode does not isolate this youth predilection for violence as a specific aspect of masculinity.

43. In contrast, a 1988 episode, "Fun with Animals," features an extended discussion of racism and implies that it may have motivated a rape among high school students. The episode ends with the revelation that the attack was not really a rape nor was it racially motivated. Effectively, the narrative shies away from confronting the ways in which rape and race are related.

44. Cuklanz, *Rape on Prime Time*, 40–41.

45. *21 Jump Street*, "Blackout," aired on July 16, 1990.

46. The class differences between the victim and her assailants are conveyed symbolically through various signifiers of social class, such as her BMW in contrast to the teenagers' weather-beaten truck.

47. The script requires the use of Fritz Lang shadows and lighting, making the teenagers appear sinister.

48. Terry Eagleton, *The Rape of Clarissa: Writing, Sexuality, and Class Struggle in Samuel Richardson* (Minneapolis: University of Minnesota Press, 1982). For an insightful criticism of his theory of the unrepresentability of rape, see Rajeswari Sunder Rajan, *Real and Imagined Women: Gender, Culture and Postcolonialism* (New York: Routledge, 1993), 64–82.

49. Brenda Silver, "Periphrasis, Power, and Rape in *A Passage to India*," in *Rape and Representation*, edited by Lynn Higgins and Brenda Silver (New York: Columbia University Press, 1991), 115–40.

50. Rajan, *Real and Imagined Women*, 64–82.

51. In an episode prior to the period examined in this chapter, "Belle of the Bald" (aired on April 14, 1988), Michael Kuzak defends a woman who murders her rapist, a man protected by diplomatic immunity. While rape is central to the narrative, the plotline focuses on the merits of diplomatic immunity and the ways in which the law fails to protect innocent victims, rather than on sexual assault.

52. *L.A. Law*, "Guess Who's Coming to Murder," aired on January 9, 1992.

53. *L.A. Law*, "Dances with Sharks," aired on February 14, 1991.

54. Projansky, "Working on Feminism" (Ph.D. diss., University of Iowa, 1995), 90.

55. Historically, especially during the Reconstruction Era, rape charges were repeatedly leveled against black men in the United States. The episode does not address the racial specificity of this issue. Instead, *L.A. Law* producer and writer Steve Bochco specifies that his intention is to deracialize Rollins's character. See Robert Lindsey, "From *Hill Street* to *L.A. Law*," *New York Times Magazine* (August 24, 1986): 31ff. Ironically, though, earlier in the season Rollins defended a white cop in a police brutality case spearheaded by a black community leader.

56. Hall, "The Mind That Burns in Each Body," in *Powers of Desire*, 329–49; Angela Davis, *Women, Race and Class* (New York: Vintage, 1983).

57. Jenny Sharpe, *Allegories of Empire: The Figure of Woman in the Colonial Text* (Minneapolis: University of Minnesota Press, 1993).

58. The 1967 movie starring Sidney Poitier and Rod Steiger located racism among police personnel and the city as a whole. The movie offered no easy solutions to racism. Originally released on television as a made-for-TV movie in March 1988, the subsequent weekly series toned down the critique of racism. None of the regular white cast of characters is shown as being racist, but the bit players who represent the townspeople are shown as being overtly racist. Actor and co-producer Carroll O'Connor said in a *TV Guide* interview that at the conclusion of the series' first season, he was redirecting the focus away from social issues and toward a more traditional dramatic structure. See Mary Murphy, "Carroll O' Connor's Sound and Fury," *TV Guide* (June 2, 1990): 15–19.

59. *In the Heat of the Night*, "Rape," aired on August 21, 1989.

60. In an earlier episode, "Accused," a white police officer, Bubba, is accused of raping an African-American woman. Her claim is supported by a white woman, who says that Bubba raped her three weeks earlier. As the narrative unfolds, it becomes clear that the two women have made the charges based on an erroneous identification. In this instance, Tibbs supports Bubba and protects him from a hostile group of African-American men. The district attorney, however, wants to prosecute Bubba to showcase the fairness of the town. In the end, Bubba is cleared, and the rapist is apprehended.

61. The final script at the Annenberg Archives lists the district attorney as a woman.

62. Adele Alexander, "'She's No Lady, She's a Nigger': Abuses, Stereotypes, and Realities from the Middle Passage to Capitol (and Anita) Hill," in *Race, Gender, and Power in America*, 3–25, 5.

63. Ibid.; Hazel Carby, "'On the Threshold of the Women's Era'," in *Critical Inquiry*, 262–77.

64. *21 Jump Street*, "Stand By Your Man," aired on October 4, 1989.

65. According to Jim Pines, on cop shows interracial tensions between police officers are resolved or held in check through the exigencies of male bonding. See "Black Cops and Black Villains in Film and TV Crime Fiction," in *Crime and the Media*, edited by David Kidd-Hewitt and Richard Osborne (East Haven, Conn.: Pluto Press, 1995), 67–77. *In the Heat of the Night* goes a step further. In episodes aired in 1994, the white police chief marries a black district attorney.

66. Lauren Rabinovitz, "Sitcoms and Single Moms," in *Cinema Journal*, 3–19.

67. In sharp contrast to this sympathetic presentation of the police, *Reasonable Doubts* presents the police force as imbued with sexism and patriarchal ideas about women. When a police officer is charged with rape, his colleagues harass the victim and try different ways to present her as an incredible claimant of rape.

68. Susan Jeffords, "Performative Masculinities," *Discourse* 13 (1991): 102–18.

69. Cuklanz has developed this argument with nuance in *Rape on Prime Time*.

70. The episodes were aired on January 4, 1990, January 11, 1990, and January 18, 1990. This is the only story line in the three-year period that addresses interracial rape, although *L.A. Law* has explored rape in at least twenty-nine episodes during its eight-season run.

71. JanMohamed, "Sexuality On/Of the Racial Border," in *Discourses of Sexuality*, 94–116.

72. In a *TV Guide* cover story by Andy Meisler, "Are They Doing Justice to Their Roles?" (April 1–7, 1989): 4–8, three of the women who act as lawyers on *L.A. Law* produce biographies for their characters that are postfeminist. The actors specify that they do not want their characters to be aggressively feminist or passively feminine. Each wants to retain aspects of the flirtatious feminine, yet show that they have been influenced by the women's movement. Here we see enacted Elspeth Probyn's concept of "choiceoise," a characteristic feature of postfeminism.

73. *L.A. Law*, "The Gods Must Be Lawyers," aired on February 21, 1991.

74. *Reasonable Doubts*, aired on October 25, 1991, November 8, 1991, November 15, 1991, and November 22, 1991.

75. Projansky, "Working on Feminism" (Ph.D. diss., University of Iowa, 1995).

76. *L.A. Law*, "From Here to Paternity," aired on March 29, 1992.

77. Judith Mayne makes a similar argument in "*L.A. Law* and Prime-Time Feminism," in *Discourse*, 30–47. According to Sarah Projansky, "Working on Feminism," on *L.A. Law*, rape often served as a bridge between episodes and seasons.

78. In the William Kennedy Smith case, prosecutor Moira Lasch revealed to the press that her client had passed a "lie detector" test. Like Grace Van Owen, Lasch was chided for trying to influence the jury.

79. *L.A. Law*, "From Here to Paternity," aired on March 29, 1992. Gregory Garrison, the prosecutor in the Mike Tyson case, presented an identical argument.

80. Grace's faith in the therapeutic solution is echoed in other story lines.

81. MacKinnon, *Toward a Feminist Theory of the State*, 92.

82. Charles McGrath, "The Triumph of the Prime-Time Novel," *New York Times Magazine* (October 22, 1995): 52–59.

83. Dawn Keetley, "*Law & Order*," in *Prime-Time Law*, 21–32.

84. According to Charles McGrath, "The Triumph of the Prime-Time Novel," *Law & Order* is renowned for its speed in responding to real-life events and incorporating them into the show's plots; sometimes it takes as little as eight weeks for a script to be developed and to make its way onto the air.

85. Spivak, "Can the Subaltern Speak?" in *Marxism and the Interpretation of Culture*, 271–313.

87. Hayden White, *The Content of Form: Narrative Discourse and Historical Representation* (Baltimore: Johns Hopkins University Press, 1987).

NOTES TO TESTIFYING IN THE COURT OF TALK SHOWS

1. In May 1993, *Jet* magazine reported that the word "Oprah" had entered teenagers' lexicon as a verb, meaning to "engage in persistent, intimate questioning with the intention of obtaining a confession; usually used by men about women, as in, 'I wasn't going to tell her, but after a few drinks, she oprah'd it out of me'." Quoted in George Mair, *Oprah Winfrey: The Real Story* (Secaucus, N.J.: Carol Pub., 1994).

2. For an extended discussion of the ways in which confessional literature produces a proto-feminist discursive space, see Felski, *Beyond Feminist Aesthetics*. Consciousness raising as a tool to mobilize people has been used by numerous social movements. For a general discussion of the liberatory potential and problematic aspects of consciousness-raising activity, see Linda Martín Alcoff and Laura Gray, "Survivor Discourse: Transgression or Recuperation?" *Signs*, vol. 18, no. 2 (1993): 260–90.

3. Donahue has said in numerous interviews that the women's movement has made him ask the "right-minded" questions. See Gloria-Jean Masciarotte, "C'mon Girl: Oprah Winfrey and the Discourses of Feminine Talk," *Genders* 11 (1991): 81–110.

4. See Laura Mulvey, "Melodrama In and Out of the Home," in *High Theory/Low Culture: Analysing Popular Television and Film*, edited by Colin MacCabe (New York: St. Martin's Press, 1986), 80–100; Lynn Spigel, "Installing the Television Set," in *Private Screenings*, 3–40; and Mary Beth Haralovich, "Sit-coms and Suburbs: Positioning the 1950s Homemaker," *Quarterly Review of Film Studies*, vol. 11, no. 1 (1990): 61–83.

5. Laurie Haag, "Oprah Winfrey: The Construction of Intimacy in the Talk Show," *Journal of Popular Culture*, vol. 26, no. 4 (1993): 115–21.

6. Ibid., 116.

7. Denis McDougal, "Donahue's Dilemma: Balancing Truth, Trash," *Los Angeles Times*, January 28, 1990.

8. In 1985, there were fourteen hours of soap operas on daytime television and only four hours of talk shows. In 1995, there were fewer than ten hours of soap-opera programming and more than twenty talk shows.

9. Winfrey's official website indicates that over 22 million people tune in every week to watch her show. See http://www.oprah.com.

10. Jeanne A. Heaton and Nona L. Wilson, *Tuning into Trouble: Talk TV's Destructive Impact on Mental Health* (San Francisco: Jossey-Bass Publications, 1995), 35.

11. Vicki Abt and Leonard Mastazza, *Coming after Oprah: Cultural Fallout in the Age of the TV Talk Show* (Bowling Green, Ohio: Bowling Green State University Popular Press, 1997), 3.

12. Ibid.

13. Walter Goodman, "Three Queens of Talk Who Rule the Day," *New York Times*, July 29, 1991.

14. Tania Modleski, "Femininity as Mas(s)querade: A Feminist Approach to Mass Culture," in *High Theory/Low Culture*, 37–52, 39.

15. Editorial in *Ms.* (September/October 1995), 45; see also Joan Barthel, "Here Comes Oprah: From the *Color Purple* to TV Talk Queen," *Ms.* (August 1986), 46ff.

16. Elayne Rapping, "Oprah, Phil, and Sally," in *Media-tions: Forays into the Culture and Gender Wars* (Boston: South End Press, 1994), 192–96; Jane Shattuc, *The Talking Cure: TV Talk Shows and Women* (New York: Routledge, 1997); Janice Peck, "TV Talk Shows As Therapeutic Discourse: The Ideological Labor of the Televised Talking Cure," *Communication Theory*, vol. 5, no. 1 (1995): 58–81.

17. See Shattuc, *The Talking Cure*; Janice Peck, "Talk about Racism: Framing a Popular Discourse of Race on *Oprah Winfrey*," *Cultural Critique* 27 (1994): 89–126; Masciarotte, "C'mon Girl," in *Genders*, 81–110; Corrine Squire, "Empowering Women?: The Oprah Winfrey Show," *Feminism and Psychology*, vol. 4, no. 1 (1994): 63–79; Alcoff and Gray, "Survivor Discourse," in *Signs*, 260–90.

18. Shattuc, *The Talking Cure*.

19. In the 1980s, some local stations characterized talk shows as information programs in their applications seeking license renewal. Ibid.

20. Robert Allen, "Audience-Oriented Criticism," in *Channels of Discourse, Reassembled*, 122.

21. Shattuc, *The Talking Cure*, 7–8.

22 . Donal Carbaugh, *Talking American: Cultural Discourses on Donahue* (Norwood, N.J.: Ablex Publishing, 1988); and Wayne Munson, *All Talk: The Talk Show in Media Culture* (Philadelphia: Temple University Press, 1993).

23. Everything about Winfrey's show is carefully scripted and controlled; the audience is screened, as are telephone calls, to fit what she wants on the program, George Mair points out. See Mair's *Oprah Winfrey*.

24. *Oprah* makes a very clear distinction between guests who narrate individual stories and experts who are invited to share their knowledge on the topic. The experts do not enter into the conversation until all of the guests have presented their stories. *Donahue*, however, blurs the distinction between guests and experts; here experts participate in the discussion from the beginning of the show.

25. Janice Peck, "TV Talk Shows As Therapeutic Discourse," in *Communication Theory*, 58–81.

26. An *Oprah* publicist describes the typical audience member as cast in the "Roseanne Connor" mold, a stay-at-home, nonwhite-collar woman with approximately a ninth-grade education. See Shattuc, *The Talking Cure*, 47.

27. Marilyn Matelski, *Daytime Television Programming* (Boston: Focal Press, 1991).

28. Mary Ellen Brown, ed., *Television and Women's Culture: The Politics of the Popular* (Newbury Park, Calif.: Sage, 1990), 7; Fiske, *Television Culture*, 179–97.

29. Peck, "TV Talk Shows As Therapeutic Discourse," in *Communication Theory*, 63.

30. Masciarotte, "C'mon Girl," in *Genders*, 94. Corrine Squire terms this tendency as psychological democracy, as Winfrey presents herself like her audience members. See "Empowering Women?" in *Feminism and Psychology*, 63–79.

31. Shattuc, *The Talking Cure*, 124.

32. Munson, *All Talk*, 10.

33. Masciarotte, "C'mon Girl," in *Genders*, 99.

34. Shattuc, *The Talking Cure*, 39. Since entering syndication in 1986 the show has remained the number one talk show for fourteen consecutive seasons. See http://www.oprah.com.

35. See Dana Cloud, "Hegemony or Concordance? The Rhetoric of Tokenism in 'Oprah' Winfrey's Rags-to-Riches Biography," *Critical Studies in Mass Communication*, vol. 13, no. 2 (1996): 115–37; Jeffery Decker, *Made in America: Self-Styled Success from Horatio Alger to Oprah Winfrey* (Minneapolis: University of Minnesota Press, 1997).

36. See Joan Barthel, "Here Comes Oprah," in *Ms.*, 48; Barbara Harrison, "The Importance of Being Oprah," *New York Times Magazine* (June 11, 1989): 28ff.

37. Martha Bayles, "Oprah vs. Phil: Warmth Wins Out," *Wall Street Journal*, January 26, 1987.

38. Jill Nelson, "The Man Who Saved Oprah Winfrey," *Washington Post Magazine* (December 14, 1986): 30–32.

39. In the pre-credits segment of "The Date Rape Controversy" (aired on July 23, 1991), Winfrey outlines a scenario of acquaintance rape and points out that the William Kennedy Smith case has facilitated debate on the subject. Beyond this cursory reference that reveals the salience of the discussion on her show, Winfrey does not address the celebrity cases that I have analyzed in Chapter 3 of this book.

40. Overall, *Oprah* runs about forty-five minutes once advertisement times are taken into account.

41. Their voices replicated many of the emotional and physical responses character-ized by scientists as rape trauma syndrome. See Ann Burgess and Lynda Holmstrom, *Rape: Victims of Crisis* (Bowie, Md.: R. J. Brady Co., 1974).

42. Elaine Scarry, *The Body in Pain: The Making and Unmaking of the World* (New York: Oxford University Press, 1985), 8.

43. Felski, *Beyond Feminist Aesthetics*, 121.

44. bell hooks, "Talking Black, Talking Back" in *Talking Back* (Boston: South End Press, 1989), 9.

45. See Chandra Talpade Mohanty, "Cartographies of Struggle: Third World Women and the Politics of Feminism," in *Third World Women and the Politics of Feminism*, edited by Chandra Talpade Mohanty, Ann Russo, and Lourdes Torres (Bloomington: Indiana University Press, 1991), 1–47; Linda Alcoff, "The Politics of Postmodern Feminism, Revisited," *Cultural Critique* 36 (1997): 5–28; Barbara Harlow, *Resistance Literature* (New York: Methuen, 1987).

46. Foucault, *The History of Sexuality*, vol. 1, 23.

47. For an extended discussion of the nature of the Protestant confessional, see Mas-ciarotte, "C'mon Girl," in *Genders*, 81–110.

48. Foucault, *The History of Sexuality*, vol. 1, 61–62.

49. Shoshana Felman and Dori Laub, *Testimony: Crises of Witnessing in Literature, Psychoanalysis, and History* (New York: Routledge, 1992).

50. Although Shoshana Felman and Dori Laub discuss the testimonial in the specific context of the Holocaust, their book provides a detailed description of its liberatory poten-tial. See ibid.

51. Squire, "Empowering Women?" in *Feminism and Psychology*, 63–79.

52. Berlant, "The Female Complaint," in *Social Text*, 237–57.

53. Butler, "Endangered/Endangering," in *Reading Rodney King, Reading Urban Uprising*, 15–22.

54. Mimi White, *Tele-Advising: Therapeutic Discourse in American Television* (Chapel Hill: University of North Carolina Press, 1992), 31.

55. For a discussion of how the talk show format reduces racism to an individual behavioral trait rather than a systemic problem, see Peck, "Talk about Racism," in *Cultural Critique*, 89–126.

56. Squire, "Empowering Women?" in *Feminism and Psychology*, 63–79.

57. Masciarotte, "C'mon Girl," in *Genders*, 100.

58. For an analysis of Ida B. Wells-Barnett's writings on black women's sexual oppression during slavery and the fear of miscegenation manifested in lynch rhetoric, see Carby, "On the Threshold of Woman's Era," in *Critical Inquiry*, 330–43.

59. Squire, "Empowering Women?" in *Feminism and Psychology*, 63–79.

60. Ibid.

61. Elspeth Probyn, "Television's *Unheimlich* Home," in *The Politics of Everyday Fear*, edited by Brian Massumi (Minneapolis: University of Minnesota Press, 1993), 269–83.

62. Sonia Livingstone and Peter Lunt, *Talk on Television: Audience Participation and Public Debate* (New York: Routledge, 1994).

63. *Talked to Death*, HBO Production (March 1997).

64. See Masciarotte, "C'mon Girl," in *Genders*, 81–115; Deborah Lupton, "Talking about Sex: Sexology, Sexual Difference, and Confessional Talk Shows," *Genders* 20 (1994): 45–65.

65. Carpignano et al., "Chatter in the Age of Electronic Reproduction," in *Social Text*, 33–55; Lisa McLaughlin, "Chastity Criminals in the Age of Electronic Reproduction: Re-viewing Talk Television and the Public Sphere," *Journal of Communication Inquiry*, vol. 17, no. 1 (1991): 41–55.

66. McDougal, "Donahue's Dilemma."

67. David Halberstam, quoted in ibid.

68. The show entitled "Central Park 'Wilding' Incident" included a journalist who was raped in Central Park as well. The host provided a brief description of the attack, but she limited her participation to enumerating factual details about the prevalence of the crime.

69. Decker, *Made in America*; Heaton and Wilson, *Tuning into Trouble*, 45.

70. Gilroy, *Problems in Anti-Racist Strategy*, 5.

71. Peggy McIntosh, "White Privilege and Male Privilege: A Personal Account of Coming to See Correspondences through Work in Women's Studies," in *Race, Class, and Gender*, 2d ed., edited by Margaret Anderson and Patricia Hill Collins (New York: Wadsworth, 1995), 76–87.

72. "Central Park 'Wilding' Incident," the *Donahue* show, aired on May 3, 1989.

73. "Crime and Punishment: Was the Jogger Defendants' Sentence Fair?" *Donahue* show, aired on September 14, 1990.

74. Peck, "TV Talk Shows As Therapeutic Discourse," in *Communication Theory*, 58–81.

75. In contrast, Mo Gaffney's *Women Aloud* on cable station Comedy Central is vocal about its feminism. A combination of stand-up comedy and the conventional talk show, Gaffney presents only the feminist view, not opposing viewpoints or debates.

76. Shattuc, *The Talking Cure*, 195.

NOTES TO FRAGMENTED COUNTERNARRATIVES

1. John Berger, *Ways of Seeing* (London: BBC, 1972).

2. Feminist film theorists have examined the ways in which the cinematic appara-tus constructs sexual difference and addresses spectators as male/masculine and female/feminine. Grounded in psychoanalytical theories of desire and difference, these studies argue that female spectators have a limited set of viewing positions: they can take up a masculine subject position, submit to a masochism of overidentification, or adopt the narcissistic position of taking the screen as a mirror and becoming one's own object of desire. Laura Mulvey is associated most closely with this concept, that the cinema solicits a male viewer. Several other scholars have developed this more fully. Specifically, Jane Gaines and Jacqueline Bobo have called for a more complex conceptualization that under-stands the specific ways in which race intersects with sex to constitute particular gendered viewing positions. Moving away from these criticisms of mainstream representational practices, Julia Lesage examines experimental films to explore the possibilities of an alter-native way of imaging rape. She outlines several characteristics as being typical of a femi-nist representational practice: the narrative is participatory and presented in a nonhierar-chical manner, the rape is depicted in a nonvoyeuristic manner, and the survivors will not be cast as object-victims but as subject survivors. See Laura Mulvey, "Visual Pleasure and Narrative Cinema," *Screen* 16 (1975): 6–18; Annette Kuhn, *The Power of the Image: Essays on Representation and Sexuality* (Boston: Routledge and Kegan Paul, 1985); Mary Ann Doane, *Femmes Fatales: Feminism, Film Theory, and Psychoanalysis* (New York: Routledge, 1991); Jane Gaines, "White Privilege and Looking Relations," *Screen* 29 (1988): 12–26; Julia Lesage, "Disarming Film Rape," *Jump Cut* 19 (1978): 14–16.

3. Lorraine Gamman and Margaret Marshment, eds. *The Female Gaze: Women As Viewers of Popular Culture* (London: Women's Press, 1988).

4. I do not intend to set up an uncritical binary between a repressive modernity and a subversive postmodernity. Feminist historians have provided ample evidence that the unified subject of modernism is itself fiction.

5. Hazel Carby, *Reconstructing Womanhood: The Emergence of the Afro-American Woman Novelist* (New York: Oxford University Press, 1987), 17.

6. See Todd Gitlin, "Movies of the Week," in *Inside Prime Time* (New York: Pan-theon, 1983), 157–200.

7. Felski, *Beyond Feminist Aesthetics*, 167–68.

8. Ibid., 171.

9. See Elayne Rapping, *The Movie of the Week: Private Stories/Public Events* (Min-neapolis: University of Minnesota Press, 1992); Gitlin, "Movies of the Week," in *Inside Prime Time*, 157–200; Browne, "The Political Economy of the Television (Super) Text," in *Quarterly Review of Film Studies*, 74–82; David Gunzerath, "*Columbo* and the Early Made-for-TV Movie: Reassessing the Origins of a Program Form," paper presented at the National Communication Association Conference, New York City, November 1998.

10. Elayne Rapping points out that these movies allow networks to produce profitable programming and simultaneously comply with FCC license requirements for public service programming. See Rapping, *The Movie of the Week*.

11. Ibid., 66.

12. Todd Gitlin argues that the desire for high ratings ensures that the movies rarely deal with issues provocatively. The story lines are cautious and pluralistic. Simultaneously, in their quest for prestige and novelty, the networks may air movies that are creative. This dialectic of sameness and difference is the signature style of the genre. See his "Movies of the Week," in *Inside Prime Time*, 157–200.

13. *A Case of Rape* (1974) explored the issue of acquaintance rape, revealing the emotional and physical trauma that accompanies sexual violence. *The Burning Bed* (1985), which focused on domestic violence, continues to be one of the most-viewed television movies. *Something about Amelia* (1984), about incest, and the aforementioned movies are considered hallmarks of the early made-for-TV movie lineup.

14. Rapping, *The Movie of the Week*. Critics and actors concur that these programs offer women the strongest roles on television. See Cliff Rothman, "Made for Television Movies at 25," *Television Quarterly*, vol. 24, no. 4 (1990): 35–41.

15. Gitlin, "Movies of the Week," in *Inside Prime Time*, 180.

16. NBC Vice President of Broadcast Standards and Practices, Dr. Rosalyn Weinman, is convinced that these movies serve an informational function. Rape counselors and sociologists find these portrayals useful, and women viewers are able to connect with the characters and take positive actions in their own lives, she asserts. Quoted in Claudia Dreifus, "Women in 'Jep'," *TV Guide* (March 14, 1992): 22–25, 24.

17. For instance, see *A Mother's Justice* (NBC), *False Arrest* (ABC), *Rape of Dr. Willis* (CBS), *Captive* (ABC), or *Sins of the Mother* (CBS). All hew closely to the women in jeopardy plotline.

18. John Leonard, "Young and Innocent," *New York* (October 23, 1989): 130–32.

19. Quoted in Dreifus, "Women in 'Jep'," in *TV Guide*, 24.

20. *The Des Moines Register* received a Pulitzer Prize for the series, and references to this event were raised in network coverage of the William Kennedy Smith and Mike Tyson cases.

21. Dreifus, "Women in 'Jep'," in *TV Guide*, 22–25.

22. John Leonard, "This Is Her Life," *New York* (March 16, 1992): 75.

23. Annette Kuhn, "The Body and Cinema: Some Problems for Feminism," in *Writing on the Body*, 195–207.

24. Officially, the film was produced by a non-network company, Tri-Star TV, and Kopple was recruited by Tri-Star's executive producer, Diane Sokolow.

25. For details of the docudrama genre, see Derek Paget, *No Other Way to Tell It: Dramadoc/Docudrama on Television* (New York: St. Martin's Press, 1998). He explains that television's requirements for dramatic narratives have altered the ways in which the documentary is constructed.

26. Several popular songs have marked Tyson's status as a folk hero and celebrate him for epitomizing the rags-to-riches dream. Notably, D. J. Jazzy Jeff and Fresh Prince's song, "I Think I Can Beat Mike Tyson" (1989), praises the boxer's extraordinary athletic prowess. An Argentine band and a salsa group also have set to music the boxer's achievements. Following his conviction, many of these popular accounts have recast the boxer as a persecuted martyr.

27. *Watch Me Now,* by Michael Marton, was about a young boxer residing at Cus D'Amato's training camp for troubled youth.

28. The movie was subsequently aired on the cable station USA. See Howard Rosenberg, "A One-Two Punch from Two Mikes," *Los Angeles Times,* February 12, 1993.

29. duCille, "The Unbearable Blackness of Being," in *Birth of a Nation'hood,* 293–338, 296.

30. I am indebted to Sarah Projansky for this insight.

31. In 1994, the cable station Arts & Entertainment produced an account of the boxer's life for their "Biography" series. A year later, HBO produced *Tyson,* recounting biographical details of the former heavyweight champion's life.

32. See Decker, *Made in America.*

33. Felicia Feaster, "Fallen Champ," *Film Quarterly,* vol. 47, no. 2 (1993–1994): 45–47, 46.

34. L. A. Winokur, "An Interview with Barbara Kopple," *Progressive,* vol. 56, no. 11 (1992): 30–33.

35. Examining media constructions of Oprah Winfrey's biography, Dana Cloud contends that African-American heirs to the Horatio Alger myth are enacting a tokenist biography. See Cloud, "Hegemony or Concordance?" in *Critical Studies in Mass Communication,* 115–37.

36. Henry Louis Gates, "Introduction," in *Black Male,* edited by Thelma Golden (New York: Whitney Museum of American Art, 1994), 11–14.

37. Randy Roberts and Gregory Garrison, *Heavy Justice: The State of Indiana v. Michael G. Tyson* (Reading, Mass.: Addison-Wesley, 1994), 162.

38. Joyce Carol Oates reminds us that one of Tyson's favorite pre-fight taunts was to boast to his opponent, "I'll make you into my girlfriend." See "Rape and the Boxing Ring," *Newsweek* (February 24, 1992): 60–61.

39. Kimberlé Crenshaw points out that the African-American community has rallied around black women only in two rape cases, the St. John's University gang rape and the Tawana Brawley rape case. In both instances, the alleged assailants were white. See Crenshaw, "Color-Blind Dreams and Racial Judgments," in *Birth of a Nation'hood,* 97–168.

40. June Jordan, "Requiem for the Champ," *Progressive,* vol. 56, no. 4 (1992): 15–16.

41. Crenshaw, "Color-Blind Dreams and Racial Judgments," in *Birth of a Nation-hood*, 150.

42. Aaronette White, "Talking Feminist, Talking Black: Micromobilization Processes in a Collective Protest against Rape," *Gender and Society*, vol. 13, no. 1 (1999): 77–100. Similarly, the publisher of *Essence* magazine wrote a letter denouncing the Free Mike Tyson rallies.

43. Quoted in Feasler, "*Fallen Champ*," 47.

44. Stuart Hall, "New Ethnicities," in *"Race," Culture, and Difference*, 252–59.

45. *ABC News* edited its coverage of the William Kennedy Smith case and marketed it through MPI Home Video as an educational video. Similarly, Courtroom Television Network abbreviated its gavel-to-gavel coverage of the case into a four-cassette instructional video geared specifically for law students. The educational programs I examine here have not been marketed separately, although ABC's *Men, Sex and Rape* is available on video.

46. See Bart and O'Brien, *Stopping Rape: Successful Survival Strategies*.

47. In sharp contrast to these programs, educational videos such as *The Vienna Tribunal* (1994) offer a global perspective on violence against women. They often link rape to a spectrum of violent acts. Even as they suggest the need for women to adopt preventive and strategic steps, they demand social, political, and legal reform.

48. *The Date Rape Backlash: The Media and the Denial of Rape* offers an extended analysis of the ways in which media representations contribute to the formation of a rape culture. It also offers a specific critique of how television representations image rape.

49. The term *rape culture* refers to cultural practices—such as media images, advertisements, and social expectations of appropriate male and female behaviors—that define gender roles and licit sex. Such a conceptualization points out that rape exists not only in people's lives but in a larger representational field, which in turn shapes the understandings and experiences of rape that people encounter in their everyday lives.

50. As in the network news narratives I analyzed in Chapter 3, here again stereotypes of nonwhite sexuality are rarely examined as resulting in a different experience of violation.

51. Earlier in 1988, HBO offered a similar hour-long examination of an Oregon-based rape prevention program in *Rapists, Can They Be Stopped?*

52. *ABC World News Tonight*, January 8, 1990; *CBS Evening News*, April 5, 1991.

53. *NBC Nightly News*, July 23, 1991; *ABC World News Tonight*, January 8, 1990.

54. Eileen Rooney, "Criticism and the Subject of Sexual Violence," *Modern Languages Notes* 98 (1983): 1269–78.

55. Anna Deveare Smith, "The Most Riveting Television: The Hill–Thomas Hearings and Popular Culture," in *Race, Gender, and Power in America*, 248–70; 253.

56. Barbara Kruger cautions us against romanticizing art. There is no uncommercial art, she asserts. In this instance, I use the awkward phrase "noncommercial art" to address

the profit-making logic that is sharply attenuated, though not absent, in the arena of art. See W.J.T. Mitchell, "An Interview with Barbara Kruger," *Critical Inquiry* 17 (1991): 434–48.

57. Through an archival analysis of newspaper accounts of the Whitechapel murderer, known as Jack the Ripper, Christopher Frayling points out the range of anxieties generated by popular cultural representations of the man. See his "The House That Jack Built," in *Rape*, 174–215.

58. Froma Zeitlin, "Configurations of Rape in Greek Myth," in *Rape*, 122–51.

59. Norman Bryson offers an insightful analysis of the different ways in which this event and the Rape of Lucretia figure in canonical art. For a more nuanced reading of the aesthetic techniques employed by the various painters, see "Two Narratives of Rape," in *Rape*, 152–73.

60. Diane Wolfthal, *Images of Rape: The Heroic Tradition and Its Alternatives* (Cambridge: Cambridge University Press, 1999).

61. See Gina Marchetti, *Romance and the "Yellow Peril": Race, Sex, and Discursive Strategies in Hollywood Films* (Berkeley: University of California Press, 1992).

62. See Lesage, "Disarming Film Rape," in *Jump Cut*, 14–16.

63. For a psychoanalytical reading of the ways in which language, sexuality, and the unconscious intersect, see Jacqueline Rose, *Sexuality in the Field of Vision* (New York: Verso, 1986).

64. Legally, a man who has intercourse with a female under the age of consent, even if it is not against her will, can be charged with rape. These laws reveal the cultural investment in childhood as an asexual period and show that female consent is meaningless when considered a juvenile.

65. Estrich, "Palm Beach Stories," in *Law and Philosophy*, 5–33.

66. Monica Chau, "Tall Tales or True Stories," in *The Subject of Rape* (New York: Whitney Museum of American Art, 1993), 79–85, 81.

67. Ibid., 85.

68. See Kim Ragusa's *Demarcations* and Soo Jin Kim's *Comfort Me*.

69. Wolfthal, *Images of Rape*, 196.

70. Thelma Golden, "My Brother," in *Black Male*, 28.

71. Kobena Mercer, "Engendered Species: Danny Tisdale and Keith Piper," *Artforum* 30 (1992): 75.

72. Frederic Jameson, *The Political Unconscious: Narrative as a Socially Symbolic Act* (Ithaca, N.Y.: Cornell University Press, 1981).

73. Melissa Deem, "From Bobbitt to SCUM: Re-memberment, Scatological Rhetorics, and Feminist Strategies in the Contemporary United States," *Public Culture*, vol. 8, no. 3 (1996): 511–37, 520.

NOTES TO CONCLUSION

1. Stuart Hall, "What Is This 'Black' in Black Popular Culture?" in *Representing Blackness: Issues in Film and Video*, edited by Valerie Smith (New Brunswick, N.J.: Rutgers University Press, 1997), 123–33.

2. Edwin Ardener, *The Voice of Prophecy and Other Essays* (New York: Basil Blackwell, 1997), 123–33.

3. Jürgen Habermas, "Further Reflections on the Public Sphere," in *Habermas and the Public Sphere*, 421–61.

4. Angela Davis, "Gender, Class, and Multiculturalism: Rethinking 'Race' Politics," in *Mapping Multiculturalism*, edited by Andrew Gordon and Christopher Newfield (Minneapolis: University of Minnesota Press, 1996), 40–48.

5. Nancy Fraser, "Rethinking the Public Sphere," in *Social Text*, 56–80.

Index